Poverty and Poverty Alleviation Strategies in North America

Edited by Mary Jo Bane and René Zenteno

Published by Harvard University David Rockefeller Center for Latin American Studies

Distributed by Harvard University Press
Cambridge, Massachusetts
London, England
2009

Library of Congress Cataloging in Publication Data

Poverty and poverty alleviation strategies in North America /edited by Mary Jo Bane
and Rene Zenteno.

   p. : ill., charts ; cm.

   Includes bibliographical references.
   ISBN: 978-0-674-03537-9

1. Poverty—Mexico. 2. Poverty—Government policy—Mexico. 3. Economic assistance,
Domestic—Mexico. 4. Poverty—United States. I. Bane, Mary Jo. II. Zenteno Quintero,
René M.

HC140.P6 P68 2009
339.46/0972

Contents

Preface

Poverty is a blight on all countries, whether it takes the form of pockets of destitution in the midst of affluence or general economic underdevelopment in countries or regions. Poverty is a blight in North America: in the Mississippi delta, in Native American reservations, among single parent families in inner cities, in U.S.-Mexico border communities, in Mexico's rural southern states, and in growing urban areas. To address this blight it is necessary to increase understanding of the roots of poverty and knowledge about effective poverty alleviation strategies. Dialogue across as well as within countries deepens knowledge and increases understanding.

This book is part of a continuing dialogue about poverty in North America, especially in Mexico and the United States. The writers recognize the economic community defined by NAFTA (North American Free Trade Agreement) and acknowledge that poverty in any one of the three NAFTA countries cannot be understood independently of conditions in the other countries. We look for solutions to poverty, in its various manifestations, wherever it occurs.

Official poverty statistics of the NAFTA partners reveal that poverty rates have been falling in all countries, most dramatically in Mexico. However, the number of people living in conditions of material scarcity has remained about the same. In general, between 85 and 90 million poor people live in North America today. Mexicans make up 55 percent of the poor in the NAFTA region.

Although all NAFTA partners recognize and face poverty and have specific policies to fight it, the contributors to this book for the most part focus on the countries with the vast majority of the poor and the most unequal income distributions: Mexico and the United States. The contrast between these two countries is important not only because of their significant differences in development, but also because the United States has been attempting to fight poverty for much longer than has Mexico. While the United States declared its war against poverty in 1964, Mexico did not have anti-poverty programs until the late 1980s. The first official account of the poor in Mexico was released in 2000, thirty-six years after the United States did so. An underlying assumption of the book is that successes and failures of the U.S. experience may be illuminating for Mexico as it develops and struggles with some of the problems the United States has also struggled with—often unsuccessfully.

The book is based on papers from a conference on "Poverty and Poverty Reduction Strategies: Mexican and International Experience" sponsored by the Kennedy School of Government of Harvard University and the Graduate School of Public Administration and Public Policy of the Tecnológico de Monterrey. The two-day conference took place in Monterrey, Mexico, in January 2005. It paid special attention to macro-policies and poverty alleviation strategies in Mexico, and how they might be improved through the Mexico-U.S. cross-national experience.

The chapters are revisions of papers first given at that conference. Researchers specializing in poverty and social policies in North America were asked to address various levels of policy aimed at helping the poor, including macro-level policies oriented toward fostering economic growth, traditional social policies such as public education, and more targeted antipoverty policies. The question that framed their analysis and discussion was: "What have we learned from experience with these policies?"

The Monterrey conference was not meant to reach agreement either on diagnosing the causes of poverty or on strategies for fighting poverty, and it did not. Neither does this book. However, the papers do provide a rich aggregation of data, evidence, and conceptual frameworks that move the debates forward.

A number of people in both Cambridge, Massachusetts, and Monterrey, Mexico, helped to make both the conference and this volume possible. We especially want to thank the session chairs and discussants at the conference: Timothy Smeeding, Bernardo González-Aréchiga, Fernando Reimers, Luis Felipe López-Calva, Fernando Cortes, Julio Boltvinik, and Merilee Grindle. We would also like to thank the leaders of the Harvard-ITESM partnership, especially Bernardo González-Aréchiga and Mary Hilderbrand. We are grateful to Harvard University's David Rockefeller Center for Latin American Studies for its support, including the publication of the volume.

Mary Jo Bane
René Zenteno

The Contributors

Sandra K. Danziger, Ph.D., Professor of Social Work and Research Professor of Public Policy, Michigan Program on Poverty and Social Welfare Policy, Gerald R. Ford School of Public Policy, University of Michigan

Sheldon Danziger, H. J. Meyer Distinguished University Professor of Public Policy and Director, National Poverty Center, Gerald R. Ford School of Public Policy, University of Michigan

Richard F. Elmore, Gregory R. Anrig Professor of Educational Leadership, Harvard University Graduate School of Education

Agustín Escobar Latapí, Research Professor at the Center for Research and Advanced Studies in Social Anthropology in Guadalajara, Mexico

Mercedes González de la Rocha, Research Professor at the Center for Research and Advanced Studies in Social Anthropology in Guadalajara, Mexico, and Director of the qualitative evaluation of *Progresa-Oportunidades* (from 1999 to 2008)

Gonzalo Hernández-Licona, Executive Secretary of the National Council for the Evaluation of Social Development Policy of Mexico

Carlos Muñoz-Izquierdo, Emeritus professor at the Universidad Ibero-Americana in Mexico City

Miguel Székely, Undersecretary for Middle Education, Government of Mexico

Guadalupe Villarreal-Guevara, Professor of the Department of Humanities at the Tecnológico de Monterrey in Monterrey, Mexico

Michael Walton, Senior Visiting Fellow, Centre for Policy Research, Delhi and Adjunct Lecturer, Harvard Kennedy School

René Zenteno, Professor of the Sociology and Demography at El Colegio de la Frontera Norte in Tijuana, Mexico

PART

I

CONTEXT

1

Poverty and Place in North America

René Zenteno, Mary Jo Bane

In this overview of poverty in North America—Mexico, the United States, and to a lesser extent Canada—we bring together the main concepts and approaches used in studying poverty in developing countries and those used in developed countries. We propose some definitions of poverty that can be usefully applied across quite different countries. We explore some correlates of poverty in the three countries, and both the similarities and the differences in the correlates of poverty across the three. We take note of the policy issues that are raised by these relationships and that frame the analyses in the rest of the volume.

We begin with an overview of growth and inequality and follow with concepts and measures of poverty and the overall incidence of poverty in the three countries, using various measures. In the third section we explore the relationship between the level of economic development and poverty, both between and within countries, followed by the relationships between household composition and poverty and between race/ethnicity and poverty in the United States and Mexico. The final section briefly raises policy issues that emerge from the analysis.

Growth and Inequality

Since the early 1990s, enormous progress has been made in conceptually linking the notions of economic growth, distribution, and poverty. Evidence has emerged on the relationships between growth, income distribution, and monetary poverty (see Chapters 3 and 4 herein; Datt and Ravaillon 1992 and Son and Kakwani 2004). As these researchers point out, initial levels of economic development and income inequality can have significant impact on poverty reductions. In addition, there is no question that long-term poverty reduction needs to be built on sustained economic growth. However, even in a context of economic growth, what happens to poverty depends on what happens to the distribution of income and consumption (Deaton 2003).

In understanding the dynamics of poverty in North America, we must first look at recent trends in economic growth and inequality in the region. The story is different depending on where you live in North America. Table 1 (tables and figures are at the end of each chapter) shows the economic and social conditions prevailing in the region. With a total of 441.6 million people, North America is one of the most populous regions in the world. Almost seven out of ten persons in the region live in the United States. Second in population size is Mexico, with 106.2 million people (24 percent). Canada accounts for less than one-tenth of the population. Most of the population in the region lives in urban settings, and the countries do not differ greatly in their levels of urbanization, ranging from 75 percent of the population in Mexico to 81 percent in Canada and the United States.

North America is one of the richest regions of the world, comprising about one-quarter of world output. By the World Bank's classification, Canada's and the U.S. economies fall into the high-income grouping. Even though Mexico ranks as an upper-middle-income economy in the world, its income per capita falls far behind those of its northern neighbors. Average per capita income is estimated to be 1.2 times greater in the United States than in Canada and 3.8 times greater than in Mexico. With a per capita income of $11,600, Mexicans have, on average, around 30 percent of the income of their NAFTA partners.

Although Canadians do not earn as much as Americans, they lead a better life in terms of other indicators of human development. A person born in Canada is expected to live, on average, 80 years and to have a chance of 5.3 in a thousand of dying before the first year of life, compared to a newborn in the United States, whose life expectancy and infant mortality rate would be of 78 and 6.5, respectively.

Since the 1930s, because of a rapid expansion of the public health system, death rates have been declining so rapidly in Mexico that by now expectations of life at birth are virtually identical in Mexico and the United States. However, the infant mortality rate—a key measure of quality of life—is still considerably higher in Mexico than north of the border: the risk of death during the first year of life is more than three times higher. A relatively high infant mortality rate in Mexico is closely related to the persistence of poverty and to high levels of economic and social inequality across regions and social groups.

Levels of educational attainment are similar in the United States and Canada, with Canada slightly higher; thus, Canada's lower gross domestic income (GDI) does not seem to result from a lower overall level of human capital. Educational opportunities are still much more restricted in Mexico. With only 22.6 percent of the adult population (25–64 years old) attending upper-secondary or higher education, Mexico exhibits significantly lower levels of education than Canada or the United States.

The magnitude of income poverty is determined by the rate of economic growth and the distribution of income (Bourguignon 2004). Figure 1 displays the trends in per capita income (PPP) for each NAFTA country from 1950 to 2004, expressed in 1996 dollars. Table 2 provides the average yearly growth rate of per capita income in these countries over the last fifty, thirty, and ten years.

Two major results emerge from this information. First, while Canada and the United States were able to sustain a positive income growth over this period, Mexico experienced income stagnation during the last twenty-five years. Second, there is strong divergence over time in per capita income between Mexico and its NAFTA partners. Long-run divergences in productivity levels and living standards between developed and developing countries have been documented by Lant Pritchett (1997). The absolute income gap between Canada and the United States has also widened since the mid-1980s, but still looks small when compared to income differences between México and the United States.

It is important to note that between 1953 and 2003, as Table 2 indicates, the Mexican economy expanded at a rate as high as those of its northern neighbors. Per capita income in Mexico grew strongly on average until the 1970s. Canada also experienced relatively high rates of economic expansion over this period. The economic expansion allowed Mexico to reduce the U.S./Mexico income ratio to around 3.0 during the 1960s and 1970s, with its lowest point in 1981–82 (2.8). The rapid economic growth of Mexico did not have a significant impact on closing the income gap with its NAFTA partners, largely because of its fast demographic growth.

However, much had changed during the next three decades. Canada experienced a decline of per capita income growth (from 2.1 to 1.9 percent) and Mexico suffered a substantial slowdown in its rate of economic expansion (from 2.1 to 1.1 percent) as a result of several economic crises. The 1993–2003 decade was not particularly prosperous for Mexico either. Although its per capita income growth averaged 1.1 percent, it experienced a major decline in living standards because of the Mexican "Tequila Crisis" of 1994–1995.[1] Per capita income in the United States grew at an annual rate of 1.9 and 2.3 percent during the last thirty and ten years, respectively. Because of diverse economic performances, the ratio of per capita income between the United States and Mexico increased substantially during the last twenty years. The absolute income gap between Mexico and its northern neighbor rose from $16,166 in 1984 to $27,933 in 2004. Not surprisingly, Mexican migrants and remittances have experienced a significant boost in the present decade.

Mexico not only fared worse than Canada and the United States over the 1980s and 1990s, but also continues to suffer a worse income distribution. Lower average income coupled with higher inequality help to explain the difference in poverty outcomes between Mexico and its NAFTA partners. Although Mexico was able to reduce income inequality between 1963 and 1984, the situation has been more uneven during the years of economic restructuring and financial crisis (Hernandez Laos 2003).

Recent trends in the distribution of income in North America, as measured by the Gini coefficient, are shown in Table 3. The table shows two important features. On the one hand, Mexico has a more unequal income distribution than Canada and the United States, while economic growth spreads its benefits more equitably in Canada than in the United States. On the other hand, the overall trend in income distribution has been rising in the three countries, particularly in Canada. As a result, differences in income inequality between Canada and the United States seem to be closing over time.

The importance of existing inequality for poverty reduction in Mexico is illustrated in a hypothetical example by Bourguignon (2004). With no change in the distribution of income, if real per capita income in Mexico would grow at an annual rate of 3 percent over a period of 10 years, poverty would be reduced by less than 7 percent. However, an absolute reduction of 0.1 on its Gini coefficient would represent a drop of more than 15 percent over the same period. Thus, it would take about 30 years to reach the same result without any change in the income distribution.

In summary, data on the level of economic development, economic growth, and income inequality show substantial differences among the United States, Canada, and especially Mexico. All three of these dimensions are related to levels and trends in poverty in the three countries.

Poverty Measures for North America

We make use of three conceptually different approaches to measure income poverty, as each makes an important contribution to understanding poverty in North America:

- For some analyses, we use the official poverty or low-income guidelines developed by and for the individual countries.

- We use the market-basket poverty lines for food poverty and basic needs poverty in Mexico, adjusted for exchange rates and purchasing power parity, to estimate the incidence of poverty across countries.

- We also use a relative poverty line, defined as 50 percent of median household income for each country.

National Poverty Lines

Each of the three countries' statistical agencies takes a somewhat different approach to measuring poverty or low income. In 2002, Mexico first developed an official poverty measure using a market-basket approach (Cortés, Rodríguez, and Zenteno 2004). Mexico uses three different poverty lines: one measures extreme, or food poverty, and is set at the cost of purchasing a minimum diet; the second line represents the cost of food plus education and health; the third represents the cost of purchasing all basic needs. The poverty lines are different for rural and urban areas, expressed as consumption per person per day, with no adjustments for household size. Mexico's official poverty lines in $U.S. are shown in Table 4.

The United States developed a market-basket approach to poverty measurement in the 1960s. The cost of a basic nutritious diet, which became known as the Thrifty Food Plan, was estimated by the Department of Agriculture on the basis of eating habits of low-income families and the prices of the foods eaten. The proportion of income that low-income families spent on food was determined empirically through consumer expenditure surveys. The reciprocal of the proportion spent on food became the multiplier of food costs. The poverty line was estimated to be about three times the cost of the Thrifty Food Plan. The poverty line is not adjusted for rural-urban residence or for region of the country. It has been updated annually using the Consumer Price Index for the country as a whole. U.S. poverty lines are normally reported as annual income measures that vary by household size and age composition.[2] The annual income poverty cut-offs and the weekly cost of the Thrifty Food Plan for household sizes 1–4 in 2000 are shown in Table 5. For comparison purposes, they are also shown in dollars/person/day.

Canada does not define an official poverty line. *Statistics Canada* does, however, define several measures of low income.[3] One is a relative measure (the Low-Income Measure), defined as 50 percent of median income, discussed below. The Low-Income Cut-offs, most commonly used in Canada as an indicator of poverty, are defined in terms of the proportion of income that families spend on the basic needs of food, clothing, transportation, and shelter. Low income is defined as having twenty percentage points less income to spend on non-basic needs. In 2000, low income was defined at the level at which families spent 54.7 percent of their income on basic needs. Canada estimates low-income levels for rural areas and for urban places of various sizes. The low-income cut-offs for rural areas and for medium-size cities (population 100,000 to 499,000) are shown in Table 6, expressed as annual income in Canadian dollars, and in $U.S./person/day at PPP.

Canada has also estimated the cost of the market basket of basic needs, which it uses as an alternative approach to measuring low income. One component of this market basket is an estimate of the cost of food. These costs are estimated separately for provinces and different community sizes. The estimated annual cost of food for a four-person family in a medium-size city in Quebec is $6,064 CAD. In $U.S. at PPP, this is equivalent to $3.43/person/day—reassuringly similar to both the United States and the Mexican lines.

These official poverty lines express each country's effort to define absolute poverty in its own context. They are meant to represent what it costs in each country to lead a minimally decent life, and they are meant to be constant over time so that progress or failure in reducing absolute poverty can be gauged. We use them in this paper to examine the relationship of poverty and place within countries, primarily because much of the data we have for this purpose uses these lines.

Comparable Absolute Poverty
Although the national poverty lines have a logic and a use for measuring poverty within each country, to examine poverty in North America we need a poverty measure or measures that can be used across countries. We use two approaches: absolute and relative. As our absolute poverty measures, we use the Mexican food poverty and basic-needs poverty lines for urban areas expressed in $U.S. at PPP. As previously discussed (see Table 4), that line is $6.76 per person per day, or $9,870 annually for a family of four—a little more than half the U.S. official poverty line and about 40 percent of the Canadian low-income cut-off for a family of four.

We looked for an absolute poverty measure for North America to use across all three countries because we believe that purely relative measures, or even allegedly absolute measures defined for each country, can lead us to misleading conclusions about the incidence, character, and location of poverty in North America. It is simply not the case that poverty is an equally serious matter in Mexico and the United States, as the relative poverty measures could lead us to believe. A comparable absolute measure allows us to recognize this and explore its implications.

It is interesting to note that the estimated cost of the basic food basket, when expressed in dollars adjusted for purchasing power parity, is about the same in Mexico, the United States, and Canada—$3.40/person/day in urban Mexico, $3.70/person/day for a four-person family in the United States, and $3.40 for a four-person family in urban Quebec. This suggests to us that the components and cost of a basic nutritious diet are being estimated in about the same way in Mexico, the United States, and Canada, and that the PPP adjustments in fact work to make the costs of the basic basket equivalent.

The basic needs poverty line in Mexico is about twice the food poverty line, reflecting the fact that families need an amount about equivalent to what they spend on food to meet their needs for shelter, clothing, health, education, and transportation at a very basic level. In the United States, the official poverty line is about 3.5 times the food poverty line as expressed by the thrifty food plan. In Canada, the low-income cut-off is almost 5 times the estimated cost of a food basket. This suggests that families in the United States and Canada are perceived to need more in the way of non-food consumption to lead a decent life, but in our view that reflects a conception of needs that is more relative than absolute. The PPP adjustments take care of differences in the costs of the same basket of goods. Fewer persons per room, central heating and air-conditioning, functioning automobiles, and various household appliances may indeed be basic in the United States and Canada, but it is still worth asking how many people in the two countries are living on an income that allows them to purchase only what would be considered basic in Mexico. Using the Mexican poverty line as one measure of poverty across all three countries allows us to estimate how many people in North America as a whole live in the conditions of material scarcity that characterize the lives of much of the Mexican population.

Relative Poverty
We also, however, look at relative poverty. The logic of this approach is the perception that what it takes to lead a decent life is defined by the standards of living in the community. Money income is a means to an end of simple material survival, but another aspect of it is inclusion and participation in the mainstream society in which one lives. To be a full member of society requires being able to purchase goods and live in conditions that

characterize the normal life of the community. To gauge this factor, relative income is the appropriate measure.

We use as our relative poverty measure half the median income for the country in which one lives. This measure is used widely in countries included in the Organization for Economic Co-operation and Development (OECD), allowing us to estimate poverty and its characteristics using the data sets for Canada, Mexico, and the United States from the Luxembourg Income Studies.[4] Whether one's country, one's city, or one's state or region is the most relevant reference group for people as they define their own relationship to the society is, of course, debatable. Nevertheless, it does seem to be the case that when people in many countries are surveyed as to what it costs to live a decent life, they tend to report a figure close to half the median income. This has become a conventional poverty measure and we employ it here.

In the United States in 2000, the relative poverty line for a family of four was $32,690, or $22.39/person/day. In Canada in 2001, the relative poverty line for a family of four was $25,570 ($US at PPP), or $17.51/person/day. The same figures for Mexico in 2000 were $4,285 ($US at PPP) and $2.93, respectively.

Mexico is the only country whose relative poverty line is lower than its officially defined absolute poverty thresholds (see Table 2). This shows that differences in income distributions between Mexico and its NAFTA counterparts are much larger than differences in absolute poverty thresholds. In other words, Canada and the United States have defined lower absolute poverty lines relative to their income distributions than Mexico, as we will see in more detail later.

Income Distribution and Poverty Lines

Figure 2 illustrates the relationships between the income distributions and poverty incidence for Mexico and the United States in 2000. It shows the density curves of the distribution of monetary income (international dollars per day per person), that is, the share of population at each level of income represented on a logarithmic scale. The figure also plots vertical lines depicting the official poverty lines of these countries, as well as the food and basic-needs poverty thresholds. The areas under the curves represent the proportion of each population that is defined as poor by the various definitions.

The income distribution differs greatly between Mexico and the United States. The overlap is minimal and the United States shows a more prominent middle class. Average daily per capita income is estimated to be 6.5 times greater in the United States than in Mexico: $57.0 and $8.7, respectively (see

Table 7).[5] The median income ratio is even higher (8.7 times). Greater inequality in Mexico than in the United States is also illustrated by the distance between the mean and median incomes in each country.

In Mexico and the United States, food budget standards are calculated independently of income distribution data. The components of a basic nutritious diet are being defined in about the same way in Mexico and the United States. The U.S. official poverty line is much higher than the Mexican one, but it is not as high as income differences. Although income is more than 6 times higher in the United States than in Mexico, the U.S. official poverty threshold is only 2.3 times higher than the Mexican one. As seen in Table 7, the official poverty threshold in the United States is only 33 percent of the median income, while in Mexico it is 23 percent above median income.

These comparisons emphasize that there is no one "right" way to define poverty and that both absolute and relative measures are useful in understanding the circumstances in which people live in different countries. We are reluctant to conclude that the official Mexican poverty line is too high, since it was constructed to represent what is perceived as a decent standard of living. It is also not unreasonable to conclude that half the country is poor under this standard, and to aspire to raise the overall standard of living such that fewer Mexicans fall below this poverty line. At the same time, in thinking about how to target public resources to the most needy, it makes a good deal of sense to use a lower poverty line, either the food poverty line or the line defined by relative income.

Poverty Incidence Using Different Poverty Measures

Table 8 shows the incidence of poverty in 2000 in Canada, Mexico, and the United States using national poverty lines; the Mexican poverty lines applied to the United States as well as Mexico and vice versa; and the relative income poverty lines for the three countries. The Canadian data come from published *Statistics Canada* and *Luxembourg Income Survey* data tables. For Mexico and the United States, we estimated poverty rates from household survey data.

The estimates are sensitive not only to the choice of poverty lines but also to the treatment of households of different sizes and to the quality of the underlying survey data. In the United States, income appears to be underreported at both the very high end, which is irrelevant to poverty rates, and at the very low end, which may lead to overestimates of poverty as measured by the Mexican lines (Weinberg 2004). In Mexico, problems of underreporting seem to be more widespread and may lead to overestimates of poverty, however measured (Székely, Lustig, Cumpa, and Mejía 2000). The seriousness of this problem can be grasped by comparing the estimate of per capita income estimated from survey data in Figure 2 ($21,587 and $2,772 for Mexico and the United States, respectively) and per capita GDP for the same year ($37,600 and $9,300 for Mexico and the United States, respectively).[6] For the United States, the ratio of the estimates is about .58, with most of the discrepancy caused by categories of income that are included in GDP but not in household income measured by the survey, and much of the rest caused by underreporting by the rich. In Mexico, the ratio is about .33. If household income in the bottom half of the income distribution is underestimated by a substantial amount, then poverty rates could be overestimated by an analogous amount.

The lack of adjustments for household size in Mexico is another way in which the estimates for the three countries are not comparable, with poverty in Mexico being relatively overestimated. Household sizes in Mexico are quite large, and most poverty scholars agree that there are indeed some economies of scale in household spending. These are taken into account in the poverty measures of the United States and Canada but not in Mexico, where they are probably more important.

Therefore we should be very cautious about drawing conclusions from the comparisons; nonetheless, they are quite striking. With a poverty rate of 11.3 percent, the United States has the lowest official incidence of poverty in North America in 2000, followed by Canada with 14.6 percent of its population living below its officially defined poverty line. In Mexico, about one of every two inhabitants is officially considered poor. The deprived economic panorama of Mexico does not change with our comparable poverty measures. Mexico has by far the highest level of absolute poverty using our comparable measure. Even if poverty in Mexico is overestimated by a factor of two, the difference between Mexico and the other two countries is very large.

When the official U.S. poverty line is used as the measure of poverty in the three countries, Mexico, as would be expected, is shown to have an extremely high incidence of poverty. Interestingly, Canada has a lower poverty rate than the United States under the common definition of poverty, even though Canada has lower per capita income. This comparison shows the importance of income inequality in determining poverty: Canada's more equal income distribution yields a lower poverty rate. Canada also has an incidence of relative poverty that is well below that of either Mexico or the United States, again reflecting its greater equality of income. About one of every four Mexicans can be classified as poor using relative standards of poverty, a figure closer to food poverty rates than to basic-needs poverty rates in the country.

Official Poverty Rates

Given the methodological complexities of adopting one standard of poverty for all countries, the last part of this section relies on the official poverty statistics of each county to paint a picture of the evolution of poverty rates and the number of poor people in North America. Table 9 displays recent trends in poverty rates and the number of poor people in Canada, Mexico, and the United States.

As we observe, the overall trend in poverty rates was towards a decline in all countries between 1992 and 2006. The three NAFTA partners had lower levels of poverty in 2005 or 2006 than in 1992. However, unlike the United States, Mexico and Canada suffered from an upsurge of poverty rates in 1996. The situation was particularly shocking for Mexico, which experienced a severe financial crisis in 1995. After peaking during the financial crisis, poverty rates began a systematic decline in Mexico, as reflected in the data. Poverty, which dipped to 69 percent of the population in 1996, has fallen to 43 percent in 2006, its lowest point since 1992. The poverty rate in Canada declined from 16 to 11 percent from 1996 to 2005. In the United States, poor people accounted for 15 percent of the population in 1992 and 12 percent by 2006.

Even when the incidence of poverty has been declining in North America, the population living in conditions of material scarcity has not varied in a significant way. In 1992, 88 million people were identified as poor by the three governments. By the middle of the current decade, the number had increased by one million, in 2005, and declined to 85 million in 2006 (using 2005 figures for Canada) as a result of a significant reduction in the number of poor people in Mexico.

In general, between 85 and 90 million poor people lived in North America circa 2006. The poverty rate of Mexicans almost quadruples that of the United States, but Americans made up 41 percent of NAFTA's poor population in 2005. Meanwhile, Mexicans account for 55 percent of the poor in the NAFTA region.

The poverty rates for the three countries are a striking illustration of the relationship, documented in many cross-country studies, between the poverty rate, the overall level of development as measured by per capita income, and the extent of inequality. They surely suggest the importance of an overall development strategy as key to poverty reduction in Mexico.

Poverty and Place within Countries

If the level of overall economic development is crucial, as suggested by the differences in poverty incidence and their relationship to overall levels and growth rates of GDP in Mexico, the United States, and Canada, then we might expect poverty within countries to be related to the overall levels of development of states or provinces. The extent to which this relationship holds, or does not hold, may help us to understand the phenomenon of poverty within each country, and in addition, may help us to understand the dramatic differences between countries.

Poverty and Place in the United States

Poverty rates in the United States vary by state, ranging in 1999 from about 20 percent in Mississippi, Louisiana, and Washington, D.C. to less than 8 percent in Connecticut, New Hampshire, and Minnesota. The variation in poverty rates is related to the overall level of per capita income in the states. Figure 3 shows that relationship.[7]

The relationship is by no means perfect: Some states, like Iowa, Nebraska, and Utah, have both relatively low per capita income and low poverty rates; and other states, most notably the District of Columbia but also California and New York, have both high per capita income and high poverty rates—in the case of D.C., very high indeed. Nonetheless, the basic relationship between the level of development and poverty rates is relatively robust.

We need to ask, though, how important is this relationship for explaining patterns of poverty in the United States and for guiding policy. Should we conclude, as development economists do when they look at poverty and economic development across countries, that per capita income differences among states or other political entities are essentially the whole story of poverty? Should we conclude, as they do, that attention to development would solve poverty problems? Three ways of approaching the problem suggest that this conclusion would not be correct.

A first approach is to look at the relationship between the number of poor in a state and its per capita income. The largest number of poor in any state is found in California, which ranks 14/51 in per capita income. Half the poor in the United States are found in eight states: California, Texas, New York, Florida, Pennsylvania, Illinois, Ohio, and Georgia. With the exception of Texas, which ranks 33rd in per capita income, all of these states are in the top half of the per capita income distribution, indeed six of the eight are in the top quarter of the per capita income distribution. This finding reflects a high level of inequality and thus relatively high poverty rates in rich states like New York and California. Moreover, many of the richer states are quite large, so that even with average or below poverty rates—as in Illinois and Michigan—they are home to large numbers of poor people.

Another way of looking at these relationships is to ask what proportion of the poor live in poor states as defined by per capita income. For this calculation, we ranked the states by per capita income, and then examined the group of low-income states whose cumulative population numbers came to about a quarter of the country. In the United States, this procedure identified twenty states, ranging from Mississippi with a per capita income of $15,853 to Iowa with a per capita income of $19,674[8] (the U.S. average in 2000 was $21,587). The group includes states in the Deep South but also Maine; and some mountain, plains, and mid-western states such as the Dakotas and New Mexico. These twenty U.S. states contained 24 percent of the population and 29 percent of the poor. In other words, the percentage of the poor living in poor states is not much higher than the overall percentage of the population (or of the non-poor) living in those states. It is also worth noting that while 29 percent of the U.S. poor live in these poor states, 71 percent do not.

A third approach is to examine two important historical divisions in income and poverty and ask what has happened to them over time: the one between rural and urban areas, and the one between the south and the rest of the country.

In 1959, the first year that the Census Bureau reported poverty data, the poverty rate for rural areas was 33 percent, compared to an overall national poverty rate of 22 percent. Residents of rural areas made up 37 percent of the population and 55 percent of the poor. By 2003, the poverty rate for rural areas was 14 percent, compared to an overall national rate of 12 percent. Eighteen percent of the population and 21 percent of the poor lived in rural areas.

The seventeen states of the south have historically been more rural and poorer than the rest of the country.[9] In 1959, the poverty rate in the south (35.4 percent) was more than half again the poverty rate in the nation as a whole (22.4 percent). Thirty-one percent of the population and 48 percent of the poor lived in the south. In 2003, the poverty rate in the south was closer to that of the nation: 15.3 percent in the south compared to 11.1 percent in the nation, and 41 percent of the poor lived in the south compared to 36 percent of the population.

This leveling trend in poverty rates reflects urbanization, convergence between rural and urban areas, and convergence between south and north in per capita income, a process which can be documented for a longer period than poverty rates. In 1940, per capita income in the south was about 68 percent of income in the country as a whole; in 1960, it was 77 percent; and in 2000 per capita income in the south was 91 percent of income in the country as a whole. The process by which the southern economy became integrated into the national economy may offer interesting insights into the economic futures of Mexico and the United States, a topic which we hope to develop in later essays.

In explaining contemporary poverty in the United States, in short, we do not get very far with an emphasis on variations in the levels of development among states. Interestingly, variations among metropolitan areas in overall level of development do not explain very much either.[10] Some isolated very poor areas persist, most notably Native American reservations, and some very poor areas along the Mexican border. Nevertheless, in the contemporary United States, poverty is more strongly related to household composition and to race and ethnicity than it is to geography.

Poverty and Place in Mexico
The story of poverty and place in Mexico is somewhat different. As in the United States, poverty rates vary by state, with the low-income states of the south having the highest poverty rates. Figure 4 shows the relationship between food poverty rates and per capita income by state. (Since basic-needs poverty is so widespread, affecting more than half of the population, we expect that it would be widely distributed geographically.) The more stringent conception of poverty is more likely to be driven by overall levels of development.

In Mexico, however, unlike in the United States, numbers of poor are also related to per capita income by states. The largest numbers of poor in Mexico live in Veracruz, which ranks 26/32 in per capita income. The next largest number is in Chiapas, which ranks second last in per capita income. Following the same procedures as for the United States, we ranked Mexican states by per capita income and identified seven low-income states, each with per capita income ranging from $1,382 in Oaxaca to $1,855 in Guerrero.[11] (Here the income data are from household surveys). Most though not all of these states are in the south. They are home to 23 percent of the Mexican population and 38 percent of the food poor.

In Mexico, then, in contrast to the United States, the poor are quite concentrated geographically in states with low levels of economic development, giving credence to the argument that local development plus migration is an important strategy for addressing poverty. At the same time, it is worth noting that while 38 percent of the very poor live in the eight poorest states, 62 percent of the poor do not. The relationship between number of poor and per capita income is by no means perfect. For example, the third largest numbers of poor are in the state of Mexico, which ranks 18/32 in per capita income and has a moderate poverty rate, but is also the most populous state. Thus in Mexico, as in the United States, large numbers of the poor live in relatively rich states. The geographical concentration of the poor is likely to decrease over time, as rural to urban and south to north migration continues. Thus it is important for Mexico to focus on urban poverty and poverty that exists alongside overall wealth, as well as on the low development levels of the southern states.

Poverty and Place in Canada

Canada presents a somewhat different story, as Figure 5 illustrates. The province with the highest GDP per capita, Alberta (with considerable oil income), has a poverty rate that is not much different from much less wealthy provinces. Alberta aside, there appears to be rather little relationship between poverty rates and overall development level.

Canada is composed of eleven provinces plus the Yukon, the Northwest Territories, and Nunavut. Two provinces, Ontario and Quebec, contain more than half the population. The four poorest provinces, Prince Edward Island, New Brunswick, Nova Scotia, and Manitoba contain only 10 percent of the population and ten percent of the poor (the poverty measure is the official Canadian low-income cut-off). Quebec is the next poorest; adding it to the list raises the percent of the population to 34 and the percent of the poor to 39. Alberta enjoys great oil wealth, as do the very sparsely populated northern territories. This means that the relationship of poverty and place in Canada is more difficult to summarize and less interesting than in the United States and Mexico.

Assessing Poverty and Place within Countries

In summary, within the countries of North America, place is not an important determinant of poverty in the United States or Canada, but is a moderate determinant in Mexico, where the lower level of development in the southern states is associated with much higher poverty rates and a concentration of the poor. In some ways, the south of Mexico looks similar to the southern U.S. states before the process of urbanization and integration into the national economy began. Moreover, there are some indications in Mexico that migration from rural to urban areas and from south to north may be blurring some of the differences even there.

However, when we look at the countries within North America, the strength of the relationship between poverty and place is stunning. Table 8 shows poverty rates using a variety of ways of defining poverty.

Obviously, one can argue about the appropriate definition of poverty for each country and for the region. However, putting aside that discussion, it is possible to specify an income cut-off expressed in a common purchasing-power-parity adjusted currency, and to see how many people in each country and in the region as a whole fall below that cut-off. Using the data in table 8 and population figures, we can calculate that between 55 and 75 percent of those who fall below the poverty lines live in Mexico.

This is not surprising, given the differences in per capita GDP that we documented in Table 1 and Figure 1. Nevertheless, the disparities ought to be shocking, and the patterns of convergence or more accurately lack thereof shown in Figure 1 ought to be extremely disturbing. As Figure 1 shows, since the early 1980s, per capita GDP in the United States and Mexico has actually diverged rather than converged.

Hispanic Communities
Is this disparity about being Mexican or about living in Mexico? About 13 percent of the U.S. population identified itself to census takers as Hispanic. About two-thirds of that number, or about 9 percent of the total, identified themselves as Hispanic and of Mexican origin. We have some information that allows us to compare this Mexican American population with the larger U.S. population, and to ask whether poverty and low income are associated more with being Mexican or living in Mexico.

We first look at poverty rates. In 1999, the U.S. poverty rate was 11.9 percent.[12] For comparison, we can look at the poverty rate for Mexican Americans, which was 24.1 percent. The poverty rate in the border states of Arizona, California, New Mexico, and Texas was 14.3 percent. However, the poverty rate for the Texas border communities with high proportion (75+) of Hispanics (McAllen, Brownsville, Laredo, and El Paso) was 30.2 percent.[13]

The poverty rate for Hispanics of Mexican origin in the United States is about twice the overall U.S. poverty rate, and higher than that in the border communities. A poverty rate of 30 percent, using the U.S. official poverty line, is shamefully high for a group within U.S. borders. However, our best estimate of what the poverty rate in Mexico would be if we used the U.S. poverty line as the poverty definition was 82 percent. Using the much lower Mexican basic-needs poverty line, the poverty rate in Mexico was 60 percent, more than twice the poverty rate for Mexican communities in the United States with their poverty measured by the U.S. line.

We can also make comparisons across the border by looking at per capita household income, adjusted for purchasing power parity. These suggestive numbers come from household survey data in the United States and Mexico. They are not adjusted for underreporting, which appears to be quite a serious problem in Mexico.

These numbers (not presented here) suggest that per capita income of Hispanics in the United States is four times that of Mexicans, and 2.8 times that of Mexicans in the relatively rich Mexican states on the U.S. border. Even if the Mexican income data is underreported by a factor of two, it appears that the per capita income of the average Hispanic in the United States is twice that of the average Mexican and half again as much as the average Mexican in the border states. Thus the data strongly reinforce the notion that poverty is related to average per capita income, and that income is strongly influenced by the presence of the Rio Grande, or by the economic, social, and political features unique to one or the other side of the river.

Poverty and People

In the United States and Canada, as we have shown, poverty is not strongly related to place. What, then, are other characteristics of the poor that might help us understand and explain poverty? One strong relationship is with education, explored in other chapters; others concern race and ethnicity and family and household composition.

Household Composition

Table 10 shows the distribution of the population in Mexico and the United States by five household types: elderly in all household arrangements; non-elderly unrelated individuals (people living alone or with other than relatives); non-elderly people, including children, in married-couple families; non-elderly people, including children, in female-headed families; and people in other household arrangements. The table also shows poverty rates for each group. For Mexico, the poverty line used to estimate poverty is the official food poverty line. For the United States, the poverty definition is the official census bureau market-basket definition.[14]

Family and household composition are clearly very different in the United States and Mexico. Poverty rates are also very different for household composition types in the two countries. The United States has a larger population of the elderly, a much larger number of people living alone or with non-relatives, and slightly more female-headed families. There seems to be a general tendency in the United States for people to form independent households when they can afford, or almost afford, to do so. Elderly couples and single elderly men and women are much more likely to live alone than with family. Young adults move out of their parents' households and live independently when they are economically independent, or close to being so. Young women, especially African American women, are more likely than in the past to have children and set up their own households when either their own earnings or transfer payments from the government allow them to do so; this tendency is exacerbated when the economic fortunes of the young men they might marry are precarious. Because of these household formation trends, the U.S. average household size is very small with a diversity of household types as illustrated in the tables. This contrasts with household composition in Mexico, where a large majority of the population lives in married-couple households, and where average household size is considerably larger.

Many of the independent, non-marital households in the United States are also economically vulnerable, as shown by the relatively high poverty rates for unrelated individuals, and especially for those in female-headed families. Women and their children living in female-headed households now make up about a third of the poor in the United States. The women who head these households tend to have low education levels and earning power. In most cases they are the only adult earners in their families, while most married-couple families have two adult wage earners. The prevalence and poverty of female-headed families in the United States is disturbingly related to race.[15]

In Mexico, in striking contrast to the United States, poverty rates for people living in female-headed families are lower than poverty rates for people in married-couple families, and poverty rates for unrelated individuals are much lower that those for other household types. Our hypothesis is that in that country independent households are formed only when those forming such households are relatively secure economically. At present, it seems that small numbers are making the decision that living independently is possible, or worth the increased economic vulnerability of living away from family. We suggest, however, that this is a trend that Mexico will need to watch, in order to avoid the situation in the United States, where female-headed families are an especially impoverished and vulnerable group.

Race, Ethnicity, and Poverty in the United States
Another important factor influencing U.S. poverty has to do with race and ethnicity. Poverty rates vary quite dramatically by race, and range from

8 percent for whites to 24 percent for African Americans. The largest difference in this area is that a much higher proportion of Blacks live in female-headed families with children. At the same time, poverty rates for Blacks and Hispanics are higher than poverty rates for non-Hispanic Whites and Asians within all family structure groups. (For details on these findings, see Tables 10 and 11.)

Research that looks for explanations for racial differences in poverty rates and family formation, and for the large and growing proportions of unrelated individual and female-headed households, has not generated particularly satisfying results. Differences in levels of education seem to explain much of the poverty gap between Hispanics (many of whom are recent immigrants) and Whites, but little of the poverty gap between African Americans and Whites. Many scholars believe that the legacy of racial stigma in the United States that dates from slavery persists in stereotyping and discrimination. Implicit discrimination and what Glenn Loury (2002) calls discrimination in contact—in neighborhoods, friendships, marriage, and other associations—remains common, even though overt discrimination has decreased since the passage of civil rights laws in the 1960s. Racial segregation may exacerbate the differences between communities in norms of behavior, many of which can be explained by lingering racial stigma in other areas.

Ethnicity and Poverty in Mexico

In Mexico, the most important racial/ethnic difference (at least the most important that we can document) is between indigenous people, who make up about nine percent of the total, and the rest of the population. Table 12 gives the basic data.

As with racial differences in the United States, the disparities in poverty rates are striking, with the indigenous poverty rate (53 percent) two and a half times that for the general population (27 percent). Unlike the United States, however, household composition differences do not explain the differences. The incidence of poverty among indigenous people must be understood in the context of the geographical and social inequality in Mexico. On the one hand, most of the indigenous population lives in southern Mexico. Only four Mexican states (Oaxaca, Chiapas, Yucatán, and Veracruz, which are among the poorest in Mexico) accounted for one of every two indigenous persons in 2000. On the other hand, indigenous people in Mexico are more economically vulnerable because they get less and worse education than an average Mexican citizen, not to mention their being exposed to higher mortality rates.

Concluding Remarks

Obviously many other aspects of poverty and its correlates in North America could be productively explored. However, some tentative conclusions can be drawn from what we have presented here.

- We believe our exploration of poverty measures for North America illustrates the possibility of using common conceptualizations to describe poverty across very different countries.

- Overall levels of economic development and inequality and patterns of economic growth go a long way toward explaining the large differences in poverty rates between Mexico and the other countries of North America. Accelerated economic development in Mexico is crucial to poverty alleviation. It is also important, though, that economic development be aimed at the poor, in the sense of generating jobs and income for the lower quintiles. Mexico, which is already highly unequal in its income distribution, must pay particular attention to this issue.

- Poverty is much more strongly related to place within Mexico than within the United States or Canada. The low-income southern states in Mexico have much higher poverty rates than the rest of the country and contain a large proportion of the country's poor. At the same time, the majority of the poor, even in Mexico, do not live in the lowest-income states. Thus, although place-specific development strategies are important in Mexico, internal migration is likely to result, as it has in the other two countries, in convergence of poverty rates. For the future, poverty alleviation strategies must also be concerned with the poor who live in urban areas and with poverty in the midst of relative prosperity.

- Poverty is related very strongly to race and ethnicity in the United States and to indigenous status in Mexico. Racial stigma and racial segregation continue to affect the African American population, with seriously harmful results. In Mexico, the indigenous population is isolated by geography, language, and education level, presenting a serious challenge for poverty alleviation efforts. Both countries need to be vigorous in combating discrimination and in making opportunities available for the disadvantaged.

The policy implications of these findings are the material of other chapters in this volume. Our findings on poverty and place motivate the discussions of development in Chapters 2, 3 and 4. To the extent poverty is not explained by place, we set the stage for the discussion of education in chapters 5 and 6 and of safety nets in Chapters 7 and 8.

Tables and Figures

Table 1. Canada, Mexico, and the United States at a Glance, 2007

	Canada	Mexico	U.S.
Population (millions)[1]	32.9	106.5	302.2
Percent Urban Population[1]	81	75	79
Gross Domestic Income in Purchasing Power Parity Per Capita, 2006 (US$)[2]	$35,900	$11,600	$44,000
Life Expectancy at Birth[1]	80	75	78
Infant Deaths per 1,000 Live Births[1]	5.3	21.0	6.5
Educational Attainment of Population 25–64 years old: % Upper Secondary or Higher, 2004[2]	84.3	22.6	87.9

Sources:
[1] Statistics of the Population Reference Bureau.
[2] Statistics of the Organisation for Economic Co-operation and Development.

Table 2. Compound Annual Growth of Real per capita Income in Canada, Mexico, and the United States, 1953–2003

	Canada	Mexico	U.S.
1953–2003	2.1%	2.1%	2.1%
1973–2003	1.9%	1.1%	1.9%
1993–2003	2.8%	1.1%	2.3%

Source: Information and authors' calculations based on Alan Heston, Robert Summers and Bettina Aten, Penn World Table Version 6.2, Center for International Comparisons of Production, Income and Prices at the University of Pennsylvania, September 2006.

Table 3. Gini Coefficients. Canada, Mexico, and the United States, 1986–2004

Canada		Mexico		U.S.	
1987	0.283	1989	0.466	1986	0.335
1991	0.281	1992	0.485	1991	0.338
1994	0.284	1994	0.496	1994	0.355
1998	0.311	1998	0.494	1997	0.372
2000	0.315	2000	0.491	2000	0.368
		2002	0.471	2004	0.372

Source: Statistics of the Luxembourg Income Study.

Table 4. Poverty Lines for Mexico in $US Adjusted for Purchasing Power Parity, per Person per Day, 2000

	Rural	Urban
Food	$2.49	$3.38
Health and Education	$3.06	$4.00
All Basic Needs	$4.55	$6.76

Source: Authors' calculations using data from Cortes, et al. (2002).

Table 5. U.S. Thrifty Food Plan and Poverty Line, 2000

Household size	Thrifty Food Plan		Poverty Line	
	weekly	per person per day	annual	per person per day
1	$32.88 [1]	$4.70	$87,942 [2]	$24.09
2	$66.33 [3]	$4.74	$11,239	$15.40
3	$76.34 [4]	$3.64	$13,738	$12.55
4	$97.3 [5]	$3.48	$17,603	$12.06
Average		$3.7 [6]		$13.8 [6]

Source: Thrifty Food Plan reported by the U.S. Department of Agriculture. Poverty lines reported by the U.S. Census Bureau.

[1] Average of adult male and adult female plus 20 percent adjustment for single person household.

[2] The Census Bureau reports poverty thresholds by household size adjusted for the age of the head (elderly or not) and for the number of children in the family. These poverty lines are the averages for household size over age-composition categories.

[3] Adult male plus adult female plus 10 percent adjustment for household size.

[4] Adult female plus two children, ages 3–5 and 9–11, plus 5 percent adjustment for household size.

[5] Adult male plus adult female plus two children, ages 3–5 and 9–11. The TFP is calculated on the base of a family of four, so the adjustments for other household sizes are meant to make them equivalent.

[6] Average calculated using the household composition captured by the Current Population Survey (March Supplement, 2000).

Table 6. Canada Low Income Cut-Offs, 2000

Household size	Cities 100–400,000		Rural areas	
	Annual $C	per person per day	Annual $C	per person per day
1	$15,757	$35.68	$12,696	$28.75
2	$19,697	$22.30	$15,870	$17.97
3	$24,497	$18.49	$19,738	$14.90
4	$29,653	$16.79	$23,892	$13.52

Source: *Statistics Canada*.

Table 7. Population Distribution of Monetary Household Income and Poverty Thresholds per Person per Day, Mexico and United States, 2000

	Mexico (US@PPP)	U.S.
Mean	$8.7	$57.0
Median	$4.8	$41.8
50% Median	$2.4	$20.9
Official Poverty Threshold (OPT)[1]	$5.9	$13.8
OPT % of Median	123%	33%

Sources: Encuesta Nacional de Ingreso y Gasto de los Hogares (ENIGH-2000) and Current Population Survey (CPS March Supplement 2000).

[1] Mexico is a national weighted average using the rural-urban population composition captured by ENIGH 2000. The U.S. is a national weighted average taking into account the household composition captured by CPS 2000.

Table 8. Incidence of Poverty Using Different Poverty Measures; Canada, Mexico, and United States, 2000

	Canada	Mexico	U.S.
Official poverty each country[1]	14.6%	53.7%	11.3%
Mexico food poverty line[2]	NA	37.1%	1.8%
Mexico basic needs poverty line[2]	NA	66.8%	3.1%
U.S. official poverty line[3]	6.9%	85.2%	11.3%
Canada LICOs[4]	14.7%	NA	NA
Relative poverty: 50% of median[5]	12.8%	21.6%	17.0%

[1] Official Statistics Canada, Mexico, and U.S., 2000. Canada and U.S. poverty statistics are based on monetary income. Mexico takes also into consideration non-monetary income.

[2] Mexican urban poverty thresholds applied to Mexico (Encuesta Nacional de Ingreso y Gasto de los Hogares, 2000) and the United States (Current Population Survey, March Supplement, 2000). Poverty rates were calculated comparing poverty lines with household monetary income.

[3] U.S. poverty thresholds applied to Canada (Statistics of the Luxembourg Income Study) and Mexico (author's calculations using the Encuesta Nacional de Ingreso y Gasto de los Hogares, 2000). Mexican poverty rate was calculated comparing poverty lines with household monetary income.

[4] *Statistics Canada.*

[5] Statistics of the Luxembourg Income Study.

Table 9. Poverty Rates and Number of Poor People According to Official Statistics in Canada, Mexico, and the United States, 1992–2006

	Poverty Rates			Poor People (millions)		
	Canada[1]	Mexico[2]	U.S.[3]	Canada[1]	Mexico[2]	U.S.[3]
1992	13.3	53.1	14.8	3.7	46.1	38.0
1994	13.7	52.4	14.5	3.9	47.0	38.1
1996	15.7	69.0	13.7	4.6	64.0	36.5
1998	13.7	63.7	12.7	4.0	60.7	34.5
2000	12.5	53.6	11.3	3.7	52.7	31.6
2002	11.6	50.0	12.1	3.5	50.4	34.6
2004	11.4	47.2	12.7	3.5	48.6	37.0
2005	10.8	47.0	12.6	3.4	48.9	37.0
2006		42.6	12.3		44.7	36.5

Sources:
[1] Statistics Canada
[2] Consejo Nacional de Evaluacion de la Politica Publica de Desarrollo Social.
[3] U.S. Census Bureau
Note: Canada and U.S. poverty statistics are based on monetary income. Mexico takes also into consideration non-monetary income.

Table 10. Household Composition and Poverty: United States and Mexico, 2000

	Mexico[1]		United States[2]	
	Population Distribution	Poverty Rate	Population Distribution	Poverty Rate
Elderly	5.4%	21.9%	12.0%	10.2%
Non-elderly unrelated individuals	1.3%	5.3%	12.5%	18.3%
Non-elderly in married couple families	78.4%	25.6%	58.5%	5.8%
Non-elderly in female headed families	11.9%	19.0%	12.6%	29.2%
Other	3.0%	18.4%	4.4%	15.5%
Total	100.0%	24.1%	100.0%	11.3%

[1] Author's calculations based on Mexican Population Census 2000 and poverty rates estimated by Cortés, Rodríguez and Zenteno (2004).
[2] Online published data from the U.S. Census Bureau.

Table 11. Race, Household Composition, and Poverty in the United States, 2003

	Non-Hispanic White	Black	Asian	Hispanic
Elderly				
Percent of group	14.6%	7.8%	8.3%	5.2%
Poverty rate	8.0%	23.5%	14.2%	19.5%
Non-elderly unrelated individuals and sub-families				
Percent of group	13.3%	14.1%	10.9%	10.8%
Poverty rate	18.3%	28.9%	24.3%	28.5%
Non-elderly persons in married-couple families				
Percent of group	61.6%	37.1%	67.1%	59.0%
Poverty rate	3.8%	8.3%	7.7%	17.0%
Non-elderly persons in male-headed families, no spouse				
Percent of group	3.3%	6.0%	5.1%	7.2%
Poverty rate	9.9%	23.9%	12.1%	18.6%
Non-elderly persons in female-headed families, no spouse				
Percent of group	8.8%	35.0%	8.6%	17.8%
Poverty rate	22.3%	39.6%	25.9%	39.3%
Overall poverty rate	8.2%	24.3%	11.8%	22.5%
Percent of group in population	62.8%	13.1%	4.5%	14.1%

Source: Online published data from U.S. Census Bureau.

Table 12. Ethnicity, Household Composition, and Food Poverty in Mexico, 2000

	Non-Indigenous	Indigenous
Elderly		
Percent of group	8.0%	7.4%
Poverty rate	32.3%	56.9%
Non-elderly unrelated individuals and sub-families		
Percent of group	1.1%	0.7%
Poverty rate	18.6%	30.2%
Non-elderly persons in married-couple families		
Percent of group	72.9%	79.2%
Poverty rate	19.5%	52.8%
Non-elderly persons in male-headed families, no spouse		
Percent of group	3.6%	3.9%
Poverty rate	19.5%	47.7%
Non-elderly persons in female-headed families, no spouse		
Percent of group	14.3%	8.9%
Poverty rate	23.3%	51.7%
Overall poverty rate	20.7%	52.5%
Percent of group in population	91.0%	9.0%

Source: Author's calculations based on Mexican Population Census 2000 and poverty rates estimated by Cortés, Rodríguez and Zenteno (2004).

Figure 1. Real Gross Domestic Product Per Capita in 1996 Constant Prices and U.S.-Canada and U.S.-Mexico Income Ratios, 1950–2004

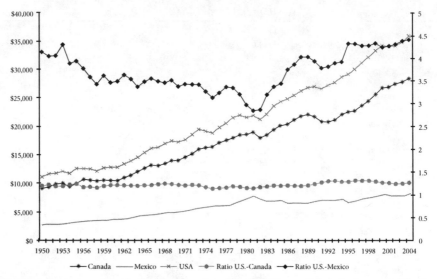

Source: Information and author's calculations based on Alan Heston, Robert Summers, and Bettina Aten, Penn World Table Version 6.2, Center for International Comparisons of Production, Income, and Prices at the University of Pennsylvania, September 2006.

Figure 2. Monetary Income Distribution in Mexico and the United States, 2000

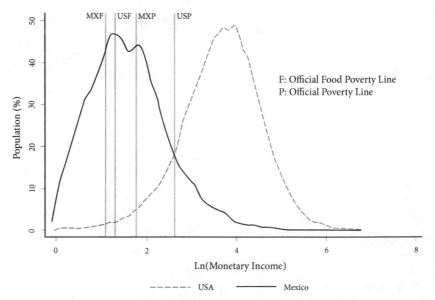

F: Official Food Poverty Line
P: Official Poverty Line

Source: Authors' calculations using ENIGH 2000 and CPS March Supplement 2001.

Figure 3. Poverty Rate by Income per capita, U.S. States

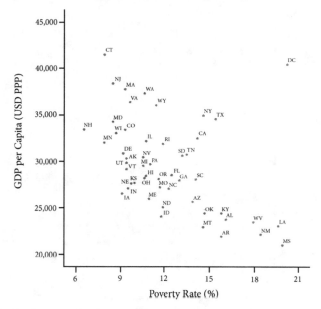

Source: Author's calculations based on data from the 2000 U.S. Census.

Figure 4. Poverty Rate by Income per capita, Mexican States

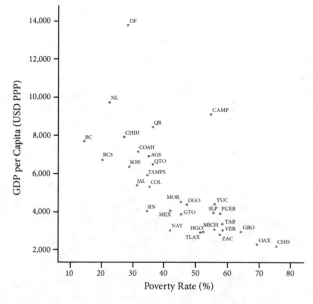

Source: Author's calculations based on Mexican Population Census 2000 and poverty rates estimated by Cortés, Rodríguez, and Zenteno (2004).

Figure 5. Poverty Rate by Income per capita, Canadian Provinces

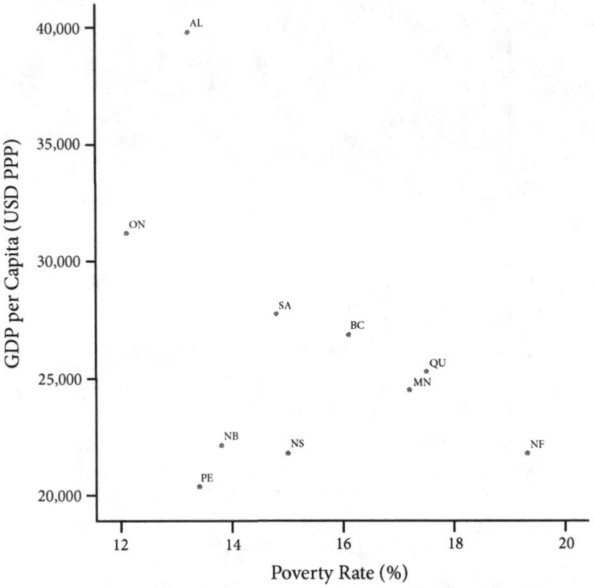

Source: Author's calculations based on 1999 data from *Statistics Canada* and the Canadian Council on Social Development.

Notes

1   The scale of the graph and the PPP comparison in Figure 1 do not clearly display the decline in per capita income in 1995.

2   An explanation of how the United States measures poverty can be found at http://www.census.gov/hhes/poverty/povdef.html. Poverty thresholds for 2000 can be found at http://pubdb3.census.gov/macro/032001/pov/new21_000.htm. The estimated cost of the Thrift Food Plan in 2000 can be found at http://www.usda.gov/cnpp/FoodPlans/Updates/foodnov00.pdf.

3   Canada's low-income guidelines are described at http://www.statcan.ca/cgi-bin/downpub/listpub.cgi?catno=75F0002MIE2004002.

4   See http://www.lisproject.org

5   Income figures come from household surveys in both countries. Numbers do not add to income statistics calculated using GDP data. The underreporting of income in household surveys seems to be worse in the case of Mexico.

6   Data not presented in any table here.

7   All the tables and graphs in this section are constructed from U.S. Census data on income and poverty rates by states, available on the census website. http://factfinder.census.gov/servlet/GCTTable?_bm=y&-geo_id=01000

US&-_box_head_nbr=GCT-P14&-ds_name=DEC_2000_SF3_U&-
_lang=en&-format=US-9&-_sse=on

8 The twenty states, in increasing order of per capita income, are Mississippi,
   West Virginia, Arkansas, Louisiana, Montana, New Mexico, South Dakota,
   Oklahoma, North Dakota, Idaho, Kentucky, Utah, Alabama, South Carolina,
   Wyoming, Tennessee, Maine, Nebraska, Texas, and Iowa.

9 South Atlantic states are Delaware, District of Columbia, Florida, Georgia,
   Maryland, North Carolina, South Carolina, Virginia and West Virginia; East
   South Central states are Alabama, Kentucky, Mississippi and Tennessee; West
   South Central states are Arkansas, Louisiana, Oklahoma and Texas.

10 Following the same procedure as for states, we can sort metropolitan areas by
   per capita income in 1999. We identified 177 metropolitan areas, from
   McAllen TX with a per capita income of $9,899 to Knoxville TN with a per
   capita income of $20,538. These poor metropolitan areas include 25% of the
   metropolitan population and 31% of the metropolitan poor. Data from the
   Census: http://factfinder.census.gov/servlet/GCTTable?_bm=y&-geo_id=
   &-ds_name=DEC_2000_SF3_U&-_caller=geoselect&-_lang=en&-redoLog=
   false&-format=US-10&-mt_name=DEC_2000_SF3_U_GCTP14_US9

11 The eight states, in increasing order of per capita income, are Chiapas, Oax
   aca, Zacatecas, Tlaxcala, Michoacán, Guerrero, Veracruz, and Nayarit.

12 This number, the numbers of Mexican-Americans, and the selected states are
   from the CPS: http://www.census.gov/population/socdemo/hispanic/
   ppl-165/tab14–2.pdf.

13 This number is not completely comparable to the others, since it comes from
   the Census rather than the CPS. Poverty rates collected by the Census tend to
   be higher than those collected by the CPS, since the CPS appears to do a better job of collecting income information. The U.S. poverty rate in 1999, as
   calculated from Census data, was 12.4%. Data reference in footnote 7, above.

14 U.S. data from detailed online tables of the CPS: http://pubdb3.census.gov/
   macro/032001/pov/new01_000.htm. We also looked at the data using other
   poverty definitions. The basic relationships among family types remain the
   same.

15 A good collection of essays on family structure in America is Moynihan et al.,
   2004.

References

Bourguignon, François. 2004. "The Poverty-Growth-Inequality Triangle." Paper
   presented at the Indian Council for Research on International Economic Relations. New Delhi.

Cortés, F. H. Rodríguez, and R. Zenteno. 2004. "Estimaciones de pobreza a nivel
   estatal y municipal en México 2000." Unpublished manuscript.

Datt, G. and M. Ravallion. 1992. "Growth and Redistribution Components of Changes in Poverty Measures: A Decomposition with Applications to Brazil and India in the 1980's." *Journal of Development Economics*, 38(2): 275–295.

Deaton, Angus. 2003. "Measuring Poverty." Princeton University. Unpublished manuscript.

Foster, James. 1998. "Absolute versus Relative Poverty." *The American Economic Review*, 88(2): 335–341.

Hernández Laos, Enrique. 2003. "Distribución del ingreso y pobreza," in *La situación del trabajo en México*, de la Garza, Enrique and Carlos Salas (ed.), pp. 97–127. Mexico City: IET-UAM-Plaza Valdez.

Loury, Glenn C. 2002. *The Anatomy of Racial Inequality*. Cambridge MA: Harvard University Press.

Moynihan, Daniel P., Timothy M. Smeeding, and Lee Rainwater (ed.). 2004. *The Future of the Family*. New York: Russell Sage Foundation.

Pritchett, Lant. 1997. "Divergence, Big Time." *Journal of Economic Perspectives* 11(3): 3–17.

Son, Hyun and Nanak Kakwani. 2004. "Economic Growth and Poverty Reduction: Initial Conditions Matter." Working Paper 2 of the International Poverty Centre of United Nations Development Programme.

Szekely, Miguel, Nora Lustig, Martin Cumpa, and Jose Antonio Mejía. 2000. "Do We Know How Much Poverty There Is?" Inter-American Development Bank, Working Paper #437.

Weinberg, Daniel H. 2004. "Income Data Quality Issues in the Annual Social and Economic Supplement to the Current Population Survey." Paper prepared for American Enterprise Institute-University of Maryland Seminar on Poverty Measurement.

PART

II

MACROECONOMIC POLICY AND HOUSEHOLD RESPONSES

Introduction

As the facts about poverty and place in Chapter 1 make clear, development is one of Mexico's major challenges for fighting poverty. In this section, Hernández and Székely, from the perspective of Mexico, and Walton, from a more comparative perspective, address the issues of economic growth, poverty, and inequality. Both approaches agree on the strong connection between economic growth and poverty reduction. Hernández and Székely (Chapter 2) first ask what kind of growth is related to poverty reduction and argue that improving labor productivity is a key aspect of poverty alleviation in Mexico. Following this line of analysis, they propose two specific sets of macro-policies that are important for poverty reduction: policies that ensure macroeconomic stability, and policies that enhance labor productivity with an emphasis on human capital as the link between macroeconomic policies and social policies.

The interconnection between economic growth and poverty is itself very dependent on the distribution of power and wealth. Michael Walton (Chapter 3) provides an analysis of the relationship between macroeconomic policies and poverty that complements and to some extent argues with that of Hernández and Székely. Walton raises a crucial point for understanding the relation between macroeconomic and market-related policies and poverty: the mediation of institutions. The poor are embedded in economic structures and institutions. Walton's analysis relies not only on a solid conceptual framework and international comparisons, but also on his knowledge of the specific Mexican case—a country that has undertaken significant economic policy reforms in the last twenty years. As he points out, macroeconomic policies in Mexico have been more oriented to stabilize the economy against internal and external shocks than to promote productive employment.

Are economic policy reforms good or bad for poverty? Walton sees a paradox in the liberalization process. On the one hand, liberalization and trade promote sustainable economic growth. On the other, since political and institutional contexts shape the distributional and efficiency effects of polices, the economic gains are captured mainly by the rich. Walton recognizes the importance of reforms to promote economic growth and reduce poverty. Nevertheless, economic reforms have ambiguous effects on income distribution and consequently on poverty. In terms of poverty reduction strategies, income distribution is more closely related to social institutions and safety nets than to markets.

How do poor individuals, households, and communities respond when macroeconomic policies do not do the job? In Chapter 4, Mercedes González de la Rocha claims that the poor have responded to economic change with innovative strategies and resourcefulness. Supported by private initiatives or survival strategies, poor households try to reduce their vulnerability to social and economic crises. By reviewing the notion of the resourcefulness of the poor to survive with scarce means, she shows that poor families and households in Mexico have been driven to a situation that is characterized more by constraints than choices.

Survival chances have been affected by trends in the labor market, given the centrality of labor for the poor. González de la Rocha argues that *Oportunidades* and other Mexican social programs have been insufficient to offset the process through which options for the poor are diminishing. She expresses concern about the costly private adjustment of the poor and its consequences for their well-being and reproduction.

2

Labor Productivity: The Link between Economic Growth and Poverty in Mexico

Gonzalo Hernández, Miguel Székely

Most people agree that the best recipe for poverty reduction is economic growth. Therefore, it follows that growth-promoting policies are also poverty-reducing policies. There has been some discussion about the *extent* to which poverty declines with growth, but few doubt that growth is practically a precondition to reduce poverty rates in a sustainable way.[1]

Although it is important and informative to acknowledge that growth reduces poverty, it is not a very relevant assertion for policymaking, because the question of what determines economic growth is far from being answered. Saying that growth reduces poverty is, in fact, almost a tautology. Some more relevant questions are, for instance, "what exactly about growth is relevant for poverty reduction?" or, "which of the elements of growth that benefit the poor are subject to be modified by policy?" Another relevant question, which has recently begun to be examined, concerns the types of growth that are related to larger poverty reduction.[2]

This chapter explores the general relationship between economic growth and other variables that characterize the macroeconomic environment and changes in poverty in Mexico. We present empirical evidence suggesting that there is a strong connection between macroeconomic stability and poverty, and evidence indicating that the underlying factor connecting growth with poverty is labor productivity. We arrive at this last conclusion by showing that the element of GDP growth that is most highly correlated with poverty is the wage bill. The wage bill is in turn determined by the level of employment and the wage rate. Of these two elements, the wage rate is the one that is most highly correlated with poverty, and among the determinants of wages, it is precisely labor productivity that is most highly associated with poverty. This conclusion has direct policy implications because it directs attention to concrete policy instruments.

It is important to stress that our analysis is subject to several caveats. Perhaps the most relevant ones are data availability and the difficulties in establishing causality. With regards to the data, the limitations of the information available impede the use of solid statistical techniques to determine the significance of the underlying relationships that we identify. As for causality, we are limited in that we are not able to test formally the relationship between poverty and macro variables. Therefore, we accept up front that our conclusions can be taken only as tentative hypotheses and general regularities in the data, to be verified in the future with more complete information and more adequate statistical and econometric techniques. We consider, however, that the exercise is worthwhile, since not much has been said about what kind of macroeconomic policies cause poverty reduction in Mexico. This chapter might be a useful starting point for this.

Our work is divided into 5 sections. Section 1 presents the stylized facts about the evolution of poverty during the past 50 years and the general relationship between poverty and economic growth. Section 2 takes a closer look at the years from 1984 to 2007, for which better data are available. Section 3 is an exploration of the factors underlying the relationship. Section 4 discusses the determinants of labor productivity from a macro perspective. Section 5 offers conclusions.

Poverty and Economic Growth: The Stylized Facts

To generate information about the relationship between macroeconomic variables and poverty that is relevant for policymaking, it is necessary to obtain the longest possible time-series data on macroeconomic performance and on poverty levels. Unfortunately, as is true in most countries in the world, a time-series of this type is not available for Mexico. There is sufficient data to document changes in the macroeconomic environment in detail, but only 17 points in time provide enough high-quality data to characterize the evolution of poverty. This constrains the possibility of using sophisticated econometric techniques and of identifying robust associations in the data over time.[3]

Because of the lack of long time-series data on poverty, it has been common practice in the poverty literature to use an indirect approach by deconstructing changes in poverty with microeconomic data, and by trying to identify elements of the change that can be linked, at least conceptually, with some macro variables.[4] The main drawback is that in most cases, it is a big leap to connect the micro with the macro variables, and it requires strong assumptions.

For our analysis, we proceed differently. We try to exploit the (very limited) time-series data available for Mexico to find direct connections between macroeconomic variables and poverty. The obvious drawback is that the data limitations do not allow for robust statistical inference, so any conclusion will be tentative and subject to future verification.

Time-series of Poverty Estimates: Data and Definitions

To engage in our exploration we use the time-series of poverty estimates recently constructed by Székely (2005) for the period 1950–1989, and for 1992–2006, those provided by Social Development Policy Evaluation National Council (CONEVAL)[5], which is the most extensive and complete compilation for Mexico. There are 17-point estimates of poverty rates for these years that are derived from household surveys for 1950, 1956, 1958, 1963, 1968, 1977, 1984, 1989, 1992, 1994, 1996, 1998, 2000, 2002, 2004, 2005, and 2006.[6]

It must be said that the data are not only limited in terms of the few surveys available, but there are also comparability problems that make the 1950–1968 data less reliable. Nevertheless, with the proper adjustments made, this is the most consistent series that can be obtained. The data between 1984 and 2006 are from the national household income and expenditure surveys, which are strictly comparable to each other. For this reason, in Section 2, we focus only on these data. In this section, we exploit the full 1950–2006 series to derive our general stylized facts.

The time-series is constructed by using the three official poverty definitions adopted by the Mexican government:[7] (a) food poverty: individuals whose income is insufficient to acquire the minimum food requirements necessary for survival (in 2006 pesos, $809.87 and $598.7 per month in urban and rural areas, respectively); (b) capabilities poverty: individuals whose income is insufficient to acquire the minimum food, health, and education requirements (in 2006 pesos, $993.3 and $707.85 per month in urban and rural areas, respectively); (c) asset (or basic needs) poverty: individuals whose income is insufficient to acquire the minimum food, health, education, housing, clothing, and transport requirements (in 2006 pesos, $1,624.92 and $1,086.41 per month in urban and rural areas, respectively).[8]

Poverty in Mexico during 1950–2006

Figure 1 presents the time-series data on poverty. The estimates show a clear decline in poverty during the 56-year period. While 61.8, 73.2, and 88.4 percent of the Mexican population were classified as poor according to the three official criteria in 1950, five decades later, in 2006, the proportions were 13.8, 20.7, and 42.6 percent for food, capabilities, and asset poverty. This implies a reduction of 78, 72, and 52 percent in each category, respectively.

The decline in poverty is quite smooth during the first 34 years—with the largest reductions between 1958 and 1968, during which real GDP per capita practically tripled. Poverty ceases to decline and remains fairly constant during 1984–1994, which coincides with the 1982 and 1986–87 years of economic contraction, where real GDP per capita increased by only 0.4 percent on average every year.

Between 1994 and 1996 there was an unprecedented increase in poverty and the greatest deterioration in living conditions. Real GDP per capita declined by 7 percent between 1994 and 1995, and poverty rates surged to levels observed 30 years earlier, during the 1960s.

Between 1996 and 2006, poverty declines continuously and by 2004 the increase observed during 1994–1996 is totally reversed. According to these data, the year 2006 shows the lowest poverty rates historically.

In sum, during the last five decades, poverty in Mexico has declined substantially, but the changes over the years, especially since 1984, have been far from smooth. Increases in poverty coincide with macroeconomic crises and years of stagnation.

Poverty and the Macroeconomic Environment

Obviously, having only 17 observations severely limits the ability of using standard statistical techniques to identify the relationship between changes in poverty and the macroeconomic environment. Here we present some descriptive elements that we propose as stylized facts for Mexico, keeping in mind the caveats already discussed.

Table 1 presents the correlation coefficients between each of the three poverty definitions (food, capabilities, and asset poverty) as compared to GDP per capita and inflation. We chose these two macro variables because they are among the only ones available since 1950, and because we would expect them to have a close connection with poverty.

According to our estimates, there is a strong correlation between all variables. As expected, the relationship between poverty and GDP is negative. Interestingly, the relationship is stronger between GDP and capabilities poverty—with a coefficient of –0.97. The association between GDP and asset poverty is somewhat smaller—a coefficient of –0.90—while the coefficient for food poverty is –0.81. The results confirm that economic growth, reflected in a higher GDP per capita, is closely associated with lower poverty rates. In fact, Figure 1 clearly illustrates that during the years where growth has been low or negative, poverty rates tended to rise.[9]

The third column in Table 1 shows the correlation between poverty and inflation. This relationship is relevant for our purposes, since inflation is a good indicator of the stability of the macroeconomic environment. It is well known that inflation tends to affect the poor most severely, on the one hand because these socioeconomic groups usually do not have access to financial systems to protect their (scarce) assets against continuous price increases, and on the other, because the poor are generally dependent on wage incomes, and inflation tends to reduce real wages.

Our results show a strong positive relationship between poverty and inflation—higher inflation rates are associated with higher poverty. The strongest associations are found to be the ones with asset and capabilities poverty—with coefficients around 0.64. The correlation coefficient between food poverty and inflation is 0.51.

The fourth column in Table 1 presents the correlation between poverty and inequality. Higher inequality is associated with greater poverty, so it is not surprising that in all cases, the coefficient is strong and positive—with values of 0.62, 0.71, and 0.73 for food, capabilities, and asset poverty, respectively.

The conclusion from these results is that the macroeconomic environment characterized by the level of GDP and the inflation rate has had a strong association with poverty in Mexico during the past 5 decades. The following section takes a closer look at the 1984–2007 years.

From 1984 to 2007: Five Periods in 23 Years

Since the time-series for poverty estimates for the years 1984–2007 are more accurate than those previously estimated because they are based on the comparability of the household surveys, we explore in more detail the connection between the macro environment and these variables for these years. We identify clearly five different sub-periods that correspond, in general terms, with years for which household surveys are available.

Figure 2 presents the evolution of GDP per capita, as well as GDP growth rates for each year. The first period, between 1984 and 1989, shows a decline in GDP per capita because of the 1986 recession. The second, for the 1989–1994 years, is characterized by high growth rates and by an expansion of GDP per capita of around 10 percent in real terms. The third period, covering 1994–1996, is characterized by a considerable reduction in GDP per capita due to the financial crisis of 1995. The fourth period, 1996–2000, is characterized by several years of high growth rates that compensate for the 1995 contraction. During these years, GDP per capita grew steadily with an increase of 17 percent. The fifth period, 2000 to 2007, covers years of moderate growth (of around 1 percent), and since 2004 higher growth rates are observed.

Figure 3 shows the three variables that reflect the stability of the economic environment (interest rates, the real exchange rate, and the rate of inflation). Periods 1 and 3 register high volatility in these three variables, mainly as consequence of the 1986 and 1995 crisis. In contrast, periods 2, 4, and 5 are periods of stability.

Figure 4 plots social expenditures and the external debt as a share of GDP, which have an inverse relationship. Periods 1 and 3 are clearly years of contraction of social expenditures, while periods 2, 4, and 5 are years of considerable expansion.

The three figures suggest the following general regularities in the data: poverty has closely followed the macroeconomic cycle by increasing in periods of economic recession, instability, and abrupt contraction of social spending (periods 1 and 3), and declining when GDP per capita grows (even modestly), in a context of stability and with the continued expansion of social expenditures (periods 2, 4, and 5). Probably the best example of the last case is 1994–1996. During these years we find an unprecedented increase in poverty rates in the country—indeed, there seems to be no other period when living standards deteriorated to such a large extent in recent history—precisely at the time of an economic contraction, high volatility, and reduced social spending.

Considering the limitations of the time-series, and that we use only very basic statistical tools and descriptive analysis, we propose that policies that guarantee growth and economic stability, and expand social spending in Mexico during the past 56 years, work in benefit of the poor.

As for GDP, saying that higher rates of economic growth have been associated with lower poverty levels is useful information, but it does not give much policy guidance. In contrast, with regard to economic stability where specific policies have been identified and tested widely (such as fiscal deficit controls or the management of the exchange rate), the determinants of economic growth and, therefore, the instruments to promote it, are far from being common knowledge. A very large share of the economics literature has in fact been devoted to answering this question, and even so, few certainties can be found. Because of this, the following sections engage in an exploration of what elements of GDP growth have been specifically associated with poverty reduction in Mexico. Our objective is to be able to shed some light on the macro policies that can promote poverty reduction through their effect on economic growth.

GDP, Wages, and Poverty

In this section we disaggregate GDP into its various components to explore the relationship between each of them and poverty.[10] We focus in the period 1989–2004, because a more thoroughly disaggregated series of GDP is available only for these years.

Disaggregating GDP

Figure 5 shows the evolution of various GDP components since 1989. The correlation coefficients between each component and total GDP reveal that the wage bill shows the closest association.[11]

Figure 6 shows the correlation in annual changes between each GDP component and poverty.[12] Here again, the wage bill shows by far the highest correlation (–0.81), indicating that increases in the wage bill are highly associated with poverty reductions. This is not surprising, since GDP is the value added in an economy, and this value is precisely the payment to all factors of production, including labor. Labor is an asset (often the only one) typically owned by the poor. In fact, according to the 2002 National Income and Expenditure Household Survey, almost 73 percent of the total income generated by households is labor income. Thus, the income generated in the labor market is perhaps the best variable that links economic growth—the growth of the value added year by year—with changes in income-poverty.

Wages and Poverty

In order to explore the poverty-wage bill relationship further, we now turn to the National Urban Employment Survey (ENEU), which is a household survey that captures the most important labor marker variables such as hours worked, monthly labor income, occupational status, and whether the individual is in the formal or informal market. This allows disaggregating the wage bill into wages (income) and labor supply.[13]

We think that the use of an urban survey is not necessarily a drawback, since there is a very close correlation between the total wage bill reported in the National Accounts and the urban wage bill from the ENEU. The correlation coefficient between both variables (in changes) is 0.68. The evolution of the two series for the period 1988–2003 is shown in Figure 7.

Figure 8 shows the association between the change in the urban wage bill from the ENEU and changes in urban (capabilities) poverty. It is clear that every time the wage bill (that is, the total labor income received by the labor force in urban areas) increases, urban poverty declines. In periods such as 1994–1996, when the urban wage bill was dramatically reduced, urban poverty increased by almost 18 percentage points.[14] The correlation between these two variables is –0.96 (the correlation with changes in food poverty and asset poverty is –0.96 and –0.95, respectively).

Table 2 illustrates the magnitude of the relationship for each year. For instance, the total wage bill increased in real terms between 1989 and 2004, which coincides with a reduction in urban food poverty from 29% to 18%. Between 1989 and 1994, poverty was greatly reduced while the wage bill increased by 33.3%. The opposite happened between 1994 and 1996; when the wage bill decreased, poverty increased substantially. Between 1996 and 2004, the real wage bill increased by 49.1% while poverty declined for the three official poverty lines. By looking at the magnitude of the changes in different periods, it is obvious that the wage bill does not affect poverty always in the same way—the wage-bill elasticity with respect to poverty varies over time.

To explore further the relationship between poverty and growth, we dis-aggregate the urban wage bill into its two components: employment and wages. Obviously, these two components are interrelated, since the balance between labor supply and demand determines not only the level of employment but also the wage level. However, the disaggregation is relevant because the policy instruments needed to affect each component are very different. If the level of employment were what largely determines poverty, policies that expand labor demand—for instance, changing the requirements for hiring and firing—would be a natural response. However, if the wage level is what matters more, other policies such as enhancing labor productivity might be needed.[15] Table 2 shows the evolution of these variables and urban poverty since 1989.

The data show that the evolution of real wages and employment differs throughout the period. In fact, due to the increasing rate of labor market participation, employment grew steadily during the 1989–2002 years, quite independently from the wage bill. In contrast, real wages behaved very much as the wage bill did: they increased between 1989 and 1994, they went down dramatically (by 28%) between 1994 and 1996, and grew until 2004 (by 23.2%). Thus, the data suggest that wages rather than employment are associated with changes in the urban wage bill. By following the argument developed above, about the connection between poverty and wages, the straightforward (although very tentative) assertion would be that the level of wages, rather than the level of employment, is the factor most highly associated with the evolution of poverty. Figure 9 illustrates these relationships; Table 3 shows the underlying data. Although lack of data prevents us from presenting a robust empirical model that relates poverty to wages and other variables (as the one estimated by J. Tobin [1994] among others), the evidence available suggests that there is a strong association between the wage level and poverty.

Aggregate Wage Determination

If the wage level in the economy has such a high association with poverty, what can we do to increase real wages to improve the income-earning capacity of the poor? From the macroeconomic point of view, apart from the straightforward connection between labor supply and demand—for instance, with an inverse relationship between unemployment and wages— the most explored connections between wages and macroeconomic variables in the literature are productivity growth, inflation, and the exchange rate.[16]

In the 18th century, Adam Smith argued that the only way to improve social well-being in the long run is by increasing the production of the worker (this has been confirmed more recently by Barro1997; Sala-i-Martin 2000; and Barro and Sala-i-Martin 2003). Theoretically, productivity positively affects wages because the demand for labor can be thought of as the price of the produced goods multiplied by the productivity of the work force—that is, the value of the marginal product of labor. If for any reason labor productivity increases, the demand for labor increases and real wages rise.[17]

As for inflation, the price level affects wages through various channels. One is backward-looking indexing (see for instance Braumann 2004). The argument is that as inflation accelerates, the adjustment of nominal wages lags behind, and real wages fall. If inflation grows every year, this phenomenon may persist for some years until workers can fully adjust their expectations. Another connection is that inflation, especially high inflation, reduces real wages through a decline in the capital stock and through shifts in relative prices. A corollary for this statement is that in periods of high inflation poverty increases and the decline in wages is higher than the decline in GDP per capita.

A third pressure on wages arises when inflation is reduced relatively quickly to low levels so it is not possible in the short run to increase nominal wages below the inflation rate due to wage-stickiness—that is, nominal wages are more rigid at lower inflation rates. The effect of the real exchange rate is also important in the process of wage determination, especially in open economies. Depreciation of the local currency makes imported goods, consumption goods, and inputs for production more expensive, reducing real wages.

The effect of the minimum wage on the distribution of wages is a more controversial issue. According to Maloney and Nuñez (2001), in Colombia and other Latin American countries, including Mexico, the setting of the minimum wage has important effects on wage distribution for minimum-wage workers and informal salaried workers. However, according to Bell (1995), in many cases minimum wages are so low that they are non-binding. Newmark (1997) obtains mixed results by showing that on the one hand, minimum wages increase the probability that poor families escape poverty, but on the other, they also increase the probability that non-poor families become poor, showing an undetermined net effect.

To understand further the determinants of aggregate wages in Mexico, we estimate a simple econometric model (with our very limited information) using urban yearly data from the ENEU for 1987–2004.[18] The econometric results in Table 4 suggest that productivity growth, the minimum wage, the percentage of informal workers (taken as the percentage of informality in urban areas), inflation, and the real exchange rate behave as theory predicts.[19] The first three variables are statistically significant—with the caveat that standard errors have to be analyzed carefully given the low number of observations. The variable combining both statistical significance and a large effect in absolute terms is productivity growth.[20] Figure 10 illustrates graphically that productivity growth and real urban wages have followed very similar trends between 1987 and 2004.

It should be mentioned that the view that productivity determines wages is controversial. For instance, Saint-Paul (2001) argues that wages increase with productivity only if they are set by monopoly unions. Hellerstein and Neumark (1996) find that productivity can explain wage differentials within the cohort of prime-age males, but the wage differential between males and females does not match the small differences in productivity between both groups. Van Biesebroeck (2003) asserts that wage premiums for worker characteristics generally equal productivity gains. Other authors, however, find a positive relationship between wages and productivity, especially with productivity growth (Orszag and Zoega 1996; Coelli, Fahrer, and Lindsay 1994; and de la Fuente and Ciccone 2002).

Table 4 shows that the effect of the minimum wage on average wages is positive and statistically significant, but it is also relatively small. This is in line with the results of Bell (1995), who explains that when the minimum wage is low, it is likely to be non-binding in some (or all) labor markets. Another explanation is that although the minimum wage set every year is the base for the other wage negotiations, many prices are indexed to the minimum wage in Mexico, so overall inflation rates move similarly.

Finally, the coefficient for the percentage of informality in the labor market (a proxy for unemployment) is negative and statistically significant. Thus, greater unemployment (or underemployment) lowers overall wages. This might be because, since the 1980s, the Mexican economy has developed an important informal labor market due to the reduced formal labor demand growth. Informality has therefore been a substitute for unemployment.

Although more informality can be seen as a proxy for unemployment, which reduces overall wages, informality does have a role in reducing poverty. In the absence of an informal labor market—informal labor demand—people who are not able to access the (limited) formal market would be either openly unemployed or out of the labor force with no labor income, as happened in countries such as Argentina in the late 1980s.

The important informal labor market in Mexico serves as a safety net for those who are not in the formal labor market. In fact, according to Maloney (1998), many formal workers enter the informal market looking for a better wage; for example, between 1994 and 1996, in the middle of the economic crisis, the reduction in formal employment was more than compensated by increases in the informal market.

It is interesting to note that the evolution of formal and informal wages is remarkably alike. Figure 11 shows that wages in both markets have had more or less the same pattern between 1989 and 2004. Although between 1989 and 1994 formal wages increased more than informal ones, the trend is more or less similar during the 1989–2004 period. The correlation coefficient of the changes between the two wages is 0.91. This implies that the correlation between the wage rate in both markets and poverty is very high and very similar to one another.

Productivity Growth, Inflation, and Reforms in Mexico

We argued above that there is a strong connection between poverty and the wage level and that the wage level is in turn determined mainly by the rate of growth of labor productivity. The implication of this assertion is that policies that enhance labor productivity are also poverty-reducing policies.

In a global economy, one obvious policy designed to increase labor productivity would enact economic reforms that eliminate restrictions to investment and improve the efficiency and competitiveness of the economic environment.[21] Indeed, since the beginning of the 1980s, Mexico has engaged in an intensive process of economic reform through trade liberalization, domestic financial liberalization, liberalization of direct foreign investments, privatizations, (limited) fiscal reforms, and deregulation and changes in monetary policy. The expectation was that these reforms would increase productivity and the competitiveness of Mexico in world markets, and that the reforms would particularly benefit the poor. Table 5 summarizes the most important changes in Mexico between 1982 and 1999, according to Clavijo and Valdivieso (2000). Figure 13 illustrates the pace of reform.

The best approach to link poverty reduction with specific reforms by using the poverty-labor productivity relationship previously suggested would consist of rigorous statistical and econometric analysis of the impact of all the reforms on the determinants of wages, and specifically on productivity. Unfortunately, we are unable to pursue this path because of data limitations and because a number of factors affect labor productivity at the same time, which makes it difficult to disentangle each effect.

Nevertheless, some descriptive evidence does point to an association between productivity and reforms in Mexico. Figure 13 shows the value of an index of economic reform developed by Lora (1997) and extended by Morley, et al. (1999) for the period 1985–1999, as well as the labor productivity index developed by Aspe (2004). The reform index summarizes information on trade reform, financial liberalization, tax reform, liberalization of external capital transactions, and privatization.[22] The productivity index is the manufacturing growth rate based on hours of work. We have smoothed the index and changed its scale to be able to compare it with the reform index.

The figure shows that reforms in Mexico accelerated between 1985 and 1994, precisely during the years when productivity increased more rapidly. There is a clear drawback in reforms between 1994 and 1996 that coincides with a turning point in the productivity trend, which diminishes thereafter. The decline in productivity from 1996 to 1999 coincides with no further progress in reforms.

Although this evidence is obviously not conclusive,[23] it is interesting that it is in line with the work of most of the researchers who have assessed the connection between productivity and reforms with various methodologies and approaches. For instance, Aspe (2004) asserts that the reforms implemented in Mexico between 1985 and 1993—especially the ones related to financial markets, the autonomy of the Bank of Mexico, the external debt, the fiscal and trade liberalizations, as well as those related to privatization and enhancement of property rights in land tenure—increased productivity growth and real wages.

The specific effect of trade liberalization has been the subject of more extensive research. Nicita (2004) finds that trade liberalization has lowered prices of most non-animal agricultural products and, while reducing the cost of consumption, has reduced households' agricultural income, widening the income gap between urban and rural areas. The author also shows that skilled workers, for whom trade liberalization has produced an increase in wages, have benefited relative to unskilled workers. Therefore, trade liberalization, although beneficial, has contributed to an increase in inequality between the south and the north of the country, urban and rural areas, and skilled and unskilled labor. From the perspective of poverty, the trade liberalization that occurred between 1989 and 2000, according to this author, has had the direct effect of reducing poverty by about 3 percent.

Hanson (2003) argues that the reforms appear to have raised the demand for skilled labor in the country, reduced rents in industries that paid their workers high wages prior to reform, and raised the premium paid to workers in states along the U.S.-Mexico border. Revenga (1999) finds that cuts in Mexico's tariff levels were associated with a small decline in employment in Mexico and with increases in average wages (perhaps reflecting improved productivity in the reformed industries and a shift toward the use of more skilled workers). The wages and employment of skilled labor were significantly more responsive to changes in protection levels than were those of non-production workers.

One of the few works going in the opposite direction is Clavijo and Valdivieso (2000), who claim that trade liberalizations helped to control inflation (with positive effects on real wages) but the appreciation of the local currency impeded industrial restructuring and improvements in labor productivity. These authors also argue that the financial liberalization helped to finance the fiscal deficit, but the excessive credit supply in Mexican markets made the external deficit surge. The reduction in marginal taxes has produced a reduction of fiscal resources, but has not increased investment in projects with high marginal returns and productivity.

Conclusions

We propose that macroeconomic variables affect poverty in Mexico in two clear ways. On the one hand, inflation, through several channels, has had an important association with poverty rates during the past two decades. High inflation has been accompanied by increases in poverty and vice versa. On the other hand, there is an apparent connection between labor productivity and poverty. Labor productivity is the most important determinant of changes in the wage level; changes in the wage level determine to a large extent changes in the wage bill (much more than do employment levels); and changes in the wage bill are very closely associated with changes in GDP, which in turn are very closely linked with poverty.

Additionally, we observe an association between changes in poverty and changes in public social expenditures over the period 1984–2007.

The main policy implications of these findings are that macroeconomic policies that guarantee stability in the environment and that enhance labor productivity are at the same time policies for poverty reduction. What is necessary to achieve stability and productivity growth? There is a large literature on these issues that identifies specific policy mechanisms which we do not discuss here (we only argue that there is an apparent association between productivity and the pace of economic reforms). However, it is worth noting that labor productivity provides a link between macroeconomic policies and social policies. On the one hand, macro policies can enhance productivity by improving the economic environment where the human capital of individuals is put to work. For instance, macro policies that promote investment, that allow for the accumulation of greater capital stocks, that improve competitiveness, that guarantee property rights and the rule of law, that create opportunities to develop and use technology, and that improve access to financial markets, among other things, make a given stock of human capital more productive. On the other hand, social policies can enhance productivity through microeconomic interventions by improving the human capital stock of individuals through investments in health, education, and nutrition, among other things. We would thus suggest that if both types of policies act in the same direction, a virtuous circle of growth and poverty reduction can be achieved through the combination of macro and social policy.

Another implication of our analysis that could be further explored is the connection between labor productivity and inequality. If productivity were in fact such an important determinant of wages, a natural extension would be that the distribution of wage incomes is, to a large extent, a mirror of the distribution of productivity among individuals. Thus, macro policies that enhance the productivity of the poor could be also defined as progressive in terms of the distribution of wages.

Perhaps the main contribution of the paper is that we try to go beyond the growth-poverty connection by identifying the elements of growth and macroeconomic performance that are relevant for reducing poverty. We are well aware of the methodological and data limitations of our analysis, but we think that this exploration is a good starting point because it proposes a clear hypothesis that can be tested with better information and econometric techniques in the future.

Tables and Figures

Table 1. Poverty Correlation Coefficients, 1950–2004

Variable	GDP per capita	Inflation rate	Inequality (Gini)
Food poverty	−0.81	0.51	0.62
Capabilities poverty	−0.97	0.64	0.71
Asset poverty	−0.90	0.65	0.73

Source: Author's calculations from INEGI and Bank of Mexico data

Table 2. Evolution of Urban Labor Market Variables and Poverty, 1989–2004

Year	Wage bill 2002 = 100	Avg. Monthly Wages 2002 = 100	Total Employment	Urban Food Poverty	Urban Capabilities Poverty	Urban Asset Poverty
1989	39,971,845,862	4,206	9,502,742	23.2	29.0	52.0
1992	47,530,729,218	4,642	10,239,352	13.5	18.4	44.0
1994	52,497,516,651	4,954	10,596,704	9.7	17.1	43.6
1996	40,277,121,751	3,563	11,305,492	26.5	35.0	61.9
1998	48,578,429,896	3,646	13,323,185	21.3	29.0	55.8
2000	57,608,892,052	4,167	13,823,069	12.6	20.2	43.8
2002	61,356,682,703	4,365	14,055,359	11.4	17.4	41.5
2004	60,061,982,027	4,389	13,684,231	11.0	17.8	41.0

Sources: Calculations from the ENEU, 16 urban areas, and the ENIGH survey

Table 3. Correlation Coefficient of Urban Labor Market Variables' Components and Urban Poverty

	Differences of poverty rates		
	Food poverty	Capabilities poverty	Asset poverty
Wage bill (% change)	−0.96	−0.96	−0.95
Employment (% change)	−0.10	−0.14	−0.10
Real wages (% change)	−0.97	−0.96	−0.96

Source: Author's calculations

Table 4. Linear Regression of Real Wages against Productivity Growth, Inflation, Real Exchange Rate, Minimum Wage, and Unemployment, 1987–2004

Source	SS	df	MS	Number of obs	18
Model	2914339.3	5	582867.9	F (4, 11)	9.28
Residual	753785.3	12	62815.4	Prob > F	0.0008
Total	3668124.6	17	215772.0	R-squared	0.7945
				Adj R-squared	0.7089
				Root MSE	250.63

Real Wages	Coef.	Std. Err.	t	P>|t|	[95% Conf. Interval]	
Constant	9894.674	3099.7	3.2	0.0	31.41.1	16648.3
Productivity Growth	198.8	48.5	4.1	0.0	93.2	304.4
Inflation	−5.7	4.3	−1.3	0.2	−14.9	3.6
Real Exchange Rate	−8.2	9.3	−0.9	0.4	−28.5	12.1
Minimum Wage	4.5	1.0	4.3	0.0	2.2	6.7
% of Informality	−145.0	72.5	−2.0	0.1	−302.9	12.8

Source: Author's calculations.

Table 5. Structural Reforms and Economic Policy in Mexico, 1982–1999

Trade liberalization

1983	Gradual reduction on tariff level and dispersion
1986	GATT incorporation
1993	Foreign Trade Law and NAFTA

Domestic financial liberalization

1982	Liberalization of leading government bonds (CETES), allowing rates and amounts to be determined by the market
1989	Legal maximum interest rates are dropped and legal tenure is changed for liquidity coefficient (30%)
1991	Voluntary reserves for bank substitute liquidity coefficients. Open Markets operations replace indirect control exchange rates
1993	Development banking and Central Bank trust funds restructure
1995–1996	Creation of Credit Information Societies (*Sociedades de Información Crediticia*)

Liberalization for Direct Foreign Investment (IED)

1984	New outlines for IED
1993	Foreign Investment Law

Privatization

1989–1993	More than 1,000 privatizations
1990	Among others, Telmex, Aeroméxico, Mexicana, and Grupo DINA were privatized
1991–1992	Commercial banks privatized

Tax Reforms

1989	Lower business and personal taxes (35%)
1990	Introduction of homogeneous tax reports (*formulario único*): Administrative and taxing
1991	Universal consumption tax (10%)
1993	Lower business and personal taxes (34%)
1995	Increase on consumption tax (from 10 to 15%)
1997	Federal Tax Bureau (SAT)

Deregulation

1989	Full transit liberty established by the Federal Commercial Transport Law
1991	Navigation and Marine Trade Law
1992	Economic Competition Law
1995	Reform of the 27th Constitutional article

Monetary Policy

1989	Band-exchange rate substitutes fix-exchange rate
1994	Autonomy of the Central Bank
1995	Market-determined exchange rate

Source: Abstract from Clavijo and Valdivieso (2000)

Figure 1. Poverty in Mexico, 1950–2006

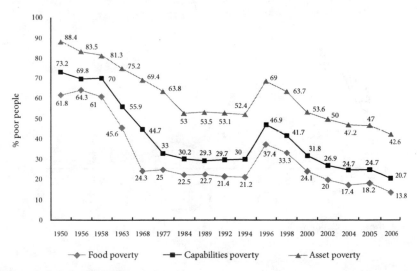

Sources: Székely (2005); CONEVAL (2007)

Figure 2. Five Periods of GDP per capita and GDP Growth (PPP US$)

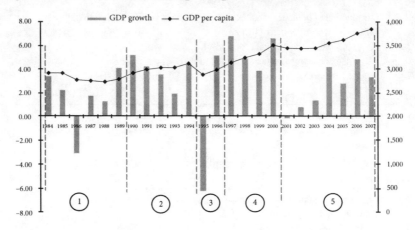

Source: Author's calculations.

Figure 3. Five Periods of Stability and Volatility

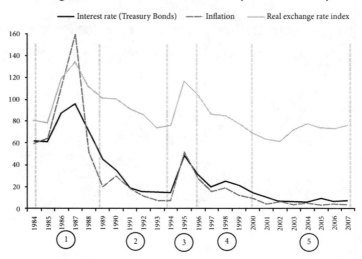

Source: Author's calculations.

Figure 4. Five Periods of Changes in Social Public Expenditure

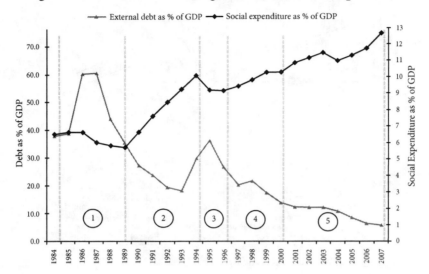

Source: Author's calculations.

Figure 5. GDP in Mexico, 1989–2004 (PPP US$)

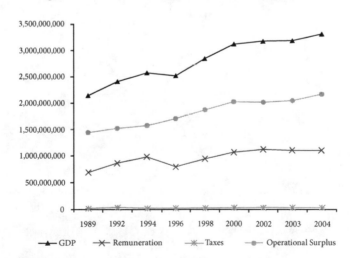

Sources: INEGI, BIE (2005), National Accounts

Figure 6. Components of GDP and Poverty

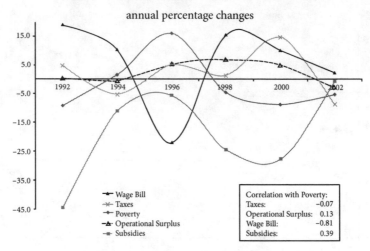

Sources: INEGI, BIE (2005), National Accounts

Figure 7. Evolution of the Wage Bill in Mexico, 1988–2003

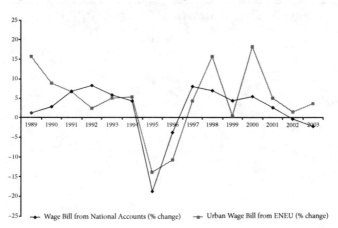

Sources: National Accounts and ENEU.

Figure 8. Changes in Urban Poverty and Urban Wage Bill in Mexico

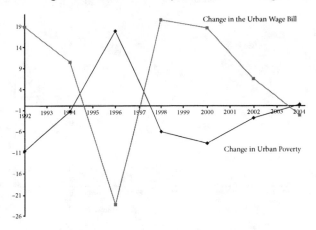

Source: Author's calculations from ENEU.

Figure 9. Changes in Poverty, Wages, and Employment in Mexico, 1992–2004

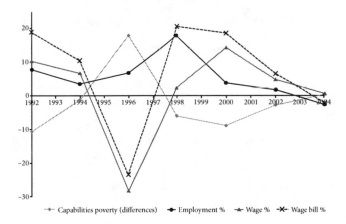

Source: Author's calculations from ENEU.

Figure 10. Real Wages and Productivity Growth in Mexico, 1987–2004

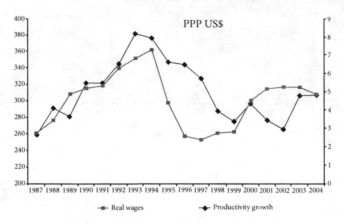

Source: Author's calculations and Aspe (2004).

Figure 11. Relative Evolution of Formal and Informal Wages, 1989–2004

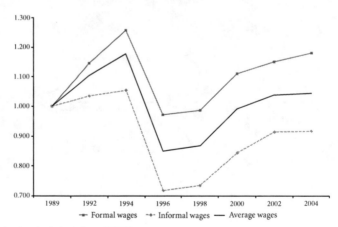

Source: Author's calculations from ENEU.

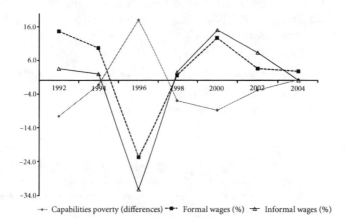

Figure 12. Changes in Poverty and Formal and Informal Wages, 1992–2004

—•— Capabilities poverty (differences)   —■— Formal wages (%)   —▵— Informal wages (%)

Source: Author's calculations from the ENEU survey

Figure 13. Productivity and Reforms in Mexico

Source: Morley et al. (1999) and Aspe (2004)

Notes

1   The literature on this issue is growing. Some of the recent papers summarizing the literature and estimating the magnitude of the relationship are by Dollar and Kraay (2000); Foster and Székely (2001); Kakwani, Prakash, and Son (2000); and Bourguignon (2004). Anand & Kanbur (1985) wrote some of the early papers on the subject.

2   The paper by Bourguignon (2004) is a good example of this strand of literature.

3   There are countries for which more data is available, and where more complete and rigorous explorations have been made (see for instance Ravallion 2000a, on India). Ravallion (2000b) discusses the typical data limitations in this analysis.

4   There are numerous examples of this indirect way. One for Mexico is Székely (1998). The paper by Loayza and Polastri (2004) for Perú is a good recent example of the efforts under this approach to understand which elements of growth are more poverty-reducing.

5   Data from CONEVAL considered the conciliation of population data by CONAPO, INEGI and COLMEX.

6   In fact all but the 1950 data are derived from household surveys. The information on income distribution used for estimating poverty for 1950 is from the National Population Census. Székely (2005) describes the data in detail and justifies the use of information from 1950.

7   See Comité Técnico de Medición de la Pobreza (2002) for a full explanation.

8   The Consumer Price Index by item is used to deflate poverty lines over time in all cases. One drawback of using the same poverty line for such a long period is that changes in consumption patterns, tastes, and needs, and changes in the availability of different goods and services, are not accounted for.

9   Of course, this is only a descriptive association. Papers analyzing the relationship more formally are Benabou (1996), Aghion, et al. (1999), Birdsall and Londoño (1997), Ravallion, Squire and Bruno (1999), Bigsten and Levin (2000), Dollar (2001), Adams (2003), and Bourguignon (2004).

10 Similar discussions can be found in Tobin (1994); Ravallion and Datt (1999); Agrawal (1999); Fallon and Lucas (2002); and Nicita (2004).

11 The wage bill includes the total amount of wage-earner payments (in cash or in kind) plus social security benefits. Cash payments include overtime hours, traveling expenses, and vacation grants.

12 We use capabilities poverty as reference for illustration, but these results and the ones we present later are almost identical when using the other two poverty definitions.

13 The labor survey with information for both urban and rural areas, the National Employment Survey (ENE), has reliable information only since 1998 and that is why we focus on the ENEU information in what follows. According to the ENE, around 50% of the population 12 years of age and older live in urban areas. For this paper, we only use information for the 16 original metropolitan areas registered in the ENEU survey since 1987.

14 Another example is the period 2002–2004, when urban capabilities poverty increased by 0.4 percentage points, while the urban wage bill declined by 2.1% in real terms. The national real wage bill from the ENE survey, which includes both rural and urban areas, increased by around 6% between 2002 and 2004, a figure that is in line with the actually observed reduction in national poverty during the same period.

15 A priori one would expect the wage bill to vary more with the wage level than with employment because, although it is possible that at a constant wage a larger labor supply can increase the wage bill—either through more working hours or through a higher rate of labor force participation—the "degrees of freedom" of employment are limited since only 24 hours are available every day to supply labor. In contrast, wages can, in principle, vary with no upper bound. This is one important reason why changes in wages are immediately translated into income-poverty changes.

16 See for instance Nickell, S. and S. B. Wadhwani (1989), Driffield, N. L. and K. Talyor (2002), Blanchflower, D., A. J. Oswald and M. D. Garrett (1990), Zweimuller, J. and E. Barth (1992), Holmlund, B. (1991). BBVA Bancomer (2004) has analyzed these relationships formally.

17 Some micro studies on this are by Ravallion and Datt (1999), who show that increasing the productivity of small farmers in India caused an important reduction in poverty because wages increased; Agrawal (1999) and Pineau (2004).

18 There are, of course, a number of econometric issues that we are not able to address, and we cannot assure causality in the interpretation.

19 The inclusion of other variables, such as capital stock, can also explain wages, but we have not included this variable here because it also determines productivity.

20 We obtained the figures for productivity growth from Aspe (2004). This author estimates productivity growth using the hours worked by employees in the manufacturing sector, from the Sistema de Cuentas Nacionales and the Encuesta Industrial Mensual from INEGI; the series reported is actually an annual moving average. Further research in this area, however, may suggest using other sources of information and methodology for productivity growth.

21 As discussed by Walton (2005), reforms can go to the heart of the causes of inequality and poverty by modifying institutions that historically exclude the

poor from the benefits of growth. By modifying such institutions the "rules of the game" of economic activity and social arrangements change, so that a larger share of the population benefits from economic opportunities.

22 Unlike proxies commonly used in the literature, these reform indices have the advantage that they are based on direct indicators of governmental policies, so that they reflect policy "effort." The trade reform index is the average of the average level of tariffs and the average dispersion of tariffs. The index of domestic financial reform is the average of an index that controls for borrowing rates at banks, an index of lending rates at banks, and an index of the reserves to deposit ratio. The index for international financial liberalization averages four components: controls of foreign investment by sector, limits on profits and interest repatriation, controls on external credits by national borrowers, and capital outflows. The tax reform index averages four components: the maximum marginal tax rate on corporate incomes, the maximum marginal tax rate on personal incomes, the value-added tax rate, and the efficiency of the value-added tax. The tax reform index is higher when the average of the marginal tax rates is lower. The privatization index is calculated as one minus the ratio of value-added in state-owned enterprises to non-agricultural GDP.

23 Several other issues not discussed here should be taken into account when looking at this relationship. One of the most important is timing: reforms are expected to have an impact on productivity, but given the nature of reforms, the impact takes some time to be realized. Therefore, we would expect the relationship to be observed with considerable lags.

References

Adams, R. H., Jr. 2003. "Economic Growth, Inequality, and Poverty: Findings from a New Data Set." Policy Research Working Paper No. 2972. Washington, D.C.: The World Bank.

Aghion, P., E. Caroli, and C. García Penaloza. 1999. "Inequality and Economic Growth: The Perspective of New Growth Theories." *Journal of Economic Literature* 37 (4): 1615–60.

Agrawal, N. 1999. "The Benefits of Growth for Indonesian Workers." Policy Research Working Paper No 1637. Washington, D.C.: The World Bank.

Anand, S. and R. Kanbur. 1985. "Poverty under the Kuznets Process." *Economic Journal* 95, pp. s42-s50.

Aspe, P. 2004. "El futuro económico de México." *Este País*, Agosto 2004, No. 161, pp. 11–20.

Banco de México. 1963. *Ingresos y Gastos Familiares*, México D.F.

——— 1968. *Ingresos y Gastos Familiares*, México D.F.

Barro, R. J. 1997. *Determinants of Economic Growth: A Cross-country Empirical Study*. Cambridge MA: The MIT Press.

Barro, R. J., and X. Sala-i-Martin. 2003. *Economic Growth*, 2nd ed. Cambridge MA: The MIT Press.

BBVA Bancomer. 2004. "La productividad en México." *Serie Propuestas*, No. 32, Junio.

Bell, L. A. 1995. "The Impact of Minimum Wages in Mexico and Colombia." Policy Research Working Paper No 1514. Washington, D.C.: The World Bank.

Bénabou, R. 1996. "Inequality and Growth." In B. S. Bernanke and J. J. Rotemberg, eds. *NBER Macroeconomics Annual*. Vol. 9. Cambridge MA: The MIT Press.

Bigsten, A. and J. Levin. 2000. "Growth, Income Distribution, and Poverty: A Review." Working Paper No. 32 in Economics. Göteborg University.

Birdsall, N., and J. L. Londoño. 1997. "Asset Inequality Matters." *American Economic Review* 87 (2): 32–7.

Blanchflower, D., A. J. Oswald, and M. D. Garrett. 1990. "Insider Power in Wage Determination." *Economica* 57 (226), pp.143–70.

Bourguignon, Francois. 2004. "The Poverty-Growth-Inequality Triangle." Paper presented at the Indian Council for Research on International Economic Relations, New Delhi, February 4, 2004 (mimeographed version).

Braumann, B. 2004. *High Inflation and Real Wages*, IMF Staff Papers, 2004, vol. 51, issue 1, p. 6.

Clavijo, F., and S. Valdivieso. 2000. "Reformas estructurales y política macroeconómica: el caso de México 1982–1999." *Serie de Reformas Económicas* 67, No. 1374. Santiago: ECLAC.

Coelli, M., J. Fahrer, and H. Lindsay. 1994. "Wage Dispersion and Labour Market Institutions: A Cross Country Study." RBA Research Discussion Paper No. 9404. Reserve Bank of Australia.

Comité Técnico para la Medición de la Pobreza. 2002. "Variantes metodológicas y estimación preliminar." Serie Documentos de investigación, Secretaría de Desarrollo Social. México,

De la Fuente, Angel, and Antonio Ciccone. 2002. "Human Capital in a Global and Knowledge-based Economy." UFAE and IAE Working Papers from Unitat de Fonaments de l'Anàlisi Econòmica (UAB) and Institut d'Anàlisi Econòmica (CSIC).

Driffield, N. L., and K. Talyor. 2002. "Domestic Wage Determination: Regional Spillovers and Inward Investment." No 02/12, Discussion Papers in Economics from Department of Economics, University of Leicester.

Dollar, D. 2001. "Trade, Growth, and Poverty." Policy Research Working Paper No. 2615. Washington, D.C.: The World Bank.

Dollar, D. and A. Kraay. 2000. "Growth Is Good for the Poor." (Mimeographed version). Washington, D.C.: The World Bank.

Fallon, P. R., and R. E. B, Lucas. 2002. "The Impact of Financial Crises on Labor Markets, Household Incomes, and Poverty: A Review of Evidence." *World Bank Research Observer* 17 (1): 21–45.

Foster, J., and M. Székely. 2001. "Is Growth Good for the Poor? Tracking Low Incomes Using General Means." RES Working Paper Series No. 453. Research Department, Inter-American Development Bank, Washington, D.C., June.

Hanson, G. H. 2003. "What Has Happened to Wages in Mexico since NAFTA?" NBER Working Paper No. 9563.

Hellerstein, J. K., and D. Neumark. 1996. "Wages, Productivity, and Worker Characteristics: Evidence from Plant-level Production Functions and Wage Equations." NBER Working Paper No. 5626.

Holmlund, B. 1991. "Unemployment Persistence and Insider-Outsider Forces in Wage Determination." OECD Working Paper No. 92.

INEGI. 1994. "Encuesta nacional de ingresos y gastos de los hogares, Documento metodológico." México: Instituto Nacional de Estadística, Geografía e Informática.

Kakwani, N., B. Prakash, and H. Son. 2000. "Growth, Inequality, and Poverty: An Introduction." *Asian Development Review*, 18 (2): 1–21.

Loayza, N., and R. Polastri. 2004. "Poverty and Growth in Peru." Background Report for Peru's Poverty Assessment. Washington, D.C.: World Bank,

Lora, Eduardo. 1997. "Una década de reformas estructurales en América Latina: qué ha sido reformado, y como medirlo." IDB-OCE Working Paper No. 348. Washington, D.C.: Inter-American Development Bank

Maloney, W. F. 1999. "Does Informality Imply Segmentation in Urban Labor Markets? Evidence from Sectoral Transitions in Mexico." *World Bank Economic Review*, 13 (2): 275–302.

Maloney, W. F. and J. Nuñez. 2001. "Measuring the Impact of Minimum Wages: Evidence from Latin America." Policy Research Working Paper No. 2597. Washington, D.C.: The World Bank.

Morley, Samuel, Roberto Machado, and Stefano Pettinato. 1999. "Indexes of Structural Reform in Latin America." *Serie de Reformas Económicas* No. 12, Santiago: ECLAC.

Nicita, A. 2004. "Who Benefited from Trade Liberalization in Mexico? Measuring the Effects on Household Welfare." Policy Research Working Paper No. 3265. Washington, D.C.: The World Bank.

Nickell, S., and S. B. Wadhwani. 1989. "Insider Forces and Wage Determination." Center for Economic Policy Research Discussion Paper No 310. London: CEPR

Orszag, J. M., and G. Zoega. 1996. "Wages Ahead of Demand." Discussion Papers from Birkbeck College, Department of Economics.

Pineau, P. O. 2004. "Productivity to Reduce Poverty: Study of a Micro-level Institution in Peru." *International Productivity Monitor*, 9: 62–75.

Ravallion, M. 2000a, "Prices, Wages and Poverty in Rural India: What Lessons Do the Time Series Data Hold for Policy?" *Food Policy*, 25 (3): 351–364.

———. 2000b, "Growth and Poverty: Making Sense of the Current Debate." (Mimeograph version). Washington, D.C.: The World Bank.

Ravallion, M. and G. Datt. 1999. "Growth and Poverty in Rural India." Policy Research Working Paper No. 1405. Washington, D.C.: The World Bank.

Ravallion, M., L. Squire, and M. Bruno. 1999. "Equity and Growth in Developing Countries: Old and New Perspectives on the Policy Issues." Policy Research Working Paper No 1563. Washington, D.C.: The World Bank.

Revenga, A. 1999. "Employment and Wage Effects of Trade Liberalization: The Case of Mexican Manufacturing." Policy Research Working Paper No. 1524. Washington, D.C.: The World Bank.

Saint-Paul, G. 2001. "Distribution and Growth in an Economy with Limited Needs." Institute for the Study of Labor (IZA) Discussion Paper No. 273. Bonn: IZA.

Sala-i-Martin, Xavier. 2000. *Apuntes de Crecimiento Económico*. Barcelona: Antoni Bosch Editorial.

Secretaría de Programación y Presupuesto (SPP). 1977. *Encuesta Nacional de Ingreso-Gasto en los Hogares*, México (Survey).

Székely, M. 1998. *The Economics of Poverty, Inequality, and Wealth Accumulation in Mexico*. London: Macmillan.

———. 2005. "Pobreza y desigualdad en México entre 1950 y el 2004." *El Trimestre Económico*, forthcoming.

Tobin, J. 1994. "Poverty in Relation to Macroeconomic Trends, Cycles, and Policies." Cowles Foundation Discussion Paper No. 1030R, Yale University.

Van Bieseboeck, J. 2003. "Wages Equal Productivity: Fact or Fiction?" National Bureau of Economic Research (NBER) Working Paper No. 10174. Cambridge MA: NBER.

Walton, M. 2005. "Macroeconomic Policy, Markets, and Poverty Reduction." Paper presented at the "Conference on Poverty and Poverty Reduction Strategies: Mexican and International Experience" sponsored by the John F. Kennedy School of Government at Harvard University, and the Escuela de Graduados en Administración Pública y Política Pública at the Tecnológico de Monterrey, Monterrey, Mexico.

Zweimuller, J., and E. Barth. 1992. "Bargaining Structure, Wage Determination, and Wage Dispersion in Six OECD Countries." Institute of Industrial Relations Working Paper No. 1074. University of California, Berkeley.

3

Macroeconomic Policy, Markets, and Poverty Reduction

Michael Walton

In examining the relationship between a set of economy-wide policies and poverty reduction, I will discuss in particular the impact of macroeconomic management and policies designed to promote market functioning, especially in financial and product markets. This is contested terrain. The question is often posed in terms of whether a set of policies—sometimes packaged as a "Washington Consensus" or "neoliberal" policy mix—is "good" or "bad" for poverty reduction. My argument is that posing the issue in this way often distracts rather than helps the analysis of the underlying patterns of interaction. In particular, it takes insufficient account of interactions between context, policy choices, and their consequences: both the nature and effects of policy choice are heterogeneous, conditional on initial asset structures, production patterns, and institutions. My own focus is on the ways in which a variety of distributions—but especially of wealth and power—shape both the choice of policy and the character of these interactions.

This chapter emphasizes the importance of explicitly bringing distribution (back) into the interpretation of policy interactions. It might be argued that a focus on poverty already does that, and in particular brings in the part of the distribution that we should be most concerned with in terms of welfare. Here I contest this view, since what is going on in other parts of the distribution, and especially in the middle and upper parts of the power and wealth distribution, are as, and sometimes more, important to the relationships that concern us. It is perhaps worthy of note that the general line of argument can be seen to fall in the tradition of Adam Smith, who, of course, is well known for his advocacy of the power of markets to improve resource allocation and growth. Yet another major strand of his thinking is of the risks of capture of policy by the powerful, with a particular concern with abuse of their influence over the state to manage markets in order to sustain protection and profits. He was also broadly concerned with the distribution of influence and behaviors in a society and how this is a complement to market functioning.[1]

Which dimensions of poverty and distribution matter to the argument? There are two issues here: the dimensions that are of normative concern to an evaluation of outcomes for social welfare, and the dimensions that matter for causative processes. With respect to the evaluative question, we recognize that well-being is multi-dimensional, encompassing incomes, health status, education status, security, dignity, and so forth.[2] As a practical matter, we focus primarily on income (or expenditure) poverty as the outcome variable of interest, though the argument would not be different in structure if other dimensions of well-being were examined, even if it would, of course, be different in the details of the mechanisms and processes. With respect to what dimensions of distribution matter for causative processes, we emphasize the importance of patterns of power and wealth, and their interactions with formal and informal institutions. Direct measures of these are often hard to come by, and we sometimes use measures of income distribution as a (highly imperfect) proxy.

One of the corollaries of the argument is to take issue with the dichotomization of policy discussions concerning growth and poverty. One line of argument is that there are well-established relations between "good" macroeconomic management, trade, and financial policy on the one hand and growth on the other. By contrast, the relations with these variables and distribution are unclear or weakly established in cross-country analyses.[3] In a version of the views on efficient instrument allocation, it might be argued that these domains of policy should be allocated to growth maximization. And since growth is (almost always) good for the reduction of income poverty, that is also a sound way to pursue the goal of poverty reduction. There is a complementary role for human capital formation and safety nets, especially in combination with growth-enhancing policies. Specific, targeted efforts to reduce poverty belong in these areas of human capital and social protection.[4] However, if, as this paper argues, the choice and effects of economy-wide policies on macroeconomic performance and market functioning are substantially shaped by distributional factors, then this dichotomization is not only incorrect intellectually, but misleading for practical policy. While there is not the space for detailed discussion of policy implications, it is argued here that effective, poverty-reducing, economy-wide policies need to take account of the pattern of power (or agency) and its institutional manifestation in interpreting policy choice and shaping policy design.

This chapter draws primarily on existing literature to discuss these issues. The next section presents some general patterns on the relationship between growth, distribution, and poverty, focusing primarily on income dimensions. The second section presents the overall argument on the relationship between distributions of power and wealth, institutions, and both policy choices and their consequences. This is in turn followed by a section that reviews issues in the application of the argument in the domains of macroeconomic policy, the financial sector, and trade liberalization, followed by the conclusions.

Patterns of Poverty Reduction, Income Inequality, Growth, and Policy across Countries

Extensive work has been done on the cross-country relationship between poverty, distribution, and growth, especially with respect to income or expenditure poverty and distribution. This section presents some of the main results.

There is a powerful association between economic growth and income poverty reduction. It is well established that greater average incomes—that is, growth—are associated with higher incomes of the poor, and thus signify a reduction in indices of poverty (see Ravallion and Chen 1997; Dollar and Kraay 2002). This is illustrated in Figure 1 for the bilateral relationship between growth in mean income or consumption from household surveys, and changes in the (log of the) poverty rate. Qualitatively similar results are found for other poverty measures that take into account the gap between the incomes of the poor and poverty line, and weighting of this gap for the poorest. Note that this is not adjusted for anything, including any changes in the distribution of income. On average, the growth of incomes of the poor is close to that of mean income from surveys. (There is also a significant, if weaker, association between poverty reduction and growth in mean income of private consumption from the national accounts.) Although the relationship is strong, growth only explains about half of the total variation in poverty changes. While old fears of growth being systematically immiserating for the poor are robustly rejected, the figure illustrates that this is not unknown: there are a few episodes where positive growth was indeed associated with poverty increases. This must have come from adverse changes in the distribution of income.

This first simple pass at the cross-country relationships might suggest that the way to tackle income poverty is via promotion of growth. There is no robust, systematic relationship between income distribution and economic growth. While immiserating growth episodes do occasionally occur, on average there is no significant association between changes in mean income or consumption and changes in inequality—as illustrated in Figure 2, which uses means from household surveys and the Gini index. Distributional change is, on average, unimportant, suggesting that reducing inequality is an unreliable route to reducing poverty. However, even if we confine our attention to income poverty, there is evidence to suggest that this assumption is incorrect, owing to the impact of income inequality on the efficacy of growth in reducing poverty, and the (probable) influence of some inequalities on the pace of growth itself. When we go beyond income dimensions of poverty to measures of health, education, access to services, insecurity, or dignity, a comparable conclusion is reached, but with greater emphasis: on average, growth is associated with improvements in these other measures, but there's typically even larger variance, and thus greater influence of other factors (see World Bank, 2004 for a synthesis). While these considerations are of immense importance, we put them to one side, to keep the focus on inequalities, overall development, and poverty.

The distribution of income does have an important effect on the strength of the relationship between growth and poverty reduction. The first way in which inequality measurably affects poverty is via the impact of both initial inequalities and changes in inequality on the efficacy of growth for income poverty declines. This can be shown mathematically: just as at a given level of income, increased inequality is associated with greater poverty (provided it is not just a product of greater inequality among the non-poor, leaving the incomes of the poor unaffected), so higher levels of inequality (under similar assumptions) mean that the poor reap a smaller share of increments of national income or consumption. Similarly, inequality *changes*, which affect the poor, will lead to greater or lower impacts on poverty declines.[5]

In addition, income inequality may be associated with the rate of growth itself. There is a great deal of literature that argues that inequality and growth can affect each other. One strand of this thinking lies at the heart of this paper and is taken up in the next section. Here we briefly comment on the cross-country relationships.

First, the Kuznetzian perspective, that inequality automatically rises and falls with the development process, is not supported by the data. There are indeed some episodes of rises and falls in inequality in some countries, but there is no relationship on average, and such changes are no more common than falls and rises in inequality (see Bruno, Ravallion, and Squire 1998). It is also worth noting that the Kuznetzian view of inequality-growth relationships is benign, viewing changes in inequality as a byproduct of the development process. Processes of industrialization and urbanization lead first to a rise in inequality as workers shift from low- to high-productivity sectors, and then a fall, as employment in relatively high productivity activities comes to dominate (with parallel patterns for education).

Second, there is not a robust empirical support for a negative influence of initial income inequality on growth from cross-country econometric analysis. Analysis in this form was motivated, in part, by concern over a less benign, causal effect of greater inequality on lower growth, working through either adverse influences on investment of incomplete capital markets, or political economy channels. Many studies did indeed find a negative coefficient of initial income inequality on growth, after controlling for a range of other factors (see Bénabou 1996 and Aghion et al. 1999 for surveys of both theoretical views and empirical results). However, these studies suffer from concerns over measurement errors in the inequality measure and over the possibility that omitted variables may be driving some relationship. Moreover, more recent work suggests the relationship is not robust.[6]

With respect to policy, the cross-country evidence on macroeconomic and market-related policies and inequality suggests that is not a robust pattern here either. As an illustrative pass at the data, Figure 5 plots the bilateral correlation of an index of policy reform and inequality in Latin America—a region known for its extensive policy reforms in the 1980s and 1990s. Using the log of the income Gini as the measure of inequality, what is most striking is the lack of any relationship with the extent of policy reform as measured by an index of policy for a number of domains, including trade liberalization, tax reform, financial sector reform, capital account liberalization, and privatization. An absence of simple correlations is also notable for individual reform indices, and between changes in the Gini and the level of reform. The same conclusions emerge from multivariate econometric exercises.[7]

While caution is appropriate on the robustness of results, we highlight additional results from López's analysis on a global data base.[8] López explores the question of net effects of polices on income poverty from the cross-country patterns. Policies that lead to greater price stability, expanded infrastructure, or more education have an unambiguous positive impact on poverty, since they appear to work through both growth and inequality channels. By contrast, policies that lead to greater trade opening and financial liberalization appear to have negative effects on poverty in the short run, but positive effects in the long term, as growth-enhancing effects come to dominate inequality impacts over the longer term.

This approach could be explored further. Some analyses are suggestive of positive impacts on inequality of greater macroeconomic stability, with negative effects of trade and financial sector liberalization. This may indicate the need for fine-tuning of policies, or ensuring that complementary policies are put in place with respect to physical and human capital, or safety nets. Although these are important lines of policy analysis to develop, we believe this approach may miss some of the bigger action on the relationship between inequality, institutions, and growth that is relevant to analysis of macroeconomic and market-related policies. We turn to this now, before returning to specific domains of policy later in the chapter.

Inequalities, Institutions, and Growth

Recent economics literature offers two broad categories of explanation for why inequality may be bad for investment and growth.[9] The first emphasizes intrinsic features of markets—in particular the role of imperfections in capital and insurance markets. Would-be investors with profitable investment opportunities are unable to borrow the funds, or insure against associated risks, owing to problems of asymmetric information and contracting. Markets for land or human capital are imperfect. As a consequence, initial wealth matters for the financing of investment. This is likely to lead to underinvestment of those with low levels of wealth, and possibly overinvestment of those with higher levels of wealth. Both the level and efficiency of investment may be affected.

The second category of explanation flows primarily from considerations of how power both shapes and is shaped by institutions. In societies with high levels of political inequality, powerful elites may have an interest in using their power for predation. Similarly, broad-based investment in physical and human capital may be against their interests—at least in the short to medium term—since this could lead to challenges to their position of power, as subordinate groups acquire greater economic leverage and form the education and social organizations that allow them to contend for power more effectively. Of course, elites may face a tradeoff between a larger share of a smaller pie, and a smaller share of a larger pie,[10] but history is replete with cases where those with power have chosen continued predation over broadening of the economic and social base of their societies. Furthermore, just as elites seek to preserve their position, so middle and poorer groups seek to improve theirs—this can lead to distributive conflicts that can also be a source of investment-sapping uncertainty over property rights and economic conditions.

The focus here is on the second category of argument, while also emphasizing the complementarity between markets and power as mediated by institutions: the combination of imperfect markets and highly unequal power is particularly pernicious for both long-run growth and inequality—and thus for poverty reduction.

The Argument: Equitable Institutions and Long-run Prosperity

The essence of the argument is that institutions necessary for long-term prosperity are more likely to be formed and sustained in the context of greater political equality.[11] Here institutions refer to the set of social arrangements and formal and informal rules of the game that shape economic, political, and social activities. The argument can be presented in two parts.

First, central to long-run prosperity are institutional arrangements that provide the rules and context to spur efficient investment, innovation, and risk-taking. We highlight three: (a) institutional arrangements that provide security of property rights for investors, and in particular, protection against abuse by the powerful (whether from the executive, employers, the court system, etc.); (b) arrangements for management of conflict over distributional shares and over institutions themselves; and (c) institutions to manage the array of risks that individuals face. An additional set of more specific economic institutions, governing financing, contracting, and employment, would provide more or less assurance to economic actors that they will receive the fruits of the efforts—in work, investment, and innovation—and that risks can be managed.

Second, institutions have distributional consequences. How they are formed, and how they change, has to be understood in terms of the interests, power, and behaviors of different groups, with conflict intrinsic to both how institutions work and how they change. Where there is a high degree of inequality of power, notably of narrow elites (but also, for example, of dominant majorities), institutions are shaped that favor the private interests of some of the population, with predatory or extractive processes and rules. This is not conducive to the provision of the property rights and economic, social, and physical security of all the population, both because predation or rent-seeking is fostered, and because there is more likely to be conflict to contest the institutional arrangements. Conflict may challenge arrangements considered exploitative or unjust—from slave revolts to peasant rebellions and social movements of industrial workers. Alternatively, it can be fights over the prize that flows from extractive structures.

In both the shaping and dynamics of institutions, interactions between power, economic conditions, and institutional histories matter. In particular, greater political equality—and more equitable economic institutions—are more likely when resource endowments and production possibilities favor the bargaining position of poorer, subordinate groups, and where institutional histories (formal and informal) favor their social and political recognition.

Evidence

While the argument is important, indeed central to development processes, only some of the evidence comes from well-identified analyses that are typical of economic hypothesis-testing. Support broadly comes from two sources: cross-country comparisons and historical narratives.

Across countries, there are contemporary associations that are consistent with the argument. These say nothing of causation, but provide some context. By way of illustration, Figure 6 plots a measure of protection against expropriation risk (from the company Political Risk Services, which assess the risk that investments will be expropriated across countries) against the log of GDP per capita. There is a strong positive association. This association is shared by many indicators of the "quality" of institutions, from a variety of sources including measures of constraints on the executive (from the Polity IV data base, see Polity IV Project, 2005), and from measures of the rule of law, corruption (with an inverse relationship), and government effectiveness (from Kaufmann, Kraay and Mastruzzi 2003). These are measures that we would expect to describe, in different ways, institutional arrangements that underpin long-run prosperity. This type of data has provided the basis for considerable empirical analysis supporting the view that "institutions matter" for long-run development, with a variety of approaches to identification of directions of causation.[12] The approach of Acemoglu, Johnson, and Robinson (2000), for instance, is based on a historical natural experiment. In a completely different approach to identification, Kaufmann and Kraay (2002) also argue that the data from the last part of the 20th century support the view that causation flows from the quality of governance to growth, not in the opposite direction.

Direct measures of the type of political inequalities we are concerned with are less easy to come by. Indices of democracy provide one important source: a democratic society is intrinsically more equal politically than an undemocratic one, despite the manifold imperfections of democracies in practice. Greater democracy is correlated with higher GDP per capita. It is also associated with greater constraints on the power of the executive branch of government. There is also a correlation with measures of economic inequality, such as the Gini coefficient for incomes or expenditures, but also substantial variation in the level of economic inequality for given levels of democracy. A similar pattern is found for correlations with measures of the quality of institutions: Figure 7 illustrates that there is negative association between an index of ethno-linguistic fractionalization (a measure of social fractures) and the rule of law, with comparable results for other indicators of social and economic inequality (including the income Gini) and measures of institutional quality. Again, there is significant dispersion around the relationship.

While these cross-country correlations say nothing about causation, they suggest that greater equalities on some dimensions are consistent with long-run prosperity. Another way to take a broad-brush look at the patterns is from the perspective of the group of highly prosperous societies. Excluding cases that are wealthy because of extraordinary levels of natural resources (notably oil-rich Gulf states), all now prosperous societies put in place equitable institutions for political, social, and economic participation to a greater extent than the bulk of the now developing world. Even the United States, commonly considered unequal and socially exclusive (see Alesina and Glaeser 2004 for a discussion), is substantially more equal than most developing countries in terms of political representation, access to schooling, and other basic services, protection from executive abuse or expropriation, gender equity, equality before the law, and action to promote the historically disadvantaged or exploited groups (notably African Americans and indigenous groups). Moreover, degrees of equality of political influence, economic opportunity, and fair process are likely to be more important than equality in outcomes (such as income) in underpinning the institutional conditions for long-run prosperity. Indeed, these equalities will typically occur alongside inequalities of outcomes owing to differences in effort, for example, ameliorating (though not necessarily eliminating) specific tradeoffs with incentives.[13]

Let us now turn to analyses that seek to identify the causal processes among political inequalities, institutions, and prosperity. We highlight the work of a series of papers by Acemoglu, Johnson, and Robinson (2000, 2001) that treats the process of colonization by European powers from around the 16th century as a form of natural experiment. This work draws on historical interpretations, notably that of Engerman and Sokoloff (1997, 2002) on the contrasting experiences within the Americas. Variation is provided not by the character of the colonizer, but by the economic and physical conditions that the colonizers found in their quest for wealth and power. Two classes of factors influenced the form of colonization: the resources found in colonized areas, and the extent to which diseases rendered the physical environment inhospitable for Europeans.[14] With respect to the first, the combination of production potential for resource-based extraction—notably in silver, gold, and sugar—plus access to pools of subordinate, unskilled labor, led to the formation of extractive, oligarchic, and socially unequal political and social institutions. In the Andes and Central America high concentrations of indigenous populations—the result of developed, semi-urbanized civilizations—were the source of subordinate labor. In other parts of Latin America, African slaves provided the labor. The institutions formed ranged from oligarchic political structures to slavery and particular institutions of land and labor management—such as the *encomienda* (rights to land and indigenous labor in assigned geographic areas) and the *mita* (forced labor of indigenous groups) in Spanish America.

By contrast, in northern America, English colonists tried to impose oligarchic structures and extractive economic institutions, but failed to do so. There was neither the natural resource base nor ready supplies of subordinate labor (Engermann and Sokoloff 2002, De Ferranti et al. 2004). The bulk of the population in governed territories was European settlers, and land was abundant. Attempts to replicate unequal structures that were known from Europe, or were being developed in Spanish America failed, and relatively equal political and economic structures evolved—complemented by less stratified social structures.

The hypothesis is that these institutional contrasts had considerable persistence, affecting the variation in the quality of institutions in the 20th century and, consequently, contemporary economic performance. These historical influences worked through a variety of institutions and policies, including voting rights, extension of education, and access to finance, as well as the particular forms of political structures that evolved in the 19th and 20th centuries.[15] To take one important area, the breadth of political influence and the expansion of education can be traced across societies and over time. This is consistent with the argument of Lindert (2004) that the broadening of social provisioning in now-rich societies was fundamentally driven by the expansion of voice to middle and subordinate groups in the population.

These historical analyses are backed by econometric results. There is a correlation between resource endowments and an inhospitable disease environment. Many resource-rich areas were in the tropics. Resource-poor areas—for example in northern America, Australasia, and the Southern Cone of South America—were outside the tropics and so less disease-prone.

There is no reason to associate such historical differences in disease conditions with contemporary economic policy, except via the association with institutional mechanisms outlined here. This allowed Acemoglu, Johnson, and Robinson to use settler mortality as an instrument for the historically determined element of contemporary institutions. They find that institutions (in this sense) can explain the bulk of differences in measures of long-run economic performance (as measured by current income levels or macroeconomic instability, for example), with competing explanations losing most of their statistical significance. While debate continues on these interpretations, this approach lends substantial support to the view that institutions matter to economic development. We have highlighted here the role of interactions between political, social, and economic inequalities in shaping institutional arrangements.

This approach suggests that historical inequalities in political, social, and economic conditions are reflected in institutional arrangements. This heritage interacts with contemporary inequalities in the shaping or reshaping of economic policies and institutions. A highly stylized representation is given in Figure 8, which suggests a chain of causation from initial economic and political conditions through political economy structures to institutions. In reality the process is, of course, continuous, with the heritage of past institutions always interacting with political and economic initial conditions. However, particular periods may experience more dramatic possibilities of change (or "rupture" in the terminology of sociologists—see Heller and Mahoney 2003).

These patterns have consequences for particular fields of action—such as macroeconomic and market-related policies and their relation to both efficiency and equity (and consequently poverty) that are the focus of this paper. It is often useful to think of two forms of influence: (a) through a causal effect on the design and implementation of public action in economic domains, in ways that affect both efficiency and equity (and consequentially poverty); and (b) through influencing how such policies work in practice in shaping distributional outcomes, both through other areas of policies (such as in human development and risk management) and in the functioning of markets.

Two Illustrations: China and Spain

Before moving to a discussion of policy domains, we will explore the overall argument further through a look at these two cases of successful transformation and poverty reduction in the second half of the 20th century. We are looking for two patterns, following the last subsection: evidence of causal relationships between moves to greater political equality and economic liberalization, and between economic liberalization, inequality, and poverty reduction. For these two countries it is useful to begin the discussion in reverse order—first looking at what happened, and then why.

China looms large in any attempt to interpret development, and especially one that seeks to understand the role of equity in development processes. Have we not seen China move from a highly equitable form of communism to extensive use of domestic and international markets? And did this not lead to *both* rising income inequality (Figure 9 below) *and* the most extraordinary pace and scale of reduction in poverty and expansion in social welfare in history? Finally, did this not occur within the context of continued concentration of political power in the Communist party? This looks, at first glance, like a brute-fact refutation of the central argument of this paper—that equity can lay the basis for prosperous development.

Yet an account along these lines is an important misreading of change in China. Take some of the major shifts in Chinese policy that the literature interprets as having driven growth and income poverty: the institutional shift to the household responsibility system allowing peasants to produce for themselves (1979–early 1980s); massive indirect effects of opening to international trade (whole period); opening to inward Foreign Direct Investment or FDI (especially in the 1990s); and huge internal migration flows. All these expanded equality of opportunity, moving society away from a situation of extensive restrictions on opportunities, especially for poorer groups. Moreover, all were part of the sources of growth. Aspects of Chinese development did increase inequity. For example, the prevalence of investment linked to connections and extensive corruption is clearly inequitable, in the sense of both unfair process and inequalities of opportunity to all potential investors. There *may* have been a tradeoff here with respect to growth in the short to medium term, if such murky deals raised investment levels—but in the long term, introducing more transparent and fairer process will be important to sustained growth.

There were also periods in which policy-related shifts were associated with biases either against inner provinces of China or against rural areas. These were the factors behind the rise in inequality in outcomes and stagnating income poverty between the later 1980s and early 1990s, and probably a source of rising inequality of opportunity. For these cases, there may have been some tradeoff—or a more balanced policy stance may have achieved greater equity without significant growth losses. In any case, few observers argue that such policy-induced biases were essential to Chinese growth, in contrast to the overall institutional change and opening.

Moreover, even using the narrower prism of income inequality, it is noteworthy that the periods when inequality fell (notably the early 1980s and the mid-1990s) actually had the highest growth rates, not the lowest. Ravallion and Chen (2004) and Ravallion (2004) examine inequality in China and India in detail during the 1980s and 1990s and document the remarkable increase in inequality in China. However, they also find that inequality grew most rapidly during periods when economic growth was slow. Moreover, provinces that experienced greater increases in inequality had lower growth. As argued by Ravallion (2004), the China example provides little support for the view that an increase in inequality is an inevitable companion to rapid economic growth. With respect to poverty reduction, the analysis of these authors confirms our expectation that poverty reduction was faster in periods when inequality was not rising. The bulk of the extraordinary reduction in income poverty can be accounted for by two periods: the initial economic liberalization and agricultural growth of the early 1980s that was associated with low levels of inequality, and the agricultural price adjustments of the mid-1990s that were associated with falls in inequality (Figure 9).

With respect to patterns, there are also rising concerns within China over the adverse consequences for development of areas of rising inequality, both in areas of social provisioning (in health for example) and the concentration of wealth through connections. There is no evidence that these brought benefits in income growth, and most observers (including the Chinese government) would see this as an area where policy could be improved.

What are the findings on the political bases for reform and their relationships to economic preconditions for prosperous growth? Here we note three important insights from the political science literature on China. First, in the wake of the Cultural Revolution and the realization that China was seriously lagging in development, the reshaping of policy under the leadership of Deng Xiaoping involved a shift in the internal political balance of power that gave greater influence to the provinces and lower levels of government, introducing checks and balances and inter-regional competition in the political system that constrained the power of the center (Shirk 1993, Montinola, Qian and Weingast 1995). Second, this was complementary to the variety of processes of economic liberalization and, especially, shifts in property rights. The latter included control rights in land for peasants, de facto ownership of Township and Village Enterprises by local governments, and increasingly mixed or private ownership of larger industrial enterprises. Moreover, while the institutions were far from the Anglo-Saxon approach to security of property rights, there was *alignment* between political conditions and economic interests in security of the returns from property, in villages, local, and provincial government (Che and Qian 1998). Third, the weakening of the political credibility of the Communist party after the Cultural Revolution made both maintenance of security of the investment and delivery of economic benefits to peasants and workers essential to its political survival. There were both powerful incentives not to expropriate investors, and a need to resolve distributional conflicts before they developed into an unmanageable form of contestation. Of course, none of these considerations are necessarily permanent resolutions: the non-disruptive management of a political opening in China is, over the long term, surely a necessary condition for sustained economic development.

Finally, it may be useful to consider China's conditions in relation to the schematic account of influences in Figure 8. China's factor endowments and domestic and international production and trading possibilities made its reliance on labor-intensive production in agriculture and industry central, rather than resource-based extraction. This combined with an ideological commitment to egalitarian political and social structures. These structures, needed to deliver economically to the mass of the population for regime credibility, at the same time reinforced the implicit negotiating position of poorer groups. External influences were also favorable with respect to the extraordinary success of East Asian neighbors (notably Taiwan) and the ready supply of capital, conditional on sufficient guarantees on property rights. Specific institutional solutions were varied and often innovative. As Rodrik (2005) has argued, what matters for effectiveness is not the particular form of institutional design but the fit within a local context and effectiveness with respect to core principles (including guarantees on property rights).

Spain provides a further illustration of the interaction between political and economic conditions, and the role of the nexus of institutions and equality.[16] It is of interest in providing an example of a transformation from a relatively backward, authoritarian, and interventionist country into a prosperous, liberalized, and democratic society. We outline a few of the major features of this transformation that are relevant to the argument in this chapter.

Spain's transformation involved a combination of: (a) extensive liberalization of product and financial markets, backed by removal of price controls and significant privatization of a large public enterprise sector; (b) a major expansion of the role of the state in social provisioning, as well as extensive provision of economic infrastructure, underpinned by a large rise in government revenues; (c) pursuit of conservative macroeconomic policies; and (d) democratization following the death of Franco in 1975.

The changes in economic and social policies occurred in two phases. The initial modernization push, backed by partial liberalization, was initiated in 1959 under Franco, in response to economic stagnation and crisis and the threat of a political crisis. This led to an acceleration of major structural shifts in the economy, with rapid growth of industrial and service production, large-scale rural-urban migration and population shifts out of the poorer south and west. It was associated with a transition from an unequal, largely agrarian society (with pockets of industrial enterprise in the Basque regions and Catalonia), to one with a significant middle and working class. The second phase occurred in the period of democratization and entry into the European Union. This major opening was politically and socially underwritten by the expansion of spending on education and a variety of risk-management mechanisms—including health, unemployment, and old-age insurance. It was also backed by an encompassing pact with unions, left-wing parties, and employers' associations in 1977 (Boix 2004) that led to the persistence of restrictive labor market policies inherited from the Franco regime. Interactions between major economic restructuring and a rigid labor market are considered an important source of high unemployment that reached over 20 percent, with much higher rates for the young and women (Bentolila and Jimeno 2003; Boix 2004).

In terms of income inequality, the major transition to moderate inequality appears to have occurred by the early 1970s, with a Gini coefficient already around 0.37. In the democratic period, the major changes were in the equalizing role of the public sphere—in line with Lindert's (2004) argument on the centrality of expansion of voice in the broadening of public provisioning and willingness to pay taxes. Figure 10 shows the share of tax revenues in relation to fitted values from an international analysis of authoritarian and democratic countries. This spending pattern was underpinned by societal attitudes: in 1979 over 70 percent of Spaniards agreed with the statement, "the distribution of wealth in this country is totally unjust" (Gunther et al. 2004, p. 173). By 1996 less than 3 percent of the population thought that the state should not be responsible for the provision of health services, pensions, housing for the poor, and regulating the environment (cited in Boix 2004).

The interactions between political conditions and economic and social policy can be looked at through the prism of the earlier part of this section (including the simplified schema in Figure 8). The transition of the second half of the 20th century can be contrasted with the early, failed transition in the 1920s and 1930s that culminated in the Spanish Civil War. Spain was then highly inegalitarian and predominantly agrarian. It was also a socially polarized society. There were strong incentives for fights over property between classes, but the subordinate groups had weak negotiating power. The existing elite won and sought to preserve the institutional bases of their privilege, albeit with some regulated protection for formal workers and housing markets inspired by Falangist (Fascist) corporatist ideology. The modernization process begun in the late Franco period then shifted the social and economic bases of the game: the middle and working classes had a stake in the system, and more to lose from conflicts over property. An industrial and service-based economy had a greater need for a productive and cooperative labor force. Social polarization had declined with urbanization. Externally there was the powerful incentive (and emblem) of successful, capitalist, social provisioning societies of the European club. These factors shifted the terms of the game to one of seeking fairer distribution within a system that supported capitalist growth. The Constitution of 1978 enshrined the existing social consensus regarding private property and a market economy on the one hand, and the need to develop a welfare state to meet social rights and manage risk on the other.

Macroeconomic and Market-related Policies, Institutions, and Poverty

Let us return to the question of policy design, but with the added prism of interactions between inequalities and institutions. We look at three areas: macroeconomic crises and associated policies, financial sector policies, and trade (and related) opening.

Macroeconomic Crises

Such crises are devastating for the poor: in the short run because of income losses that are often complemented by declines in public services induced by fiscal problems; and in the long term because of foregone gains and possible permanent losses in investment, including in the human capital of children.[17] For example, in Mexico the 1994–95 Tequila crisis led to a sharp increase in income poverty, and not until 2002 was the level back down to the pre-crisis level (Figure 11). Moreover, this occurred despite a small reduction in inequality in the wake of the crisis (consistent with cross-country results found in López, see Table 1). We are interested in what determines crises, and in their distributional (and so poverty) consequences. The perspective of the previous section illuminates both questions.

Institutional conditions and political inequalities affect the propensity for crises. The extensive macroeconomic literature emphasizes a variety of causes, depending on the nature of the crisis. These range from fiscal imbalance, herd-like movements of investors behind exchange-rate crises, and interactions between external liabilities, exchange rate, and financial-corporate conditions, especially under conditions of crony capitalism.[18] We emphasize a complementary line of argument that is closely related to the discussion of the preceding section. This is developed by Acemoglu et al. (2003) based on the political science literature (see, for example, Bates 1981 on Ghana). The authors argue that crises reflect underlying distributional struggles and social fractures, as well as the absence of effective institutional arrangements for managing these. Acemoglu et al. note that macroeconomic crises are both positively correlated with common indicators of "bad" macroeconomic policies, such as high inflation, exchange-rate overvaluation, and high fiscal deficits, and negatively correlated with measures of the quality of institutions, such as a measure of the constraint on executive power (see Figure 12 for an illustration of the latter relationship). The researchers use the same identification strategy as was applied to influences on long-run incomes, using settler mortality data as an instrument for the historically determined component of contemporary institutional quality. Macro policies are either treated as exogenous or instrumented by their lagged values. The analysis indicates a strong, causal influence of the historically determined component of institutions and, once this is controlled for, little or no influence from macro policies (there is weak support for the role of exchange-rate overvaluation, but not for the role of inflation or public spending/fiscal deficits). The interpretation is that the underlying sources of crises lie in institutional and social arrangements that may manifest themselves via macro policies or alternative fields—if macro policies become too tightly controlled for whatever reason, they will spill over into macroeconomic instability via other channels.

In related work on the relationship between macroeconomic instability and interactions with inequality and institutions, Rodrik (1999) argues in a cross-country empirical analysis that the effects of external shocks in the 1970s were significantly worse for subsequent growth in societies where latent distributional conflicts (as proxied by income inequality or ethno-linguistic fragmentation) were severe, and conflict-management mechanisms (proxied by institutional strength and indicators of democracy) were weak.

The *effects* of crises can also be highly regressive, and are shaped by unequal influences. Analyses of the effect of crises on income inequalities find a variety of effects: according to household income surveys, crises are sometimes associated with rising inequality (a common pattern in the 1980s in Latin America, see De Janvry and Sadoulet 2000) and sometimes with falling inequality. As previously noted, López (2004) finds that high inflation is associated with increased inequality, but banking crises are associated with falls in inequality (as occurred in the Mexican Tequila crisis).

However, analyses that utilize household income surveys miss important parts of the action. In particular, there is additional evidence of regressive effects from factor shares, and case study evidence from banking crises, that are probably highly regressive in the case of banking crises.

Diwan (2001, 2002) finds that labor shares systematically fall during crises and do not fully recover afterward; Figure 13 illustrates a cross-country result for three countries in Latin America. In Mexico, for example, the labor share fell sharply in 1982, steadily recovered during the following decade, weathered the more moderate macroeconomic setback of 1989, and then fell significantly following the 1994–95 crisis. The flip side of this pattern, of course, is that the shares of profits rise relative to wages, though some of the effect may be due to rises in informal enterprise income. There are also significant interactions with structural variables. In particular, closed trade, capital controls, and fiscal deficits are associated with higher labor shares in normal times, but also with larger falls in labor shares when crises occur. Diwan interprets crises as mechanisms for the resolution of distributional conflicts that are not tackled during good economic times. Labor is relatively immobile and so typically bears a higher proportion of the cost.

When macroeconomic crises also involve banking crises, additional mechanisms play a role. This works both through the cost of fiscal bailouts of financial losses and through patterns of gains and losses within the financial system. The fiscal costs of banking crises are large (Table 2). In analyses of a number of Latin American case studies, Halac and Schmukler (2003) argue that the beneficiaries of such bailouts are primarily those in the upper ranks of the income and wealth distribution, including depositors, bank owners, and corporate borrowers. While some depositors are in the middle of the distribution, poorer groups are systematically excluded, since they participate much less in the formal financial system. There are possible gains for poorer groups through indirect employment effects, but Honohan and Klingebiel (2000) find no relationship between the extent of bailout and economic activity. Moreover, Halac and Schmukler find that large borrowers with close connections with banks particularly benefited from bailouts associated with crises in Chile, Ecuador, and Mexico.

In addition to effects of bailouts, there can be significant effects from within a financial system. In Argentina, large foreign depositors were moving out their money earlier than small depositors. Indeed, in terms of the value of Argentine assets, on average capital *gains* may have been reaped, as illustrated by the huge rise in the value of foreign assets in relation to domestic GDP (Figure 14).

Interpretation and Policy Implications

We can relate the patterns of interaction between institutions, inequality, and crises to the schematic account of influences presented earlier. Fundamental to high crisis proclivity and regressive workouts are institutional arrangements that do a poor job in constraining the exercise of influence of the rich and powerful. In unequal societies, incentives to extract benefits in crises from existing structures (financial, fiscal, property) and to shift assets out of the country are strong. The costs of doing so may be low, given histories of holding assets abroad. The bargaining position of poor and subordinate groups may be weak, despite pockets of influence in parts of the formal sector, and is further weakened by a crisis. Indeed, an implicit function of a crisis is as a mechanism to resolve distributional conflicts, including through the weakening of the influence of labor, given the inadequacy of conflict-management and commitment mechanisms for prudent custody of the economy in normal times. Spending expansions in "good" times are a classic instrument of populist macro policy that, far from being a means of redistribution between groups, is a means of shifting distributional conflicts to the future—as recognized in some of the literature on hyperinflation (Bruno 1993; Morales and Sachs 1988).

What does this interpretation mean for the formulation of a more poverty-oriented policy while seeking to prevent and manage crises? There is no space to go into design specifics, but we can outline some principles. These are summarized in Table 3, which highlights the complementarity between policy design and political and social accountability structures. In terms of policy design, some features are familiar: the need to build stronger regulatory and supervisory structures for the financial system and comprehensive insurance mechanisms *out of crisis*. Once a crisis hits, it is practically hard to design and implement such measures, and politically difficult to implement more equitable outcomes.

Less obvious is the emphasis on fiscal prudence. In public debates, adopting a less stringent macroeconomic stance is often portrayed as a pro-poor, equalizing approach, whether in good times or bad. While there will always be specific judgments made about the distributional impacts of fiscal and monetary policy options, the analysis here suggests that taking a "superprudent" position over the course of the cycle provides greater hope of supporting a more equal development pattern (De Ferranti et al. 2004). At one level, this sharply reinforces the common prescription to break away from pro-cyclical policy positions (that is, fiscal expansion when the economy is growing and fiscal tightening when it is contracting). Macroeconomic restraint in good times will facilitate automatic stabilizers and allow a sensible, contra-cyclical easing of policies when adverse shocks occur. Building fiscal rules and institutions that help overcome both the political economy-related pressure to deplete potential surpluses in good times and informational asymmetry problems—and hence improve credibility in countercyclical fiscal policies during downturns—therefore becomes a top priority (Perry 2003). This strategy would in particular provide the macroeconomic foundation for broad-based, self-expanding safety nets.

Finally, there is a case for different forms of accountability. Over the long term, the most effective approach is to move to new fiscal and social contracts built on deeper accountability structures in a better political equilibrium (Robinson 2003). The case of Spain is a good example of such a shift. This needs to be effected with strong regulatory accountability that is shielded from short-run political pressures from all sides—more independent central banks and financial sector supervision—and greater transparency and debate over the overall design of macro policy and the incidence of workouts.

Financial Sector Development, Inequality, and Poverty[19]
Unequal access to finance is associated with unequal opportunities to produce, invest, and manage risk. Poorer households face lower access to finance or less favorable terms. External finance is needed for new investment of economic entrants and for expansions, and can play a role in overcoming other barriers. For these reasons, financial reform is often judged to be part of the solution to both constraints on productive investment and broader access. There is indeed an association between financial depth and income inequality: Beck, Demirgüç-Kunt, and Levine (2004) find a relationship that appears to flow from deeper finance to lower inequality in a cross-country analysis (this seeks to control for reverse causation, but does not control for possible common influences on both factors).

There is a growing body of evidence on the importance of barriers to entrepreneurial activity (Djankov, La Porta, López-de-Silanes, and Shleifer 2001; World Bank 2003). These obstacles are generally more onerous in poorer countries and particularly costly for small- and medium-sized businesses and the self-employed. They are an important reason for small firms and the self-employed choosing to remain informal. Yet informality further undermines their access to finance, limits trading opportunities, and reduces their capacity to expand.

Various economic, technical, and institutional reasons explain unequal access to finance, including the fixed costs of loan provision, high costs of enforcement of repayment of small loans, and weak property rights in the informal sector (De Soto 2000). However, such reasons only form part of the story. Access is unequal for areas of finance for which enforcement is not a concern—such as deposit taking. In addition, both the micro-credit movement, and large banks such as Bank Rakyat Indonesia and ICICI Bank in India have shown how to reach poorer customers profitably. Barriers to entry are, at least in part, outcomes of underlying inequalities in power.

Inequality of influence can be a source of unequal financial sector policies and institutions. The causation from unequal influence to a narrower financial system is probably of greater importance than the effects in the other direction. This is borne out by a variety of case studies, from the historical experience of developed societies (see Rajan and Zingales 2004) and from contemporary developing countries. Table 4 provides a selective list of results from recent studies of developing countries (from Claessens and Perotti 2004) that range from low-income societies such as Pakistan to middle income countries such as Korea, Malaysia, and Mexico, and transition societies such as the Czech Republic and Russia.

These findings are supportive of the view that political influence, when unchecked by societal institutions, is an important source of inequitable distortions in financial systems. This conclusion is also consistent with more general cross-country evidence that the level of enforcement of barriers to entry rises with both lower political accountability and higher inequality of income. Figure 15 (Graphs 15a and 15b) illustrates the patterns for income inequality (which is, of course, only a very weak proxy for unequal power).

Banking systems with concentrated ownership structures are associated with weaker institutional environments (Caprio, Levine, and Laeven, 2004). They are also associated with lower long-term growth. Such adverse long-term effects can be magnified in crises, with further adverse effects for growth, equity, and poverty, both because connected lending lowers asset quality and renders financial systems more vulnerable, and because the powerful gain disproportionately in crises, through looting or securing greater protection and bailouts.

While broadening of the financial sector can be good for growth, equity, and poverty, rapid and premature liberalization can *also* be captured. The policy implications of the pathology of capture by the few would seem to be for greater financial liberalization to ensure broader access. However, there is an apparent paradox: rapid or premature liberalization can bring two new sets of problems: undermining of the intent of the reforms by the powerful, and creation of a backlash against reform.

There are many examples of liberalization and privatization of financial systems leading to concentration of benefits. As a result of privatization, many state-owned banks went to powerful insiders or corporate groups: in Chile in the 1970s, Mexico in the early 1990s; and Russia in the 1990s.[20] Provision of licenses has been directed to insiders in Indonesia and Thailand. In Korea only *chaebols* (large conglomerates) were allowed to open non-bank financial institutions, and there is evidence that this social and cultural circle has maintained the unequal patterns, with the daughters of *chaebols* marrying promising bureaucrats in the Ministry of Finance (Haggard, Lim, and Kim 2003; Siegel 2003). Capital-account liberalization in developing countries has occurred more frequently in countries with higher income inequality (Quinn 2000). Mass privatization in the Czech Republic led quickly to high levels of concentration of ownership and delays in the establishment of a securities and exchange commission (Cull, Matsova, and Shirley 2002). In Pakistan, reform of mutual funds has favored a few individuals (see Khwaja and Mian 2005).

Inequalities in the liberalization process can be sources of inefficiency and increased financial vulnerability. In the 1990s, large-scale connected lending has been documented in the wake of the financial liberalization and privatization in Mexico, for East Asian conglomerates, and in Russia.[21] With respect to Russia, where there had been four state banks, within a couple of years of liberalization around three thousand banks were created. One could argue that this was evidence that no elite was blocking entry. In practice, though, such rapid entry in a regulatory power vacuum precluded any chance of regulatory oversight and compromised the public perception of what a bank is and how it operates, undermining the very foundation required for the development of the domestic banking sector. Indeed, many of these "banks" were not banks but private fund-management entities used to channel capital flight. Those that raised deposits from the public proceeded to lend the cash to insiders, gamble it irresponsibly, or simply ship it abroad, leaving the banks as empty shells full of liabilities.

Banks could get away with such behavior not just because rapid entry overwhelmed the (rather unprepared) bureaucrats, but also because the banking lobby further promoted laws that granted banks an extraordinary freedom to operate and dispose of other people's money. Russia endorsed the "universal bank" model, for example, hardly a structure suited to a legal and regulatory vacuum. Bank lobbyists also ensured that banks were exonerated from the new commercial bankruptcy code (the bankruptcy code established before the 1998 crisis vaguely stated that banks would be subject to a specific bankruptcy legislation, which was not even tabled before 1998). The universal banking structure and lack of bankruptcy system contributed to the severity of the financial crisis of August 1998, resulting in massive losses to depositors, foreign investors, and the state budget (as many liabilities were transferred to the state-owned Sberbank).

A second risk is of reform backlash, if the benefits are perceived to be concentrated in a few powerful groups. While there is little specific evidence for the financial system, it forms part of a broader pattern of reaction against liberalizing processes. It is evident in the dramatic fall in support for privatization in Latin America between the mid-1990s and early 2000s (Latinobarómetro 2003) and in evidence of capital account liberalization leading to subsequent de-democratization (Quinn 2000). Such a backlash is likely to be particularly sharp when associated with gains for particular groups, for example, "economically dominant minorities" in the interpretation of a series of case studies by Chua (2003) that can heighten the sense of horizontal inequities amongst other groups in the population.

Interpretation and Policy Implications
If both established systems and financial liberalizations are often captured, what does this imply for the design of reform? This is a complex and in some ways highly technical question, but we can outline some principles here. Reforms that are both good for efficiency and access involve tackling the entrenched influence of incumbents. This is likely to require strengthening the accountabilities surrounding the reform, combined with attention to the design of the financial reform itself. Technological innovation and competition can play important facilitating roles (see Rajan and Zingales 2004), but are unlikely to be a substitute for building accountabilities for the reform process to assure the long-run robustness of the system.

A contrast between the stock markets of Poland and the Czech Republic illustrates the role of regulation and disclosure.[22] After the transition of 1989, the Czech Republic allowed a radical voucher-based privatization of state-owned assets, convinced of the power of the market to organize itself. Poland pursued a more gradual approach, starting with the introduction of strict disclosure standards, and then creating an institution that regulated these standards and protected minority shareholders. The results were very different: the stock market in the Czech Republic started larger, but quickly became dominated by insiders—with corporate insiders capturing "58 percent of the values of companies over and above their legitimate shareholding, compared to an insignificant 1 percent in the United States" (Rajan and Zingales 2004 p. 159). Eventually the Polish market grew beyond the size of the Czech market, Polish authorities showed their willingness to prosecute violations, and there was significant raising of capital.

The specific design of financial sector reform also matters. There is often an emphasis on the more complex and sophisticated aspects of financial systems in reform efforts. Both from an equity and political economy viewpoint, we argue for a different approach—reforming from the basics first, starting with broadening of payments systems, building secure deposit-taking institutions (narrow banks, limited deposit insurance); then relatively safe loans, including consumer loans; and finally broader commercial loans and more complex risk-management instruments. Such management of reform with quantity-based segmentation is likely to be more effective and less susceptible to capture.

Micro-credit is best viewed as a promising element within this approach to broadening the financial sector—a complement, not a substitute, for more equitable overall financial sector reform. It is obviously no substitute for core financial system development, but it also appears to be only one part of a strategy for broadening access. In most countries of the world, micro-credit and similar micro-finance institutions reach less than 2 percent of the population; only in a few countries is it really extensive— Bangladesh, Indonesia, and Sri Lanka stand out with coverage ratios on the order of 8 percent (Honohan 2004). Maintenance of a segmented system makes sense until the micro-credit sector matures, with a gradual bringing in of the stronger micro-credit institutions into the core supervisory and regulatory net as they evolve.

Last but not least, external commitment has a potential role to play: for example, through the salutary effects of following the rules of the particular club that countries decide to join. EU accession countries pursued effective reforms in strengthening of regulatory accountability as part of the process of preparing for joining. The relative success of Central European countries has been attributed to the constraint on abuse induced by the need to prepare for accession (Roland and Verdier 2000). Slovakia is an example where, following a decade of slow reform and influence peddling, financial sector reform began only as the date of possible EU-accession approached (Claessens and Perotti, 2004).

Trade Opening

The third area we examine is that of trade liberalization. This is sometimes associated with opening to foreign direct investment, in which case we do not observe the independent effects of trade opening per se. Increased inward foreign investment can accelerate the production transitions generated by trade opening.

The traditional view of trade among economists is that opening would be pro-poor—see for example, the position in the World Bank's 1990 report on poverty (World Bank 1990). This conclusion was consistent with a simple reading of standard Hechschler-Ohlin theory (and in particular the Stolper-Samuelson theorem) predicting that trade opening would be associated with an expansion of production and increase in factor prices in activities intensive in the relatively abundant factor. Since developing countries are typically abundant in unskilled labor (the major resource of the poor), trade should be good for unskilled wages (including labor incomes in labor-intensive self-employed production) and for the incomes of the poor. This perspective was also consistent with the great successes of growth and poverty reduction of the 1970s and 1980s in East Asian countries that supported labor-intensive agriculture and industrial expansion through major export growth and insertion in the global economy. This was *the* model of growth with equity or "shared growth" (World Bank 1993).

More recent experience and analysis has updated this perspective. Trade expansion (and FDI) can be good for growth and can be associated with labor-intensive growth, but the effects are more heterogeneous between and within countries than was expected in the earlier view. Under some conditions trade opening can be associated with rising inequalities (at least in labor markets). It can also be linked to horizontal inequities between groups; for example, with respect to differences in geographic location or initial production activity. Much of this heterogeneity is explicable in terms of the variety and complexity of economic interactions. However, it is also of value to see trade as embedded within the political and institutional considerations highlighted in the sections above. We provide illustrations of both here.

Labor Markets, Skill-biased Technical Change, and Household Activity

There is a striking contrast between the apparent pattern of relative equal, or equalizing, growth of the early East Asian successes, and rising wage inequalities in liberalizing Latin American countries in the 1980s and 1990s. As described earlier, greater inequality substantially reduces the "effectiveness" of growth in reducing income poverty.[23] Part of the reason may be caused by the position of Latin America in global markets (Wood, 1997). Whereas the East Asian countries were entering effectively at the bottom of the global labor hierarchy in terms of wages, Latin America is decidedly in the middle—and especially so given the massive and continuing insertion into global markets of labor-intensive giants such as China and India, as well as Bangladesh, Indonesia, and Vietnam. Some Latin American countries are also relatively resource- rather than labor-intensive. However, there is growing evidence that the patterns within Latin American societies are not reflective of simple versions of Heckscher-Ohlin theory, but are more like processes of skill-biased technical change across industries and sectors.[24] In terms of timing, these have tended to follow transitions to more open trade and foreign investment regimes, suggesting that liberalization has mediated processes of technological upgrading or workplace reorganization that led to the observed skill-biased technical change. Moreover, the two countries that liberalized earliest and furthest, Chile and Mexico, saw a leveling off and slight reversal of the skill-biased trend in the late 1990s—even after allowing for supply-side effects on skills in the workforce. This is consistent with theories that times of transition and change temporarily increase the premium to skills (Pissarides 1997).

Whatever is happening in countrywide labor markets, the position of particular households will vary with respect to their initial labor market activity (when there is not perfect labor mobility between activities) and consumption patterns. Trade opening affects both production possibilities and consumption price vectors, and households integrate these effects. As one example, a Computable General Equilibrium and household survey-based simulation analysis of reducing the protection on cereal production in Morocco found that rural families would tend to lose, while urban ones would gain. Overall, there would be an adverse impact on poverty as "the losses to the net producers of cereals outweigh the gains to the net consumers amongst the poor" (Ravallion 2004, pages 21.–22; see also Ravallion and Lokshin 2004).

Geography, Infrastructure, and the Workings of Product Markets
Internal geographic patterns of infrastructure and the workings of product markets are also sources of heterogeneous effects. Economic distance to new production opportunities from trade affects the extent to which

benefits at the border are passed through. An analysis of Mexico illustrates a significant gradient in the impact of trade opening on household welfare, with higher effects closer to the U.S. border (Figure 16, from analysis by Nicita 2003; see also Hanson 2003 for similar results on the role of economic distance).

Comparable effects can occur through interactions with imperfect domestic products. In the agriculture sector, either public marketing agencies or monopsonistic private traders can reduce the pass-through of gains to farmers. In Vietnam, the rice marketing system is controlled by a small number of state enterprises that have high transaction costs that limit the transmission of border prices to producers (Minot and Goletti 1998; cited in Winters et al. 2004). In Mozambique, the state trading company for cashews was privatized in the late 1980s, but this left a private market with a high degree of monopsonistic power. When cashew export restrictions were lifted in the early 1990s, much of the gain was appropriated by these intermediaries, who enjoyed 50 percent margins from farm to factory (Rodrik and McMillan 2002).

Links to Political and Institutional Structures, and Implications for Policy

Both the design of trade and related liberalization and interactions with other influences are shaped by a given political and institutional context. The design of protection is closely linked to patterns of influence, including the connections of the powerful and the negotiating ability of organized workers. Similarly, the pattern of infrastructure provision is, in part, a product of historical patterns of influence. In addition, protection within domestic markets can be subject to preferences, as vividly illustrated by the granting of clove monopoly to a family member under the Suharto regime in Indonesia.

We briefly outline the implications for policy, drawing four conclusions. First, the heterogeneity of effects of trade opening needs to be recognized, with no guarantees that the poor, or at least all the poor, will automatically benefit, especially in the short to medium term. This degree of variation needs to be taken into account for reasons of social welfare and because of the risk of reform backlash.[25] Second, the complementarity between trade opening and other considerations is fundamental, with respect to policies affecting labor supply, the functioning of labor markets, safety nets and adjustment assistance, infrastructure, and the workings of domestic product markets. Third, there may be a case for sequencing of trade opening itself, providing temporary protection for sectors likely to be adversely affected, with consequent effects on poverty. This carries risks of delaying needed liberalization, and the tradeoff between clean liberalization (with complementary measures) and sequenced reform has to be assessed in light of political considerations. Fourth, both in the design of any sequencing and the management of complementary measures, and also in the political and institutional context, patterns of concentrated influence and power are likely to bias the reform process, and these need to be countered by mechanisms of societal accountability that represent poorer groups.

Conclusion

This chapter has been a review of the relationship between policies and poverty in a core set of areas for developing economies: macroeconomic management and market-related policies, focusing on the financial sector and trade opening. A general theme is that posing the question in terms of whether such policies are "good" or "bad" for poverty is misleading. There is indeed some regularity in the cross-country patterns, of which the most robust is that between overall growth and growth in the incomes of the poor. Consequently, policies that are good for growth—and good at reducing the risk of crises—are good for poverty. However, the robustness of this relationship does not imply that concerns over the influence of inequalities are misplaced. At a proximate level, the level of inequality has a powerful mediating influence on the efficacy of growth in reducing poverty. Even if episodes of immiserating growth for the poor are infrequent, societies that are more unequal or experience rises in inequality do experience a much lower impact of growth on poverty reduction than their more equal counterparts.

At a deeper level, there is increasing recognition that some forms of inequality can be detrimental to the overall process of development and growth. While the contemporary literature on this is relatively new, and so conclusions are still somewhat tentative, a case can be made that there are first-order effects between political inequalities, the functioning of economic, social, and political institutions, and development paths. This links thinking on poverty and inequality with the burgeoning interest in the role of institutions in development. The central hypothesis is that high levels of inequalities of power can help shape, and become crystallized in, institutional arrangements that place inadequate checks on the action of the powerful and wealthy, as well as in inadequate conflict-management institutions and weak institutions of inclusion in social and economic life. Such social arrangements typically *also* do a bad job of providing broad protection of property rights for all, offering complementary public investments that open investment opportunities for the population, assuring the rule of law, and delivering macroeconomic stability. The poor suffer twice over, from relatively weak overall growth and development paths, and from relative exclusion from the benefits of growth.

This perspective is relevant to macroeconomic management and the conduct of market-related policies such as financial sector liberalization and trade opening. The consequences of such policies are also shaped by the institutional context, and should be interpreted within this frame. A particular paradox is the following: while financial and trade restrictions typically benefit the powerful and wealthy, rapid liberalization can also be captured by the few. This can be a source of greater inequity (sometimes horizontal equities between distinct groups), weaker poverty impacts, and reform backlash. At the broadest level, policy needs to focus on reducing the influence of the few and strengthening overall political and social accountabilities in a society. In addition, within particular domains of policy, there is a need for policies to take account of the heterogeneity of effects and to be designed specifically in ways that increase accountabilities, as well as promote efficiency. This can involve a mixture of measures that promote social accountability (for example, through more transparency), more indirect forms of internal accountability via horizontal regulatory structures with some independence, and through the use of external commitment mechanisms.

Tables and Figures

Table 1. Estimated Effects of Policy Reforms on Inequality from Existing Cross-Country Studies

Study	Morley/ECLAC	Berhman, Birdsall, and Székely	López
Variable	Gini index	Wage differentials	Gini index
Trade liberalization	+	0	+
Financial liberalization	0	+	+
Capital account liberalization	–	+	n.a.
Tax reform	+	+	n.a.
Privatization	0	–	n.a.
Inflation	n.a.	n.a.	+
Banking crises	n.a.	n.a.	–
All	0	+	n.a

Note: + means inequality increasing, – indicates inequality declining, 0 means no robust effect. Morley (2001) and Behrman, Birdsall, and Székely (2001) address Latin America; López (2003) uses a global database. See De Ferranti et al. (2004).

Table 2. Fiscal Costs of Selected Banking Crises

Country and episode	Fiscal cost (in percent of GDP)
Argentina, 1980–82	55.1
Brazil, 1994–96	13.2
Chile, 1981–83	41.2
Ecuador 1996–	13.0
México, 1994–	19.3
Venezuela, 1994–97	22.0
Korea, 1997–	26.5
Indonesia, 1997–	50.0
United States 1981–91	3.2

Note: Costs refer to the present value of the future stream of costs. Banking crises in Korea and Indonesia were ongoing at the time of study.
Source: Honohan and Klingebiel 2000. Costs refer to both fiscal and quasi-fiscal outlays.

Table 3. Areas of Policy Design and Complementary Accountability Structures to Reduce Macroeconomic Instability and Manage Crises

	Policy design	Accountability structures
Fiscal	Fiscal prudence over the cycle, with contracyclical tax-spending; use of fiscal rules	Move to new tax contract, democratic deepening and other societal mechanisms for management of distributional conflict
Monetary	Greater autonomy for monetary management (e.g. independent Central Banks)	Societal understanding of monetary autonomy
Financial	Ex ante stronger supervision, precautionary regulation, deposit insurance restricted to small depositors	Greater regulatory accountability and public information for financial systems
Crisis workouts	Greater equity in loss allocation; inclusive risk-management mechanisms (built out of crisis); stronger safety nets; potential use of temporary tax instruments	Transparent public debate, backed by technocratic analysis of loss incidence

Table 4. Case Study Evidence of Financial Policy and Institutions Being Captured by the Few

Country	Evidence	Paper
Brazil	Public financial institutions in Brazil appear to have served larger firms more than private banks have.	Kumar, et al. (2004)
Chile	Following liberalization in the late 1970s, groups played a perverse role in the privatization process with many privatizations of state-owned banks to groups of insiders.	Larrain (1989)
Czech Republic	Mass-privatization in the Czech Republic delayed the establishment of a securities and exchange commission, facilitating tunneling.	Cull, Matesova, and Shirley (2002)
Indonesia	Market attributes large financial value for political connections, suggesting politics rather than economics determined access or rents.	Fisman (2001)
South Korea	The opening up of new segments of financial services provision was limited to insiders. Increasing openness primarily expanded and strengthened the politically most connected firms (2003); Siegel (2003).	Haggard, Lim, & Kim
Malaysia	The imposition of capital controls benefited firms with ties to the ruling party (may have benefits to all from interest rates).	Johnson & Mitton (2003)
Mexico late 1800s	There was capture of the financial sector in Mexico in the late 19th and first half of 20th century.	Haber et al. (2003)
Mexico 1990s	Related lending in the 1990s was prevalent (20% of commercial loans) and took place on better terms than arms'-length lending (annual interest rates were four percentage points lower). Related loans were 33% more likely to default, and when they did, had lower recovery rates (30% less) than unrelated ones.	La Porta, López-de-Silanes, & Zamparippa (2002)
Pakistan	Mutual funds reform in Pakistan seems to have benefited only a few individuals. In the banking sector, insider lending was related to political motives as political firms borrow 40% more and have 50% higher default rates, with economy-wide costs of the rent-seeking identified are estimated to be 0.3% to 1.9% of GDP per year.	Mian & Khwaja (2005)
Russia	Russia's choice of a universal banking system provided great rents to the insiders through the loan for shares scheme. There was capture of state resources or protected rents, which weak institutions could not stop.	Perotti (2002); Black, Kraakman, & Tarassova (2000)

Source: Claessens and Perotti (2004).

Figure 1. The Relationship between Changes in Poverty and Growth

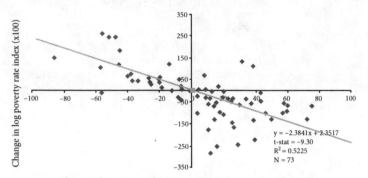

Change in log mean consumption or income between surveys (x100)

Source: World Bank data.

Figure 2. The Relationship between Changes in Inequality and Growth

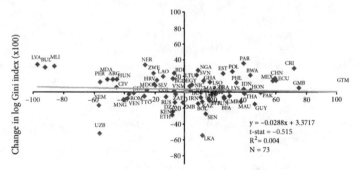

Change in log mean consumption or income between surveys (x100)

Source: World Bank data.

Figure 3. The Relationship between the Elasticity of Poverty Reduction with Respect to Mean Income Growth and Initial Income Inequality (on the Basis of a Poverty Line of $1US at PPP)

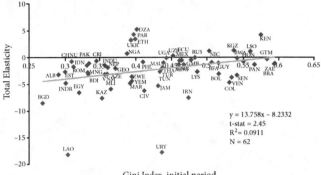

Gini Index, initial period

Source: World Bank data.

Figure 4. Predicted Total Growth Elasticity of Poverty Reduction

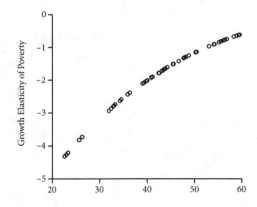

Source: Ravallion (2004).

Figure 5. The Correlation between Changes in Reform and Changes in Income Inequality in Latin America

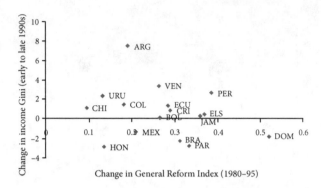

Source: De Ferranti et al. (2004) with calculations based on Morley 2001.

Figure 6. Protection against Expropriation Risk and GDP per Capita

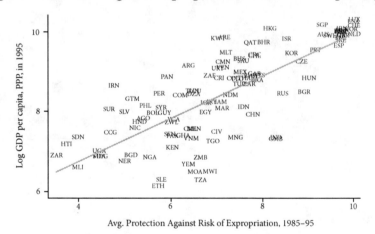

Source: Political Risk Services, International Country Risk Services (ICRG) and World Bank data.

Figure 7. The Bivariate Relationship between the Rule of Law and Ethno-linguistic Fractionalization

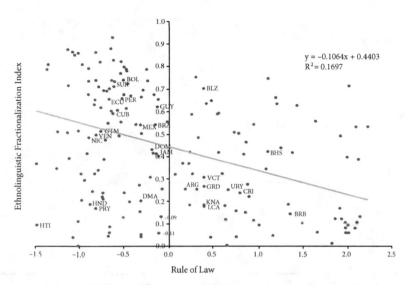

Source: World Bank Institute Governance Data Base for rule of law; Alesina and others (2002) for ethnic fractionalization.

Figure 8. A Stylized Representation of the Influence of Political and Economic Conditions on Institutions

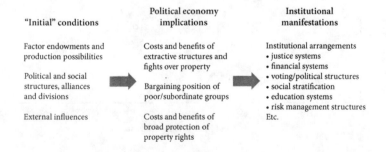

Figure 9. Two Decades of Income Inequality in China

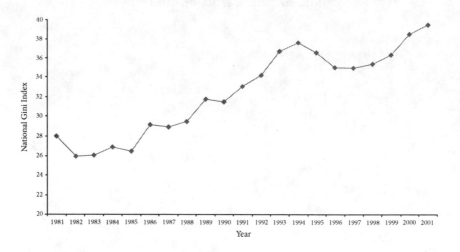

Source: Ravaillon and Chen, 2004.

Figure 10. Public Revenue and per Capita Income in Spain

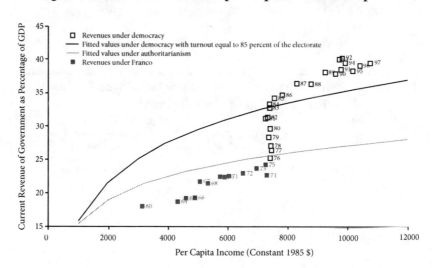

Source: Boix (2004).

Figure 11. The Effect of Macroeconomic Crisis on Poverty in Mexico

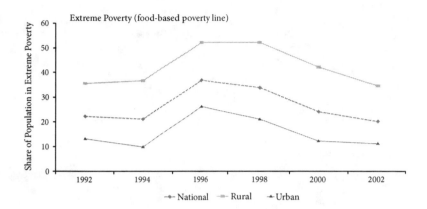

Source: World Bank (2004).

Figure 12. The Bivariate Relationship between Macroeconomic Volatility and a Measure of Constraints on the Executive

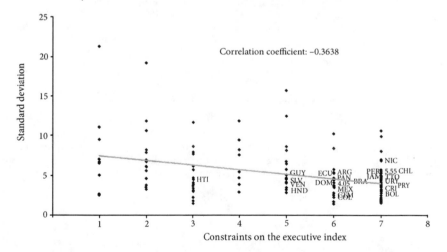

Source: Authors' calculations, using World Bank statistics and the Polity IV database for constraints on the executive index.

Figure 13. The Evolution of the Labor Share in Chile, Mexico, and Peru

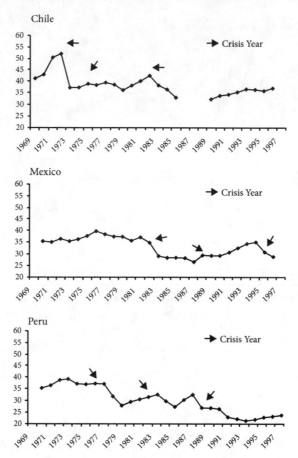

Note: Crisis years are defined as years in which at least two out of three of the following occur: a 25 percent nominal devaluation, negative growth, and 50 percent inflation.

Source: Authors' calculations, based on national accounts.

Figure 14. Patterns of Changes in Foreign Asset Holdings during the Argentine Crisis

A. Private foreign asset holdings, Argentina (in billions of U.S. dollars)

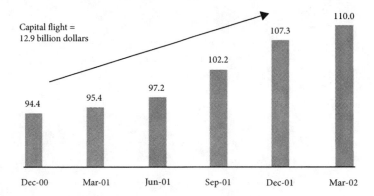

B. Net private foreign assets (in percent of GDP)

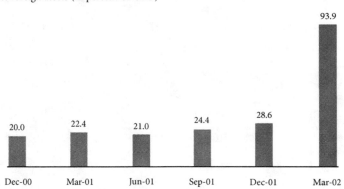

Source: Halac and Smukler (2004) and Ministry of the Economy, Argentina.

Figure 15. Higher Inequality and Enforcement of Barriers to Entry

Fig. 15a: Enforcement and income inequality ($R^2 = 0.374$)

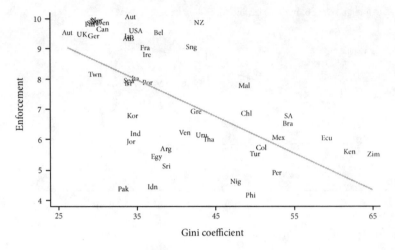

Fig. 15b: Enforcement and inequality, controlling for political accountability ($R^2 = 0.628$)

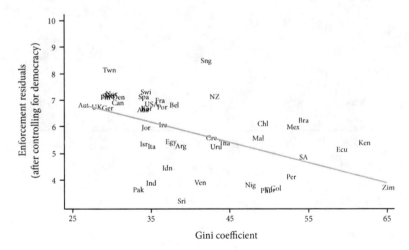

Source: Perotti and Volpin (2004); Claessens and Perotti (2004).

Figure 16. The Relationship between Location and the Benefits from Trade in Mexico

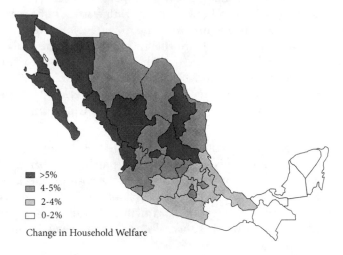

- ■ >5%
- ▨ 4-5%
- ▨ 2-4%
- □ 0-2%

Change in Household Welfare

Source: Nicita, 2003.

Notes

1   See Rothschild (2001) for a broad discussion.

2   There are various ways to answer the evaluative question, and reference to "multi-dimensionality" is loose shorthand for different approaches. Amartya Sen emphasizes the capability, or freedom, of an individual to lead a life of her choosing—to do things that she has reason to value (Sen, 1985, 1999). Others have more straightforwardly noted that, at the level of both individuals and societies, what is considered of value to life—and by extension what is a minimally acceptable standard of living—includes a variety of dimensions of living, from access to schooling to a minimum private consumption level. See World Bank (2000) for one typical discussion.

3   Dollar and Kraay (2002) present an empirically based version of this approach. However, the broader dichotomization is more generally pervasive in mainstream development circles.

4   While simply put, this view is not far from that of the World Bank's 1990 World Development Report on Poverty, and, at least from the late 1990s, the formal position of the IMF as well.

5   This is also illustrated by patterns in the data. Figure 3 shows the elasticity of poverty reduction with respect to growth (the percent reduction in a poverty index relative to a percent increase in mean incomes) for the same set of

growth episodes as were used in the previous figures. At low levels of inequality—a Gini of 0.3—the elasticity is about –4, while at high levels—a Gini of over 0.55—it drops to almost zero. In a comparable exercise, Ravallion (2004) estimated the relationship between the growth elasticity of poverty and the initial Gini index using the following equation: Rate of poverty reduction = [$a * (1 - \text{Inequality Index})^q$] * Growth rate of the mean. The total elasticity of poverty reduction is the term in square brackets. The non-linear least squares estimates were –9.33 for a, and 3.03 for q, both highly statistically significant. Figure 4 presents the predicted values for the total elasticity, using the estimated value of a, and $q = 3$, on the basis of initial Gini coefficients from the data set in the original paper.

6   Using shorter frequency data from 5-year intervals, Li and Zou (1998) and Forbes (2000) find a positive coefficient on inequality, and Barro (2000) finds a negative association for poor countries but a positive association in rich countries. Banerjee and Duflo (2003), on the basis of a non-parametric analysis of the relationship between growth and inequality, find an inverted U-shaped pattern, in which either falls or rises in inequality are associated with lower growth.

7   Figure 6 summarizes the results of three recent studies: by Morley (2001) and Behrman, Birdsall and Székely (2001) for Latin America data; and López (2004), using a global data base. Note the absence of a common pattern. Indeed, for analyses of Latin America, two stylized facts from the 1990s are of a generalized tendency for rising wage differentials, but no strong overall pattern of changes for the household per capita distribution of income (De Ferranti et al. 2004).

8   It is also useful in that he uses a common data base and methodological approach (Generalized Method of Moments) to a closely related, and state-of-the-art, study of growth from a cross-country econometric perspective—see Loayza, Fajnzylber, and Calderón (2002).

9   For surveys, the reader is again referred to Bénabou (1996) and Aghion et al. (1999).

10 See Bourguignon and Verdier (2000) for a model of this tradeoff.

11 See also Glaeser, Scheinkman, and Schleifer (2003) for a general model and discussion in the context of justice systems.

12 See the sources in the references by Acemoglu, Johnson, and Robinson, and also Rodrik for examples of analysis from the perspective of cross-country analysis.

13 These important considerations warrant much more than a couple of sentences; they are developed further in World Bank (2005).

14 For a historical discussion of the role of resource endowments see Engermann and Sokoloff (2002). The vulnerability to disease of Europeans and indigenous populations were typically very different. Whereas indigenous

groups proved extraordinarily vulnerable to diseases imported from Europe (such as measles and influenza), they had greater resistance to certain tropical diseases, such as malaria and yellow fever, to which the settlers were more vulnerable. See Diamond (1997).

15 See De Ferranti et al. (2004) for a summary account of mechanisms of persistence.

16 This section draws primarily on Boix (2004)

17 Such irreversible effects depend on the particular conditions and behavioral responses: for example, examining Peru's severe economic crisis 1988–92, Schady (2002) and Paxson and Schady (2004) find *increases* in school attendance (probably due to the decline of alternative income opportunities of children) but potentially permanent *losses* in child health.

18 For a brief survey of the different generations of models of crises see Krugman 1999 and for selected references see Aghion and others 2001, Chang and Velasco 2001, Krugman 1979, Obstfeld 1996, and Velasco 1996.

19 This section draws in particular on Claessens and Perotti (2004).

20 See Haber and Kantor 2004; Claessens and Pohl 1994.

21 See Claessens et al. 2000, Perotti 2002.

22 See Rajan and Zingales (2004).

23 As already noted, the transmission of inequalities from the labor market to households is complex. Yet a significantly equalizing development pattern in the labor market would have imparted a significant tendency for equalization for households too, other things being equal.

24 There is a small literature of country case studies. See Sánchez-Páramo and Schady (2003) and De Ferranti et al. (2003) for overviews of results across several Latin American countries.

25 Chua (2003) is again relevant here: she argues that reform is particularly vulnerable to backlash and even violence when the initial beneficiaries are disproportionately amongst "economically dominant minorities," such as the ethnic Chinese in Indonesia or Lebanese in West Africa.

References

Acemoglu, Daron, Simon Johnson, and James Robinson. 2000. "Why Did the West Extend the Franchise? Growth, Inequality, and Democracy in Historical Perspective." *Quarterly Journal of Economics*, 115(4): 1167–99.

———. 2001. "The Colonial Origins of Comparative Development: An Empirical Investigation." *American Economic Review*, 91(5): 1369–401.

Acemoglu, Daron, Simon Johnson, James Robinson, and Yunyong Thaicharoen. 2003. "Institutional Causes, Macroeconomics Symptoms: Volatility, Crises, and Growth." *Journal of Monetary Economics*, 50(1): 49–131.

Aghion, Philippe, Philippe Bacchetta, and Abhijit Banerjee. 2001. *A Corporate Balance Sheet Approach to Currency Crises* (Discussion paper 3092). London: Centre for Economic Policy Research.

Aghion, Philippe, Eve Caroli, and Cecilia García-Peñalosa. 1999. "Inequality and Economic Growth: The Perspective of the New Growth Theories." *Journal of Economic Literature*, 37: 1615–60.

Alesina, Alberto, Arnaud Devleeschauwer, William Easterly, Sergio Kurlat, and Roumain Wacziag. 2002. "Fractionalization." National Bureau of Economic Research Working Paper 9411. Cambridge, MA.

Alesina, Alberto, and Edward Glaeser. 2004. *Fighting Poverty in the US and Europe: A World of Difference*. Oxford: Oxford University Press.

Banerjee, Abhijit, and Esther Duflo. 2003. "Inequality and Growth: What Can the Data Say?" *Journal of Economic Growth*, 8(3): 267–99.

Barro, Robert J. 2000. "Inequality and Growth in a Panel of Countries." *Journal of Economic Growth*, 5(1): 5–32.

Beck, Thorsten, Asli Demirguc-Kunt, and Ross Levine. 2004. "Finance, Inequality, and Poverty: Cross-country Evidence." Washington, D.C.: World Bank Policy Research Working Paper Series 3338.

Behrman Jere, Nancy Birdsall, and Miguel Székely. 2001. "Economic Policy and Wage Differentials in Latin America." Washington, D.C.: Inter-American Development Bank.

Bénabou, Roland. 1996. "Inequality and Growth." In Ben Bernanke and Julio J. Rotemberg (eds.), *National Bureau of Economic Research Macroeconomics Annual 1996*. Cambridge, MA: MIT Press.

Bentolila, Samuel and Juan F. Jimeno. 2003. "Spanish Unemployment: The End of the Wild Ride." CEMFI Working Paper, # 0307. Madrid.

Black, Bernard, Reinier Kraakman, and Anna Tassarova. 2000. "Russian Privatization and Corporate Governance: What Went Wrong?" *Stanford Law Review* 52(6): 1731–808.

Boix, Carles. 2004. "Spain: Development, Democracy, and Equity." In Anthony Bebbington, Anis Dani, Arjan de Haan, and Michael Walton eds. *Institutional Pathways to Equity: Addressing Inequality Traps*. Washington, D.C.: World Bank.

Bourguignon, François and Thierry Verdier. 2000. "Oligarchy, Democracy, Inequality and Growth." *Journal of Development Economics*, 62(2): 285–313.

Bourguignon, François, Francisco H. G. Ferreira, and Nora Lustig. 2004. *The Microeconomics of Income Distribution Dynamics in East Asia and Latin America*. Washington, D.C.: World Bank.

Bruno, Michael. 1993. *Crisis, Stabilization and Economic Reform: Therapy by Consensus*. Oxford: Oxford University Press.

Bruno, Michael, Martin Ravallion, and Lyn Squire. 1998. "Equity and Growth in Developing Countries: Old and New Perspectives on the Policy Issues." In Vito

Tanzi and Kyung Ye Chu, *Income Distribution and High-Quality Growth.* Cambridge MA: MIT Press.

Caprio, Gerard, Ross Levine, and Luc Laeven. 2004. "Governance and Bank Valuation." Policy Research Working Paper No. 3202. Washington, D.C.: World Bank.

Chang, Roberto and Andrés Velasco. 2001. "A Model of Financial Crises in Emerging Markets." *Quarterly Journal of Economics* 116(2): 489–517.

Che, Jiahua, and Yingyi Qian. 1998. "Insecure Property Rights and Government Ownership of Firms." *Quarterly Journal of Economics*, 113(2): 467–96.

Chua, Amy. 2003. *World on Fire: How Exporting Free Market Democracy Breeds Ethnic Hatred and Global Instability.* New York: Anchor Books.

Claessens, Stijn, and Enrico Perotti. 2004. "The Links between Finance and Inequality: Channels and Evidence." Washington, D.C.: World Bank.

Claessens, Stijn, and Gerhard Pohl. 1994. "Banks, Capital Markets, and Corporate Governance: Lessons from Russia for Eastern Europe." Policy Research Working Paper Series 1326. Washington, D.C.: World Bank.

Claessens, Stijn, Simeon Djankov, and Larry H. P. Lang. 2000. "The Separation of Ownership and Control in East Asian Corporations." *Journal of Financial Economics* 58(1–2): 81–112.

Cull, Robert, Jana Matesova, and Mary Shirley. 2002. "Ownership and the Temptation to Loot: Evidence from Privatized Firms in the Czech Republic." *Journal of Comparative Economics*, 30(1): 1–24.

De Ferranti, David, Guillermo Perry, Francisco H. G. Ferreira, and Michael Walton. 2004. *Inequality in Latin America: Breaking with History?* Washington, D.C.: World Bank.

De Janvry Alain and Elisabeth Sadoulet. 2000. "Growth, Poverty and Inequality in Latin America: A Causal Analysis, 1970–1994." *Review of Income and Wealth*, 46(3): 267–87.

De Soto, Hernando. 2000. *The Mystery of Capital: Why Capitalism Triumphs in the West and Fails Everywhere Else.* New York: Basic Books.

Diamond, Jared M. 1997. *Guns, Germs and Steel: The Fate of Human Societies.* New York: W. W. Norton.

Diwan, Ishac. 2001. "Debt as Sweat: Labor, Financial Crises, and the Globalization of Capital." Washington, D.C.: World Bank

———. 2002. "The Labor Share during Financial Crises: New Results." Washington, D.C.: World Bank.

Djankov, S., R. La Porta, F. López-de-Silanes, and A. Shleifer. 2003. "The Regulation of Entry." Centre for Economic Policy Research Discussion Paper Series 2953. London.

Dollar, David, and Aart Kraay. 2002. "Growth Is Good for the Poor." *Journal of Economic Growth*, 7(3): 195–225.

Engerman, Stanley L., and Kenneth L. Sokoloff. 1997. "Factor Endowments, Institutions, and Differential Paths of Growth among New World Economies." In S. H. Haber (Ed.), *How Latin America Fell behind*. Stanford, CA: Stanford University Press.

————. 2002. "Factor Endowments, Inequality, and Paths of Development among New World Economies." *Economía*, 3: 41–109.

Fisman, Raymond. 2001. "Trade Credit and Productive Efficiency in Developing Economies." *World Development*, 29(2): 7311–21.

Forbes, Kristin J. 2000. "A Reassessment of the Relationship between Inequality and Growth." *American Economic Review*, 90(4): 869–87.

Glaeser, Edward L., Jose Sheinkman, and Andrei Shleifer. 2003. "The Injustice of Inequality." *Journal of Monetary Economics*, 50(1): 199–222.

Gunther, Richard, José Ramón Montero and Joan Botella. 2004. *Democracy in Modern Spain*. New Haven: Yale University Press.

Haber, Stephen, and Shawn Kantor. 2004. "Getting Privatization Wrong: The Mexican Banking System, 1991–2003." Stanford, CA: Stanford University.

Haber, Stephen, Noel Maurer, and Armando Razo. 2003. *The Politics of Property Rights: Political Instability, Credible Commitments, and Economic Growth in Mexico: 1876–1929*. New York: Cambridge University Press.

Haggard, Stephan, Wonhyuk Lim, and Euysung Kim (eds.) 2003. *Economic Crisis and Corporate Restructuring in Korea*. Cambridge, U.K.: Cambridge University Press.

Halac, Marina, and Sergio L. Schmukler. 2003. "Distribution Effects of Crises: The Role of Financial Transfers." Policy Research Working Paper Series 3173. Washington, D.C.: World Bank.

Hanson, Gordon. 2003. "What Has Happened to Wages in Mexico since NAFTA? Implications for Hemispheric Free Trade." Working Paper Series 9563. Cambridge, MA: National Bureau of Economic Research.

Heller, Patrick and James Mahoney. 2003. "The Resilience and Transformability of Social Inequality in Latin America." Providence, RI: Brown University.

Honohan, Patrick. 2004. *Financial Sector Policy and the Poor: Selected Findings and Issues*. Washington, D.C.: World Bank.

Honohan, Patrick, and Daniela Klingebiel. 2000. "Controlling the Fiscal Costs of Banking Crises." Policy Research Working Paper Series 2441. Washington, D.C.: World Bank.

Johnson, Simon, and Todd Mitton. 2003. "Cronyism and Capital Controls: Evidence from Malaysia." *Journal of Financial Economics*, 67(2): 351–82.

Kaufmann, Daniel and Aart Kraay. 2002. "Growth without Governance." *Economía*, 3(1): 169–229.

Kaufmann, Daniel, Aart Kraay, and Massimo Mastruzzi. 2003. "Governance Matters IV: Governance Indicators for 1996–2004." Policy Research Working Paper No. 3630. Washington, D.C.: World Bank.

Krugman, Paul. 1979. "A Model of Balance-of-payments Crises." *Journal of Money, Credit, and Banking*, 11(3): 311–25.

———. 1999. "Balance Sheets, the Transfer Problem and Financial Crises." In P. Isard, A. Razin, and A. K. Rose (eds.), *International Finance and Financial Crises: Essays in Honor of Robert P. Flood*. Dordrecht, Netherlands: Kluwer Academic Publishers and Washington, D.C.: International Monetary Fund.

Kumar, Anjali, Thorsten Beck, Cristine Campos, and Soumya Chattopadhyay. 2004. *Assessing Financial Access in Brazil*. Washington, D.C.: World Bank.

La Porta, Rafael, Florencio Lopez-de-Silanes, and Guillermo Zamarripa. 2002. "Related Lending." Working Paper Series 8848. Cambridge, MA: National Bureau of Economic Research.

Larrain, Mauricio. 1989. "How the 1981–1983 Chilean Banking Crisis Was Handled." Working Paper 300. Washington, D.C.: World Bank.

Latinobarómetro. 2003. *Informe-Resumen: La Democracia y la Economía* [Summary report: democracy and the economy]. Santiago.

Li, Hongyi, and Heng-fu Zou. 1998. "Income Inequality Is Not Harmful for Growth." *Review of Development Economics*, 2(3): 318–34.

Lindert, Peter H. 2004. *Growing Public: Social Spending and Economics Growth since the Eighteenth Century* (vols. 1 and 2). Cambridge, U.K.: Cambridge University Press.

Loayza, Norman, Pablo Fajnzylber, and César Calderón. 2002. "*Economic Growth in Latin America and the Caribbean: Stylized Facts, Explanations, and Forecasts*." Washington, D.C.: World Bank.

López, J. Humberto. 2004. "Pro-growth, Pro-poor: Is there a Tradeoff?" Policy Research Working Paper Series 3378. Washington, D.C.: World Bank.

Mian, Atif and Asim Ijaz Khwaja. 2005. "Do Lenders Favor Politically Connected Firms? Rent Provision in an Emerging Financial Market." *Quarterly Journal of Economics* 120(4): 1371–1411.

———. 2005. "Unchecked Intermediaries: Price Manipulation in an Emerging Stock Market." *Journal of Financial Economics*, 78(1): 203–41.

Minot, Nicholas, and Francesco Goletti. 1998. "Rice Market Liberalization and Poverty in Vietnam." Research Report 114. Washington, D.C.: IFPRI.

Montinola, Gabriela, Yingyi Qian, and Barry Weingast. 1995. "Federalism Chinese-style: The Political Basis for Economic Success in China." *World Politics*, 48(1): 50–81.

Morales, Juan Antonio, and Jeffrey D. Sachs. 1998. "Bolivia's Economic Crisis." Working Paper Series 2620. Cambridge, MA: National Bureau of Economic Research.

Morley, S. 2001. *The Income Distribution Problem in Latin America and the Caribbean*. Santiago: Economic Commission for Latin America and the Caribbean.

Nicita, Alessandro. 2003. "The Effects of Mexican Trade Liberalization on Household Welfare." Washington, D.C.: World Bank.

Obstfeld, M. 1996. "Models of Currency Crises with Self-fulfilling Features." *European Economic Review*, 40: 1037–47.

Paxson, Cristina H., and Norbert Schady. 2004. "Child Health and the 1988–1992 Economic Crisis in Peru." Policy Research Working Paper Series 3260. Washington, D.C.: World Bank.

Perotti, Enrico. 2002. "Lessons from the Russian Meltdown: The Economics of Soft Legal Constraints." *International Finance*, 5(3): 359–99.

Perotti, Enrico, and Paolo Volpin. 2004. "Lobbying on Entry." London, U.K.: Centre for Economic Policy Research Discussion Paper Series 4519.

Pissarides, Christopher. 1997. "Learning by Trading and the Returns to Human Capital in Developing Countries." *World Bank Economic Review*, 11(1): pp. 17–32.

Polity IV Project. 2005. *Political Regime Characteristics and Transitions.* Available at http://www.cidcm.umd.edu/inscr/polity/.

Quinn, Dennis. 2000. "Democracy and International Financial Liberalization." Seminar Series 2001–04. Washington, D.C.: International Monetary Fund.

Rajan, Raghuram G., and Luigi Zingales. 2004. *Saving Capitalism from the Capitalists: Unleashing the Power of Financial Markets to Create Wealth and Spread Opportunity.* New York: Crown Business.

Ravallion, Martin. 2004. "Why Should Poor People Care about Inequality?" Washington, D.C.: World Bank.

Ravallion, Martin, and Michael Lokshin. 2004. "Gainers and Losers from Trade Reform in Morocco." Policy Research Working Paper Series 3368. Washington, D.C.: World Bank.

Ravallion, Martin, and Shaohua Chen. 1997. "What Can New Survey Data Tell Us about Recent Changes in Distribution and Poverty?" *World Bank Economic Review*, 11(2): 357–82.

———. 2004. "China's (Uneven) Progress against Poverty." Policy Research Working Paper Series 3408. Washington, D.C.: World Bank.

Rodrik, Dani. 1999. "Where Did All the Growth Go? External Shocks, Social Conflict, and Growth Collapses." *Journal of Economic Growth*, 4(4): 385–412.

———. 2005. "Growth Strategies." In Philippe Aghion and Steven Durlauf (eds.), *Handbook of Economic Growth.* Vol. 1A, Amsterdam: Holland.

Rodrik, Dani, and Margaret McMillan. 2002. "When Economic Reform Goes Wrong: Cashews in Mozambique." Working Paper Series 9117. Cambridge, MA: National Bureau of Economic Research.

Roland, Gérard, and Thierry Verdier. 2000. "Law Enforcement and Transition." Discussion Paper Series 2501. London, U.K.: Centre for Economic Policy Research.

Rothschild, Emma. 2001. *Economic Sentiments: Adam Smith, Condorcet, and the Enlightenment.* Cambridge, MA: Harvard University Press.

Sánchez-Páramo, Carolina, and Norbert Schady. 2003. "Off and Running? Technology, Trade, and the Rising Demand for Skilled Workers in Latin America." Policy Research Working Paper Series 3015. Washington, D.C.: World Bank.

Schady, Norbert. 2002. "The (Positive) Effect of Macro Crises on the Schooling and Employment Decisions of Children in a Middle Income Country." Policy Research Working Paper # 2762. Washington, D.C.: World Bank.

Sen, Amartya. 1985. *Commodities and Capabilities.* Amsterdam: Elsevier.

———. 1999. *Development as Freedom.* New York: Knopf.

Shirk, Susan. 1993. *The Political Logic of Economic Reform in China.* Berkeley, CA: University of California Press.

Siegel, Jordan. 2003. "Is Political Connectedness a Paramount Investment after Liberalization? The Successful Leveraging of Contingent Social Capital and the Formation of Cross Border Strategic Alliances Involving Korean Firms and Their Global Partners (1987–2000)." School Working Paper Series. Cambridge, MA: Harvard University.

Velasco, Andrés. 1996. "Fixed Exchange Rates: Credibility, Flexibility and Multiplicity." *European Economic Review,* 40: 1023–35.

Winters, L. Alan, Neil McCulloch, and Andrew McKay. 2004. "Trade Liberalization and Poverty: The Evidence So Far." *Journal of Economic Literature,* 42(1): 72–115.

Wood, Adrian. 1997. "Openness and Wage Inequality in Developing Countries: The Latin American Challenge to East Asian Conventional Wisdom." *World Bank Economic Review,* 11(1): 33–57.

World Bank. 1990. *World Development Report 1990: Poverty.* New York: Oxford University Press.

———. 1993. *The East Asian Miracle.* New York: Oxford University Press.

———. 2003. *Doing Business in 2003: Understanding Regulation.* Washington, D.C.: World Bank and Oxford University Press.

———. 2004a. *World Development Report 2004: Making Services Work for Poor People.* New York: Oxford University Press.

———. 2004b. *Mexico: Poverty Reduction and Government Strategy.* Washington, D.C.: World Bank.

———. 2005. *World Development Report 2006: Equity and Development.* New York: Oxford University Press.

4

Social Isolation: Economic Constraints versus Strategic Choices in Mexico

Mercedes González de la Rocha

Research concerning household responses to economic change is part of a long-standing tradition in Latin America. In Mexico, social scientists have devoted considerable attention to the understanding of rural households and the peasant economy; to the impact of migration, urbanization, and industrialization on urban household dynamics; and to the mechanisms of survival or how the urban poor cope with poverty and economic disadvantage.

From marginality theory during the 1960s and early 1970s to the estimates of the new poverty of today, Latin American scholars have carefully assessed the impacts of social and economic change on the private space of families and households (Duque and Pastrana 1973; Bilac 1978; Cinira Macedo 1979; Jelin and Feijoó 1981; Haguette 1982; García, Muñoz, and Oliveira 1982, 1983; González de la Rocha 1986, 1988, 1991, 1994, 2001; Benería and Roldán 1987; Duarte 1988; Gabayet, Escobar, García, González de la Rocha, and Lailson, 1988; García and Oliveira 1993; González de la Rocha 2004). As household-focused research developed in the region, the emphasis on household strategies and adaptation capacities[1] disseminated rapidly. As a participant in this tradition, I have both benefited from and contributed to the knowledge of the choices and constraints of the poor in Latin American societies.

When the Mexican economic crises of the 1980s and the 1990s triggered major reforms, it was necessary to revisit previous studies, including mine, which had emphasized the resourcefulness of the poor. During the eighties, empirical research enabled us to understand poverty and household arrangements as dynamic, changing realities, and the poor as active participants in the making of their own lives and livelihoods, in spite of major economic changes (García et al. 1982; Pastore, Zilberstajn, and Pagotto

1983; González de la Rocha 1984, 1994; Escobar and González de la Rocha 1995; Chant 1991; Selby, Murphy, and Lorenzen 1990). As mechanisms of social protection disappeared, the tasks of survival and reproduction of the poor, in contexts shaped by low wages and scant support from the state, were left in the hands of the poor themselves. In these studies, households were seen as the main places for the implementation of survival strategies, while families and social networks were understood as the archetypal resources for protection against misfortune and economic distress. But our research and conclusions were abused by Mexican and international aid and development agencies, which referred to our findings as providing proof that the poor could and would cope with additional reforms that lowered wages and decreased wage-earning opportunities, replaced general price-based subsidies with targeted transfers, and otherwise impacted their ability to extract incomes from an economy transiting from a given model of development to an uncertain something else.[2]

What is at stake here is a model of development that extols the virtues of private initiative and private solutions to macroeconomic problems while, at the same time, it cripples individuals' and families' ability to carry out successful strategies of adaptation to change and contribute to their own growth and well-being. In this chapter, I draw from my own long-standing research interests and findings on the shifting dynamics of household organization to examine the process that has led to social isolation among the poor in Mexico. In so doing, I re-examine the widespread notion of the resourcefulness of the poor: their assumed endless capacity to work more, to consume less, and to take part in mutual help networks. According to this notion, aggressive and violent economic shocks make little difference. The always-good poor keep on working, reciprocating, and relying on their own safety nets (Narayan 2000; Chiarello 1994; Durston 2003; Gershuny 1994).

This view had disastrous consequences for Mexico and for many other Latin American societies. From the mid-1980s onwards, the retreat of the state from a number of social security functions, the privatization of social services, and the dismantling of provisions and subsidies aimed at lowering the cost of living for the poor, together with poor economic performance, produced the most serious worsening of poverty in Latin America during the 20th century.

As a result, Latin American governments and international institutions such as the World Bank have begun to reappraise their views and policies. Once again, the state is seen as responsible for the design and implementation of policies that should reduce poverty and, ideally, enable the poor to participate more fully in national development. New policies are in place in a number of countries, and some analysts believe social policy has undergone a paradigm change, from a liberal perspective to one that provides a renewed role for the state.

Social scientists, and particularly those working on household economies, played a role in both trends, first by their emphasis on the ability of the poor to cope under duress, and more recently by insisting that this ability was not without limit and that it had reached a dead end. This is an account of how, in the span of twenty years, research in Mexico responded to a changing reality and moved from one emphasis to the other.

During these twenty years, I argue, the poor have undergone a process leading to social isolation. This process can be understood as the outcome of three distinct, but related phenomena: (a) the erosion of work, (b) a paradoxical de-diversification of household work strategies, and (c) the private adjustments that have taken place at the household level, and their limits.

Changing Realities and Perspectives

Twenty years ago I started doing research in Guadalajara, the second largest city in Mexico, on the ways in which households are shaped by labor-market dynamics. I argued that the agency of the poor is framed by labor-market opportunities, development strategies of societies, and social and economic policies that either facilitate or constrain survival, social mobility, and reproduction. That research was conducted during the last years of import-substitution industrialization, and one year before the onslaught of the severe economic crisis that led to the Latin American lost decade. I proposed that the resources of poverty, or the ability of the poor to survive, depended on a household strategy of diversification of income sources and multiple income earners. Labor markets offered low wages, but informal and formal employment coexisted and acted as viable options. Workers could choose formal or informal jobs (in many cases a combination of both) according to their needs and the advantages among different jobs: time schedules, flexibility, benefits, salaries, and so forth. The informal sector represented, in the early 1980s, an attractive, viable alternative, with similar or even higher wages than those offered by formal jobs (Escobar 1986; Selby, Murphy, and Lorenzen 1990; González de la Rocha 1994). Income derived from wages constituted an important source for nourishing livelihoods, but household economies relied heavily on petty commodity production and petty trade, domestic production of goods and services for consumption, and assets and income from social exchange through networks and informal systems of support. A collective and diversified income-generating strategy, not free of conflicts, negotiations, and uneven workloads and rewards, was documented (Chant 1991; González de la Rocha 1986, 1994). Questioning how crises, adjustment policies, and restructuring of labor markets would affect the lives of the working poor in urban Mexico and other countries, I have devoted my research and thinking to understanding household responses to economic change, or the private adjustments taking place at the household level (González de la Rocha 1994, 1995, 2000, 2001).[3]

In the early 1980s, I found a few socially isolated households and individuals. These were considered deviant cases since the majority of the poor formed strong, though flexible, constellations of social relationships of kin, neighbors, and friends. Since socially isolated households were empirically the poorest of the poor, these deviant cases were analyzed to demonstrate the devastating consequences of social isolation and the crucial uplifting effect of socializing on the well-being of the poor (González de la Rocha 1986, 1994). In the context of poverty, everyday life and social involvement could be explained only by taking account of the effect of social exchange within social networks (Stack 1974; Lomnitz 1977; Roberts 1995; González de la Rocha 1994).

Today, social isolation is one of the outstanding characteristics of large segments of the poor in Mexico and the rest of Latin America (Bazán 1998, 1999; Estrada 1999; González de la Rocha 1999, 2001; Auyero 2000; Kessler 1996; Feijoó 2001). According to a recent Mexican survey,[4] fifty-one percent of the poor do not have anybody to rely on for childcare support; more than sixty percent think that friends do not influence well-being, and only six percent accept that belonging to civil associations brings some kind of benefit. Almost twenty percent think that nobody would help them in case of unemployment, and similar numbers of individuals declare they have no support from relatives, neighbors, or friends when they go hungry or homeless. It seems that social networks have become, for an increasing number of people, drained and fragile. My interpretation of social isolation as a growing phenomenon has been enlightened by a perspective that explores the limits and constraints for the implementation of survival strategies, instead of stressing the resources of poverty as endless and unlimited.

The Erosion of Work

I argue that wage income constitutes a major ingredient in poor people's livelihoods, not simply one among several types of resources.[5] By presenting the reality of the growing deterioration of wages and work conditions, my aim is to show the large extent to which livelihood opportunities are being affected by the erosion of work.

During the last twenty-five years, Mexico has gone through processes of economic and social change characterized by severe economic crises, adjustment policies, economic restructuring, and a rapid and relatively successful integration of the Mexican economy to world markets, with a growing emphasis in export-oriented production. Export-oriented production, however, is highly concentrated both geographically and in terms of economic sectors and branches of manufacturing. The opening to both imports and exports has had a dramatic impact on Mexican firms, especially small and medium-sized manufacturing enterprises, which found the competition with foreign commodities' producers a challenge too difficult to overcome (Escobar and González de la Rocha 1995). As a result, many firms have closed, and many jobs have been lost. According to Escobar (1996), the 1994 financial crisis signaled a watershed for Mexican labor markets because, for the first time since 1982, the population did not respond with a general intensification of work and informal employment.[6] Instead, unemployment soared, and its abatement after 1995 may be due to withdrawal altogether from the job search rather than success in finding work, since male employment continued to fall.

Integration to world markets has entailed a diminishing capacity of the Mexican government to regulate and control prices, wages, and job creation.[7] In this context, formal employment has become leaner and insufficient to meet the needs of a population whose average age, in 2003, was 27 years old, and whose working-age segment—people between 15 and 64 years old—is rising rapidly and will continue doing so. However, the creation of new jobs is as critical as it is a projection of wishful thinking. Employment creation is rare; it is concentrated in certain economic niches, is highly specialized, and earmarked for workers and employees with special credentials, except during certain periods.[8]

As a result, most workers have no employment options but casual labor, and choices are, for a growing number of them, no longer possible. Nonpermanent, unreliable, casual labor has become a critically important source of household income. It is characterized by very low and irregular wages, especially in urban areas where the market has become saturated and there is a high degree of competition for jobs.[9] Unemployment had reached unprecedented levels (particularly during the 1994–1996 period), while its extension had increased.[10] At the same time, the number of people at work in unsatisfactory conditions (unemployed and individuals with wages below the minimum who work less than 35 hours per week for market reasons) is also high, and growing.[11] An essential change that must be noted is that individuals and households are no longer able to choose alternative forms of employment. Moreover, choice is an essential component of strategy-making.

Changes taking place in the employment structure have drastically affected poverty levels in Mexico. From 1983 to 1988, the worst years of the 1980s economic crisis, formal employment decreased in absolute and relative terms and minimum wages lost 56 percent of their purchasing power, by far the largest decrease in Latin America during that period (Benería 1992). Government spending on health and social security in 1987 was lower than in 1970, and state subsidies were reduced significantly. Therefore, there was a palpable decrease in income levels and a rise in the number of the poor, both rural and urban. While the country's population expanded from 71.4 to 81.2 million between 1981 and 1987, the poor increased their numbers from 32.1 to 41.3 million, and almost half of them were considered to be extremely poor (Tello 1991).

As one crisis succeeded another, household responses became progressively weaker. After the onset of the first Mexican crisis, the rates of employment of women and the young increased by 35 percent in just 3 years (1982 to 1985), and after the crises of 1986–1987 (González de la Rocha 1991), employment of women and the young rose again until 1992; however, after the crisis of 1994, it barely changed. The ability of households to cushion the blows of each successive crisis and to elude falling into poverty had worn out for the most part.

After a few years of economic recovery (the late 1980s and early 1990s), a recovery that was insufficient to heal the wounds and cuts that the previous disastrous years had produced, another distressing decade came along, with more risks and insecure horizons for the already debilitated poor. Real wages decreased during the 1990s, and in the year 2000, per capita monetary income did not attain the levels it had reached in 1992 (Cortés, Hernández, Hernández Laos, Székely, and Vera 2002); consequently, absolute and relative poverty rose between 1992 and 2000 (see Table 1). In the year 2000, the Mexican economy was the tenth largest in the world; however, a quarter of Mexico's population did not have enough income to buy a basic basket of food, and 54 percent of the Mexican people could not afford food, education, health services, housing, clothing, or transportation.[12] Not only did the number of poor people increase during the 1990s, but also the poor became poorer during this period (Cortés et al. 2002). Poverty is one of the country's most extended and profound problems, not simply a matter of income; it is related to precarious employment, very low wages, and, in general, to very scarce and increasingly narrow economic opportunities. In spite of the impressive fall of poverty figures from 2000 to 2006 which, in my view, is the result of the absence of economic crises since the mid-nineties and the sustained effort of the Federal Government to provide five million households with cash transfers (through the *Oportunidades* program), almost 10 million households and 45 million people live in poverty conditions (below line 3), or 44 percent of the total population. Of these, 14.4 million people do not have enough income to obtain a food basket (line 1). In other words, they cannot eat or feed their families adequately even if they devote all income to food.

A Paradox: The Limits of Diversification

Alongside the previously described process of work erosion—increasing unemployment, precariousness, and insecurity in labor markets—a paradoxical de-diversification of household work strategies has been taking place. The erosion of work has seriously affected household livelihoods, traditionally nurtured by the collective participation of household members in diverse tangible and intangible income producing activities. I have argued that wages not only fuel households' consumption economies but also trigger other income-generating activities, including self-employment, self-provisioning, and social exchange (González de la Rocha 2001). This closely corresponds to Pahl and Wallace's findings during the early 1980s in de-industrializing Britain, to the effect that "employment and self-provisioning go together, rather than one being a substitute for another" (Pahl and Wallace 1985, 215). My research has documented the increasing constraints that growing numbers of men and women face in order to start (or to continue) self-employment and self-provisioning when regular income (from wages) stops flowing into the household economy. They simply do not have money to buy materials or to cover transportation expenses. This means that self-provisioning activities and, in general, income from sources other than wages diminishes in contexts of growing unemployment and labor-market precariousness. As a result, the diversity of income sources, through participation of household members in various waged and unwaged activities, which was the traditional base to achieve survival, fades away.

Precarious employment was present in the pre-crises and restructuring periods, but it coexisted with formal employment and autonomous income sources and, most importantly, was one of various options open to the poor. Today's context is characterized by a combination of a lack of jobs (that is, unemployment) and precarious employment for the majority of workers, while permanent employment has become rare and available only to an increasingly reduced number of the poor. A new type of segmentation seems to be emerging, not along "formal" and "informal" lines, but between a privileged group of permanently employed workers and the vast majority who struggle to survive with very scarce resources amidst precarious employment and unemployment. The absence of regular income from at least one household member makes it more difficult to start or to continue autonomous projects; conversely, in households where monetary income flows in regularly, people have a wider scope to devote time and other resources (including money) to self-provisioning and household production.

Paradoxically, while the number of people who experience the erosion of work is growing, household economies largely depend on money coming from wages in order to satisfy consumption needs and to implement household survival strategies that require the participation of household members in diverse income-earning activities, including social exchange. According to a recent analysis, household expenditure practices and consumption patterns are largely monetary in rural as much as in urban areas, with a very small part of total consumption being covered by non-monetary sources, such as gifts, self-provisioning, or in-kind payments (Hernández and Pérez García 2003).[13] This picture appears troubled indeed: wage income has become a major ingredient in poor people's livelihoods at a time when waged employment is less available to major groups of the population.[14] Labor force, the most abundant and traditionally crucial resource in the hands of the poor, has become the most redundant, leading to unfeasible diversification strategies. This is what I have called the shift from the *resources of poverty*, as a model of survival, to the *poverty of resources* (Gonzalez de la Rocha 2001). It is not surprising, then, that the process of de-diversification of household strategies has meant severe private cuts and adjustments.

Private Adjustments and Social Isolation

By private adjustments I mean the array of changes that have taken place within households as they face crises, restructuring, and the erosion of employment opportunities. Private responses implemented at the household level are intended to compensate for the loss of individual wages during structural economic crises and to help overcome family emergencies, with (frequently unequal) collective effort and deprivation. I have argued that along processes of economic adjustment and restructuring of production, households have also been adjusted and restructured (González de la Rocha 1988, 1994, 2001). Although urban poor households have attempted to intensify the use of their labor force, especially the work of women,[15] the deteriorated labor markets have not rewarded such attempts. Therefore, adjustment at the private level takes place.

Compared to the non-poor, poor households devote a considerably larger proportion of their income to food expenses and a substantially lower proportion of it to education, healthcare, clothing, and leisure.[16] Consumption and expenses figures alone show the great disparities produced by the very unequal distribution of income as well as the actual restrictions that compel poor households. Ethnographic research has documented the shifts and trade-offs that household members work out as households adjust to economic change. In fact, research conducted in the 1980s and 1990s shows the types of restrictions—and not simply transformations—that the poor have been obliged to implement in their lives. I stress that changes taking place within households have suppressed or limited household members' social practices. Consumption of goods and services has been modified, with painful cuts and reductions in the areas of food (by reducing the number of meals per day and the amount and types of food), education, health, clothing, transportation, and social intercourse.

Household adjustment, however, has been enforced not only in consumption, but also through a general withdrawal from the market and an overall strategy of "tightening the belt." As a growing number of individuals are rejected from formal regulated employment and experience longer spans of unemployment or have no other alternative but precarious jobs, households experience the lack of monetary income that is, in my view, a key ingredient for social exchange. Increasing economic and social pressures on households are leading to premature separation of their members, decreasing solidarity and co-operation within the family, increasing gender conflicts and domestic violence (usually over scarce resources), masculine drug-addiction and depression, and social isolation. In sum, the reduction in the flow of monetary income decreases the "social fund" of households' economies, since it undermines households' and individuals' capacities to maintain the cost of reciprocity. Therefore, although I highlight the importance of social networks for survival, I also emphasize that such networks might crumble under the pressure of poverty, leading to social isolation.

Social isolation is a growing phenomenon that has sparked little attention from social scientists even though it appears to be an important outcome of poverty. The few studies that document and interpret this phenomenon have recently showed that social isolation manifests itself in two ways in Latin American cities. First, the unfolding process of social and physical segregation that, according to some studies, is taking place in urban contexts. Here, the links that the poor have with the non-poor are gradually diluted until flagrant "de-linkage from larger society and the confinement of shantytown dwellers to nether zones of accumulated and self-reinforcing joblessness, violence, and vulnerability" is reached (Auyero 2000, 111; see also Wilson 1987, 1997; Kaztman 1999; Wacquant, 1999). This might be interpreted as a collective process of social isolation in which the poor become isolated or segregated from the rest of society.

A second manifestation of social isolation is observed when considering a lower level of analysis, that of households and individuals within poor urban settlements. Here, the scant but growing literature points out the weakening social links among the poor themselves that gradually leads to a loss of social exchange among equals. In order to understand this type of social isolation, we ought to consider that reciprocity, the cultural norm that is at the base of networks and informal support systems, is not costless nor is it a virtue but, on the contrary, it implies costs, it is socially constructed, and it has limits (González de la Rocha 1999, 2004). As Auyero (2000) puts it, the blood of reciprocal networks is the monetary flow that enters the household and the poor neighborhood. When blood ceases to circulate, or is severely diminished, the social system of reciprocal exchange with its mutual favors and aid—the traditional mechanism among the poor to make ends meet—is debilitated. Resources running through social networks in the context of the erosion of work are fewer, weaker, and more sporadic. Vulnerability of the poor increases, as individuals and households are left without the crucial income (both tangible and intangible, monetary and non-monetary) that traditionally has been moved around in the forms of gifts, favors, crucial information, services, emotional support, and care.

According to my recent research on social isolation in urban contexts, both manifestations of the phenomenon (segregation of the poor from the non-poor, and crumbling networks of poor individuals and households) are sharpened by factors such as aging, chronic disease, and drug addiction (González de la Rocha 2005). All these factors are gaining ground in Mexican society as demographic transition advances, diabetes and high-blood pressure increase,[17] and drug consumption rises dramatically among poor and unemployed young males and, to a lesser extent, females. Growing fears, decreasing solidarity, and a general weakening of the social fabric are all reinforcing social isolation and vulnerability throughout the poor, workless, or precariously employed population.

Conclusion: Cumulative Disadvantages

In using the term "cumulative disadvantages," I allude to the "downward spiral of economic and social detachment" (Pahl and Wallace 1985, 224); that is, the snowballing impact that the erosion of work has had in various dimensions of the lives of the poor. As a concept, cumulative disadvantages refers to the intertwined and reinforcing links between factors that promote and perpetuate poverty, minimizing the capacities of the poor to face risks and to cope with insecurity and life precariousness. In other words, the poor are more vulnerable when joblessness, precariousness, and social isolation are combined in a perverse ensemble of disadvantages.

The majority of poor households have not followed a path towards recovery after crises and adjustment. Household assets have diminished, deteriorated, and become impaired. "Cumulative disadvantages," then, refers to a continuous deficit, to the gradual but real exhaustion of the resources of poverty. In this process, former comparative advantages that favored large, extended households going through the consolidation stage of the domestic cycle (compared to small, nuclear, and young or old households) are gradually lost. These households' comparative advantages were based on the existence of an abundant labor force and the capacity of households to use it. This erosion of social systems of support and self-help is linked directly to labor markets that increasingly exclude the poor. Persistent crises and current economic policies have diluted the resourcefulness of the poor, by eroding their ability to use their most important asset, their labor force.

Asserting that poor individuals, households, and communities have responded to economic change with innovative strategies and resourcefulness is an accurate conclusion. The survival of the poor has been supported mostly by private initiatives. However, it is crucial to acknowledge that households are very sensitive to economic and social change. Households' social organization is affected intimately by trends in the labor market, given the centrality of labor, including wage employment, for the survival of the poor. I have argued that economic policies bear upon the dynamics of the wage labor market and are a major determinant of household well-being. Employment policies are badly needed to restore the dimension of work if a surmounting survival problem is to be avoided. So far, however, the Mexican government's social policy, in spite of its aggressive attempts to reduce poverty,[18] has not been able to solve the crucial problem of employment precariousness and loss of labor options.

In conclusion, the much-heralded elasticity of the poor has its limits. The notion of resourcefulness of the poor that contributed to our understanding of their lives, their survival mechanisms, and their daily struggles to make it amidst scarce resources should not obscure the fact that the actions implemented by the poor to secure a livelihood take place in a context of increasing structural constraints. Households have been forced to make costly private adjustments, with serious and cumulative implications for their well-being and sustainable reproduction.

Table

Table 1. Evolution of Poverty from 1992 to 2006

	1992		2000	2006
LINE 1	21.4%	(population)	24.1%	13.8%
	16.4%	(households)	18.5%	10.6%
LINE 2	29.7%	(population)	31.8%	20.7%
	23.1%	(households)	25.2%	16.1%
LINE 3	53.1%	(population)	53.6%	42.6%
	44.5%	(households)	45.7%	35.5%

Line 1: Income is less than 15.4 and 20.9 pesos a day, per person, in rural and urban areas respectively; the minimal income to obtain a food basket. This means that those who fall in this category cannot eat or feed their families properly even if they devote all income to food.

Line 2: Income is less than 18.9 and 24.7 daily pesos, per person, in rural and urban areas respectively. This is the minimal income to obtain a food basket plus minimal expenses in education and healthcare.

Line 3: Income is less than 28.1 and 41.8 pesos a day, per person, in rural and urban areas respectively. This amount corresponds to the minimal income to cover expenses in food, healthcare, education, clothing, housing, and transportation.

Source: CONEVAL, based on ENIGH 1992–2006 http://www.coneval.gob.mx/coneval/medicion.html, (consulted 2nd of June, 2008).

Notes

1   To work harder for increasingly lower wages, to restrict consumption, and to be part of support systems of mutual help.

2   An economic and social reorganization rooted in a free-market development approach.

3   See, as well, Benería, 1992; Moser, 1996; Benería and Feldman, 1992; Escobar and González de la Rocha, 1995; and González de la Rocha, 1988 and 1991.

4   A survey conducted by the Mexican Federal Government in 2003 that claims to be representative of three Mexican regions (north, central, and south) and of two types of settlements (urban and rural): *Lo que dicen los pobres.*

5   As has been stressed by the World Bank and other international aid and development agencies.

6   While women's participation rates continued to rise, men's fell for the first time since the 1982 crisis. Escobar's analysis shows that 700,000 women entered the

labor force between 1993 and 1995—compared to only 300,000 men. Unemployment among male youth reached unprecedented levels in 1995 and was almost 30 percent in the main metropolitan areas during that year.

7 As the Director of the Subsecretaría de Prospectiva, Planeación y Evaluación, from SEDESOL, clearly points out: "Now, it is increasingly difficult to influence the evolution of poverty and inequality since, in the world of today, the salaries of Mexican workers ... increasingly depend on decisions that are made in the rest of the world" (Székely 2003).

8 Such as the period 1996–2000, when Mexico generated 730,000 formal jobs per year.

9 Escobar and González de la Rocha (1995) argued that informal employment and incomes were stagnating at the end of the Salinas period (the early 1990s). This stagnation resulted from the saturation and economic marginalization of the sector. External trade and the influx of low-priced Asian products drastically affected Mexican labor-intensive industries, subcontracting, and informal work.

10 According to data from INEGI (Instituto Nacional de Estadísticas, Geografía e Informática), less than 18 percent of the unemployed population had been unemployed during January to March 2002 for nine weeks or more (the category for the longest period). In 2004, that category of unemployed had increased to 22.85 percent, in the period January to March, and to 30.34 percent from April to June. Although unemployment rates actually decreased after 1996, from 5.9 percent in 1994–1996 to 2.9 in the period between 1996–2000 (Cortés et al. 2002), the span of time while being unemployed rose dramatically during the last two years (INEGI, Encuesta Nacional de Empleo Urbano, Distribución Porcentual de la Población Desempleada Abierta, según Duración del Desempleo, Trimestral, Total, Cobertura Actual; 32 ciudades).

11 The majority of manual workers and employees in services and trade, who make up the largest part of the active population, is, according to a recent analysis, *critically employed*. This means that 55.5 percent of the economically active population was unemployed, underemployed, or working in the increasingly deteriorated informal sector in 2000 (Cortés et al. 2002). In order to contrast the present context with past scenarios, it is useful to consider that in 1978–1979, more than three quarters of male heads of households in urban areas (or 78 percent) earned more than the minimal wage while more than half (59 percent) were formally employed, 81 percent had achieved job stability (they held their jobs for more than a year), and 69 percent enjoyed fringe benefits (Selby et al. 1990; see also González de la Rocha for the specific case of Guadalajara).

12 These two figures correspond to two of the three official poverty lines: (a) food line, or 15.4 and 20.9 pesos a day per person in rural and urban areas respectively, and (b) "patrimony" line, or 21.1 and 41.8 pesos a day per person in

rural and urban settings respectively. Between these two lines, the Mexican government considers another line, called "capacities" line, which has been calculated for those whose income is not sufficient for food, and minimal expenses in health and education. The calculated income to cover such expenses is, for rural areas, 18.9 pesos a day, and 24.7 pesos for urban inhabitants (Székely 2003).

13 Consumption has been measured through monetary and non-monetary income that is spent in areas such as food, health, education, etc. Although the weight of non-monetary expenses is reduced (it is present only in food and health expenses and covers very low percentages of them), the importance of gifts increases among the very poor when compared to better-off groups of the population. Longitudinal statistical analyses about the decreasing or increasing coverage of gifts, over a period of time, do not exist.

14 Perception surveys conducted among beneficiaries of social policy programs indicate that the lack of employment is mentioned as reason number one within various poverty causes, followed by poorly paid jobs. The same sources show that most beneficiaries of social programs think that the government should provide poor households with job opportunities, rather than nutritional support (food). Most of them think that in order to combat poverty, programs to generate employment should be created. It should be mentioned that among the various programs that the Mexican government is currently operating, none is devoted to enhance employment opportunities for the poor. Programs such as *Oportunidades* have been launched to support poor families in the domains of education, health, and food intake (see Escobar Latapí and González de la Rocha 2003 for the analysis and discussion of the impact of *Oportunidades* in households' vulnerability).

15 During the 1980s crisis, most adult men were already participating in the labor market, and households responded mostly through the entrance in the market of adult women who were poorly schooled, married, and with domestic responsibilities. Young men and boys also intensified their participation. Increasing male unemployment in the following decade has severely affected men's breadwinner role, and a feminization of household economies has become more visible.

16 According to Hernández and Pérez (2003), the poorest ten percent of rural households devote 52.2 percent of their total income to food expenses while the richest ten percent allot only 15.4 percent. The wealthiest urban households spend 15.8 percent of their income in food, compared to 42.4 percent of the poorest urban households. Expenses in education and leisure activities, however, as a proportion of total income, are greater among the richest households (urban and rural, who devote 19.2 percent of their income, compared to only 8.7 percent of the poorest total household income).

17 These chronic diseases are, according to medical studies, linked to—among other factors—childhood under-nutrition and "bad" diets (high in fats and sugars).

18 Mexican policy's main program, *Oportunidades*, is human-development oriented and aims at improving health, education, and nutrition of poor families. For an assessment of the program's impacts, see Escobar and González de la Rocha 2003.

References

Amado, Felipe. 1994. *As condições de sobrevivencia da população pobre em Angola.* Luanda: Africa Databank, The World Bank Group.

Auyero, Javier. 2000. "The Hyper-shantytown: Neo-liberal Violence(s) in the Argentine Slum." *Ethnography*, 1 (1): 93–116.

Bazán, Lucía. 1998. "El último recurso: las relaciones familiares como alternativas frente a la crisis." Paper presented at the International Congress of LASA (Latin American Studies Association), Chicago.

———. 1999. *Cuando una puerta se cierra cientos se abren. Casa y familia: los recursos de los desempleados de la refinería 18 de Marzo.* México, DF: Centro de Investigaciones y Estudios Superiores en Antropología Social.

Benería, Lourdes. 1992. "The Mexican Debt Crisis: Restructuring the Economy and the Household." In L. Benería and S. Feldman (eds.), *Unequal Burden: Economic Crises, Persistent Poverty, and Women's Work.* Boulder: Westview Press.

Benería, Lourdes, and Martha Roldán. 1987. *The Crossroads of Class and Gender: Industrial Homework, Subcontracting, and Household Dynamics in Mexico City.* Chicago: University of Chicago Press.

Bilac, Elisabete. 1978. *Famílias de trabalhadores: Estratégias de sobrevivência, a organização da vida familiar em uma cidade paulista.* São Paulo: Coleção Ensaio e Memória, Edições Símbolo.

Chant, Sylvia. 1991. *Women and Survival in Mexican Cities.* Manchester: Manchester University Press.

Chiarello, Franco. 1994. "Economía informal, familia y redes sociales." In R. Millán (ed.), *Solidaridad y producción informal de recursos.* Mexico City: Universidad Nacional Autónoma de México.

Cinira Macedo, C. 1979. *A reprodução da desigualdade: o projeto de vida familiar de um grupo operário.* São Paulo: Editora Hucitec.

CONEVAL (Consejo Nacional de Evaluación de Política Social), 2006. *Poverty Measure.* http://www.coneval.gob.mx/coneval/medicion.html, (consulted June 2, 2008).

Cortés, Fernando, Daniel Hernández, Enrique Hernández-Laos, Miguel Székely, and Hadid Vera. 2002. *Evolución y características de la pobreza en México en la última década del siglo XX. Serie Documentos de Investigación, 2.* Mexico City: SEDESOL.

Duarte, Isis. 1988. "Crisis, familia y participación laboral de la mujer en la República Dominicana." Paper presented at the 37th Annual Latin American

Conference Demography of Inequality in Contemporary Latin America, University of Florida, Gainesville, February 22–24.

Duque, Joaquín, and Ernesto Pastrana. 1973. *Las estrategias de supervivencia económica de las unidades familiares del sector popular urbano (una investigación exploratoria)*. Santiago de Chile: Facultad Latinoamericana de Ciencias Sociales (FLACSO).

Durston, John, 2003. "Capital social: Parte del problema, parte de la solución, su papel en la persistencia y en la superación de la pobreza en América Latina y el Caribe." In Raúl Atria and Marcelo Siles (eds.), *Capital social y reducción de la pobreza en América Latina y el Caribe: en busca de un nuevo paradigma*. Santiago de Chile: CEPAL/Michigan State University.

Escobar Latapí, Agustín. 1986. *Con el sudor de tu frente: Mercado de trabajo y clase obrera en Guadalajara*. Guadalajara: El Colegio de Jalisco.

———. 1996. "The Mexican Labor Market, 1976–1995." Unpublished manuscript.

Escobar Latapí, Agustín, and Mercedes González de la Rocha. 1995. "Crisis, Restructuring and Urban Poverty in Mexico. *Environment and Urbanization, 7* (2) (April): 1.

———. 2003. "Evaluación cualitativa del programa de desarrollo humano Oportunidades. Seguimiento de impacto 2001–2002, comunidades de 2,500 a 50,000 habitantes." *Serie Documentos de Investigación, 3*. Mexico City: SEDESOL.

Estrada, Margarita. 1999. *1995: Familias en la crisis*. México, DF: Centro de Investigaciones y Estudios Superiores en Antropología Social.

Feijoó, María del Carmen. 2001. *Nuevo país, nueva pobreza*. Buenos Aires: Fondo de Cultura Económica.

Gabayet, Luisa, Agustín Escobar, Patricia García, Mercedes González de la Rocha, and Silvia Lailson (eds.). 1988. *Mujeres y sociedad. Hogar, salario y acción social*. Guadalajara: El Colegio de Jalisco/CIESAS.

García, Brígida, and Orlandina de Oliveira, 1993. *Trabajo femenino y vida familiar en México*. Mexico City: El Colegio de México.

García, Brígida, Humberto Muñoz, and Orlandina de Oliveira, 1982. *Hogares y trabajadores en la Ciudad de México*. Mexico DF: El Colegio de México/UNAM.

———. 1983. *Familia y mercado de trabajo: Un estudio de dos ciudades brasileñas*. Mexico DF: El Colegio de México/UNAM.

Gershuny, Jonathan. 1994. "La economía informal: su papel en la sociedad postindustrial." In René Millán (ed.), *Solidaridad y producción informal de recursos*. Mexico DF: Universidad Nacional Autónoma de México.

González de la Rocha, Mercedes. 1984. "Domestic organization and reproduction of low-income households: The case of Guadalajara." Ph.D. Thesis, Faculty of Economic and Social Studies, University of Manchester.

————. 1986. *Los recursos de la pobreza: Familias de bajos ingresos de Guadalajara.* Guadalajara: El Colegio de Jalisco/CIESAS/SPP.

————. 1988. "Economic Crisis, Domestic Reorganisation and Women's Work in Guadalajara, Mexico." *Bulletin of Latin American Research* 7 (2): 207–223.

————. 1991. "Family Well-being, Food Consumption, and Survival Strategies during Mexico's Economic Crisis." In M. González de la Rocha and A. Escobar Latapí (eds.), *Social Responses to Mexico's Economic Crisis of the 1980s.* La Jolla: Center for U.S.-Mexican Studies, University of California, San Diego.

————. 1994. *The Resources of Poverty: Women and Survival in a Mexican City.* Oxford: Basil Blackwell.

————. 1995. "The Urban Family and Poverty in Latin America." *Latin American Perspectives, 85* (22) (2): 12–31.

————. 1999. "La reciprocidad amenazada: un costo más de la pobreza urbana." In E. Rocío (ed.), *Hogar, pobreza y bienestar en México.* Guadalajara, Mexico: Instituto Tecnológico de Estudios Superiores de Occidente.

————. 2000. *Private Adjustments: Household Responses to the Erosion of Work.* New York: UNDP.

————. 2001. "From the Resources of Poverty to the Poverty of Resources? The Erosion of a Survival Model." *Latin American Perspectives,* 119 (28) (4): 72–100.

González de la Rocha, Mercedes, Elizabeth Jelin, Janice Perlman, Bryan. Roberts, Helen Safa, and Peter Ward. 2004. "From the Marginality of the 1960s to the New Poverty of Today: A LARR Research Forum." *Latin American Research Review,* 39 (1): 183–203.

González de la Rocha, Mercedes. (With Paloma Villagómez Ornelas). 2005. "Nuevas facetas del aislamiento social: un acercamiento etnográfico." In M. Székely Pardo (ed.), *Desmitificación y nuevos mitos sobre la pobreza: escuchando lo que dicen los pobres.* Mexico DF: SEDESOL.

Haguette, Teresa María. 1982. *O mito das estratégias de sobrevivência. Um estudo sobre o trabalhador urbano e sua família.* Fortaleza: UFC.

Hernández, Daniel, and María de Jesús Pérez García. 2003. *En el año 2000, gasto de los hogares y pobreza en México. Cuadernos de desarrollo humano.* Mexico DF: SEDESOL.

Jelin, Elizabeth, and Mara del Carmen Feijoó, 1981. *Presiones cruzadas: trabajo y familia en la vida de las mujeres.* Research Report. Buenos Aires: Centro de Estudios de Estado y Sociedad (CEDES).

Katzman, Ruben (Ed.). 1999. *Activos y estructuras de oportunidades: Estudios sobre las raíces de la vulnerabilidad social en Uruguay.* Montevideo: CEPAL/PNUD.

Kessler, Gabriel. 1996. "Algunas implicaciones de la experiencia de la desocupación para el individuo y su familia." In Beccaria, Luis and Néstor López (eds.), *Sin trabajo: Las características del desempleo y sus efectos en la sociedad argentina.* Buenos Aires: Losada.

Lomnitz, Larissa. 1977. *Networks and Marginality: Life in a Mexican Shantytown.* New York: St. Martin's Press.

Moser, Caroline. 1996. "Confronting Crisis: A Comparative Study of Household Responses to Poverty and Vulnerability in Four Urban Communities." *Environmentally Sustainable Development Studies and Monographs* (Serial No. 8). Washington, D.C.: The World Bank.

Narayan, Deepa (with Raj Patel, Kai Schafft, Anne Rademacher, and Sarah Koch-Schulte). 2000. *Voices of the Poor. Crying out for Change.* Washington, D.C.: The World Bank.

Pahl, R. E., and Claire Wallace. 1985. "Household Work Strategies in Economic Recession." In Redclift, Nanneke and Enzo Mingione (eds.), *Beyond Employment. Household, Gender and Subsistence.* Oxford: Basil Blackwell.

Pastore, José, Helio Zylberstajn, and Carmen Silvia Pagotto. 1983. *Mudança social e pobreza no Brasil: 1970–1980 (O que ocorreu com a família Brasileira?).* São Paulo: Fundação Instituto de Pesquisas Económicas/Libraría Pionera Editora.

Roberts, Bryan. 1995. *The Making of Citizens: Cities of Peasants Revisited.* London: Arnold.

Selby, Henry, Arthur Murphy, and Stephen Lorenzen. 1990. *The Mexican Urban Household: Organizing for Self-Defense.* Austin: Texas University Press.

Stack, Carol B. 1974. *All Our Kin: Strategies for Survival in a Black Community.* New York: Harper and Row.

Székely Pardo, Miguel, 2003. "Es posible un México con menor pobreza y desigualdad." *Serie Documentos de Investigación (5).* Mexico DF: SEDESOL.

Tello, Carlos. 1991. "Combating Poverty in Mexico." In González de la Rocha, Mercedes and Agustín Escobar Latapí (eds.), *Social Responses to Mexico's Economic Crisis of the 1980s.* La Jolla: Center for U.S.-Mexican Studies, University of California, San Diego.

Trapenciere, Ilze, Ritma Rungule, Maruta Pranka, Tana Lace, and Nora Dudwick. 2000. *Listening to the Poor: A Social Assessment of Poverty in Latvia.* Riga: Ministry of Welfare and United Nations Development Programme.

Wacquant, Loic. 1999. "Urban Marginality in the Coming Millennium." *Urban Studies, 36* (10): 1639–1647.

Wilson, William Julius. 1987. *The Truly Disadvantaged: The Inner City, the Underclass, and Public Policy.* Chicago: The University of Chicago Press.

———. 1997. *When Work Disappears: The World of the New Urban Poor.* New York: Vintage Books.

PART

III

EDUCATION POLICY

Introduction

Education has long been seen as a cornerstone of poverty reduction, and it is a major challenge for Mexico on two fronts: attainment and achievement. As described in the chapter by Bane and Zenteno in this book, only 23 percent of the Mexican population 25 to 64 years old had access to secondary or higher education, while 88 percent of the U.S. population in the same age group did have it. International comparisons also show that educational achievement of Mexican children and youth is the lowest among OECD countries.

Education creates the human capital—skills, knowledge, and habits—which enables workers to be more productive. Greater productivity leads to increased income and lower poverty. Most countries (including the United States and Mexico) have seen education as an economic development strategy and as a way to decrease the gap between rich and poor. They have tried to increase school enrollment at all levels, and have tried, with less success, to improve student learning and tailor learning to the needs of a dynamic economy and a democratic society.

The paper by Muñoz and Villarreal reviews the evidence on the effects of various educational policy interventions in Mexico. One problem that educational policy addressed there was school attendance, through the *Oportunidades* Program, an innovative and widely imitated cash transfer program in which receipt of benefits is conditional on children's attending school and receiving health care. The logic of the program is that children are often kept out of school because of the costs of attendance, both the direct costs of school fees, clothes and so on, and the opportunity costs of children's lost contributions to the household through work, childcare, or home production. Cash transfers are directed at families with school-age children and are set at levels meant to encourage those most in danger of dropping out, such as girls and older children, to stay in school.

Oportunidades has been carefully evaluated, and there is now reasonably good evidence that it has indeed been successful in increasing school attendance. Indeed, it may have done about as much as can be done in that regard. Primary attendance is now close to universal, and secondary schooling is enrolling substantial proportions of its age cohort.

However, there is almost no evidence that *Oportunidades*, or the national-level compensatory programs that Mexico has put in place, has narrowed the achievement gap between rich and poor. This finding is quite consistent with evidence from the United States. Indeed, a long tradition of educational policy research has found little indication that policy interventions of a general sort have much impact on achievement. The class-size experiments are in some ways the exception that proves the rule.

Richard Elmore's chapter suggests why. He makes the obvious (but usually ignored) point that learning takes place in classrooms because of the interaction of teachers, students, and contents. Only when high-level content is taught effectively to students with the skills and motivation to learn does learning take place. Policy makers who seek to improve education, therefore, whether in the United States, Mexico, or anywhere else, have to pay close attention to the design of demanding curriculum, to educating teachers capable of dealing with the students, and to the circumstances of the students. Incentives and accountability play a role, but building capacity may be even more important. This is hard, demanding work, and may pay off only after a relatively large investment of time and effort. Nevertheless, as Elmore shows, it is possible to achieve real improvements in the education of disadvantaged children when these basic insights are put into practice.

5

Interpreting the Educational Effects of Compensatory Programs in Mexico

Carlos Muñoz-Izquierdo, Guadalupe Villarreal-Guevara

Our purpose in this chapter is to answer the following questions:

- What is the extent of inequality in the distribution of educational opportunities for Mexican children in relation to their families' poverty levels?
- What do we know about the nature and results of government programs that have been implemented to combat this inequality?
- What factors can explain the results of these programs and what implications do these results have for designing policies aimed at distributing the educational opportunities more justly?

The chapter is laid out in four sections. In the first, we discuss data that reflect the inequalities arising from the interdependence that exists between poverty levels and the distribution of educational opportunities. In the second section, we describe some programs that the Mexican government has enacted to combat such interdependence.

In view of the strategies that these programs follow to achieve their objectives, they may be classified into two categories. One set of programs was designed to improve quality of school inputs. To reach this goal, the programs have distributed various types of aid to schools located in regions whose inhabitants live in poverty. The programs in the second category, on the other hand, are dedicated to strengthening students' socioeconomic capacity to attain basic education. To this end, they offer a variety of subsidies to economically disadvantaged families.

In the third part of this chapter, we discuss a series of analyses that we made in order to evaluate the results of some programs of the first type. We also summarize the research findings that evaluate the effects of one program of the second type, which has been implemented under a variety of titles.

Next, we interpret the results of these programs. To achieve this, we describe one of the models that best reflects the present state of knowledge in this matter, and we present the results of two research projects that seek to apply this knowledge to the Mexican situation.

Finally, in our conclusions, we point out some implications for public policies aimed at improving the distribution of educational opportunities in Mexico.

The Magnitude of Educational Inequalities

During the last decades of the twentieth century, Mexico had taken important steps to distribute equitably opportunities for children to enter the school system and stay in it. To this end, the CONAFE (acronym in Spanish for National Council of Educational Promotion) was created in 1971. This institution's original purpose was to promote access to primary education for children who lived in economically disadvantaged areas.

As a result of the institute's actions, among others, the government was able to announce in 1981 that, according to primary school enrollments, all Mexicans between the ages of six and fourteen had the opportunity to receive a primary education. However, some students in primary school were enrolled in lower grades than those that normally corresponded to their ages. Thus, the relationship between the number of enrollments in primary schools and the size of the population between the ages of six and fourteen did not really indicate that the primary schools were satisfying demographic demand.

Several research projects have demonstrated that these disparities between a student's age and the grade he or she is enrolled in are related to the socioeconomic conditions of his or her family as well as to the probability that the student will stay in school.[1] This indicates that there is a strong relationship between the distribution of educational activities and poverty levels in the different social strata.

Table 1 (all tables are at the end of the chapter) shows some indicators of the repercussions of that relationship in the Mexican educational system; the values of eight indicators reflect different dimensions of this phenomenon. The first three indicators refer to the situation 19 years after Mexico achieved an equal number of students enrolled in elementary schools in the demographic cohort corresponding to the appropriate educational level (i.e., indicators that correspond to the demographic cohort whose ages in 1981 were between 6 and 10 and whose ages in the year 2000 were between 25 and 29). The rest of the indicators refer to the students who in 2006 were enrolled in elementary and junior high schools.

1. Indicators reflecting the situation 19 years after achieving the number of students enrolled in elementary schools were equal to the size of the corresponding demographic demand.
   a. In the year 2000, the illiteracy rate corresponding to the above-mentioned demographic cohorts was 1.0 percent in the Mexican state that had achieved the highest level of socioeconomic development, and 16.1 percent in the most disadvantaged state.[2]
   b. The proportion of the demographic cohorts that did not complete their primary education represented 3.6 percent in the richer states and 24.2 percent in the poorer.
   c. In the former states, 14.4 percent of demographic cohorts did not complete their basic[3] education, which contrasts with the 25.8 percent that did not reach that goal in the latter states.
2. Indicators referring to the students enrolled in elementary education in 2006.
   a. The probability of completing primary education in 6 years ranges from 0.58 (in the most disadvantaged state) and 0.86 (in the most developed)[4];
   b. The proportion of 13-year-olds who have completed 6th grade varies between 81.4 percent and 96.4 percent in these states, respectively;
   c. The proportion of 16-year-olds who have completed 9th grade varies between 67.7 percent and 83.9 percent in these states, respectively.

Academic achievement is also clearly related to poverty. In fact, the percentage of students who in 2006 reached a high level of achievement in Spanish was 2.0 percent in the poorest state, and 16.2 percent in the richest one. In addition, the proportion of students who were high achievers in mathematics ranged from 2.8 percent to 14.8 percent in those states.

The need to create programs aimed at improving the distribution of educational opportunities—in access to the school system and staying in school, along with having the ability to achieve academic competence—is thus evident. This is the reason that Mexico has implemented so many different compensatory programs.

Nature and Goals of Compensatory Programs

Programs Aimed at Improving Quality of School Inputs

Starting in 1992, CONAFE has also assumed the responsibility of contributing toward the improvement of the elementary education offered in impoverished areas. For this purpose, it implemented compensatory programs through which a variety of resources (material, economic, educational, and teacher-training) are distributed among rural, indigenous, and disadvantaged urban schools, whose records show a lower academic achievement than the one obtained in other schools.

In order to strengthen the supply of educational services, CONAFE uses two types of components. The first seeks to improve the material conditions of the schools and the offices of supervisors (installations, furniture, equipment, and materials) and the second is directed toward the development of faculty, supervisors, principals, and administrative personnel of the state boards of education.

Within this framework, in 1992 CONAFE created PARE (a Spanish acronym for Program to Overcome the Educational Gap). This program was implemented in the four poorest states of the country (Chiapas, Guerrero, Hidalgo, and Oaxaca). Subsequently, CONAFE has launched similar programs in several states. Financial resources assigned to those programs—which amounted to 352 million $U.S. (MD) in 1991—should meet the goal of 760 MD in 2006. It is expected that contributions of the Mexican government will increase from 102 to 155 MD, whereas those of international organizations that contributed to the financing of these programs will do so from 250 MD to 625 MD (see Table 2).

On the other hand, as seen in Table 3, during the last decade of the twentieth century, the elementary school population served by these programs increased from 1.02 to 4.34 million students (this last number represents 29.4 percent of the total enrollment in this educational level).

Programs Aimed at Strengthening Students' Socioeconomic Capacity to Attain Basic Education

It is important to point out that the compensatory educational programs also propose, albeit minimally, to strengthen students' socioeconomic capacity to attain basic education, since they have proposed to promote the timely distribution of free textbooks. However, the programs that specifically pursue this goal concern themselves more with distributing subsidies among poverty-stricken families.

The first of these programs was called *Progresa* (Spanish acronym for Program of Education, Health, and Food). It currently goes by the name *Oportunidades*, and its goal is to support marginalized families through diverse strategies in order to develop their abilities to reach higher levels of well-being by arresting the causes of poverty in their lives. In the educational realm, this program's aim is to support children and youths so they may enter school and stay there until they have completed their basic education.

This program's coverage has become extensive. The number of benefited families grew from 400,000 in 1997 to 4,939,400 in 2004. Of those, 72.3 percent are rural, 12.9 percent live in semi-urban areas, and the remaining 14.8 percent live in urban marginalized areas.[5] In view of its importance, the program receives 46.5 percent of the Secretary of Social Development's (SEDESOL) budget assigned to combat poverty.[6]

Scholarships go to students under eighteen who are enrolled in grades 3–12. To keep their scholarships, students must attend at least 85 percent of their classes. Scholarships increase with grade levels, and women in secondary school receive more money as an encouragement to stay in school.

CONAFE believes that by zeroing in on families and communities in need, its services benefit approximately 85 percent of these communities with programs aimed at strengthening educational opportunities in rural and indigenous zones, thus increasing the efficiency and effectiveness of formal education.[7]

Indirect Assessments of Program Outcomes

Effects on Course Repetition and Terminal Efficiency

According to CONAFE (see Tables 4 and 5), the indexes of course repetition and finishing school in communities with access to compensatory programs improved more rapidly than those of the rest of the school population.

Table 6 shows the improvement these indexes had in each of these subpopulations as well as in the whole population. The difference between the changes that occurred among the indicators corresponding to each of the school population segments is in part caused by the fact that these indicators do not evolve linearly but rather asymptotically. In 1991, the indicators corresponding to communities not in need of compensatory programs were better than those communities that did benefit from them, therefore, the "ceiling" these indicators had for improving was smaller than that for the communities receiving the programs.

It is impossible, however, to discard the hypothesis that the speed with which course repetition and terminal efficiency indicators for recipient communities improved is that these changes are a result of the educational strategies designed by compensatory programs.

Effects on Student Achievement

Mexican primary and junior high schools are grouped into categories (called modalities) according to their source of financing, to their socio-geographic location[8] and to their curriculum. Primary school modalities include private schools, urban public schools, rural public schools, community centers that operate in small communities and follow CONAFE's curriculum, and schools for the indigenous population, commonly called "indigenous schools." Junior high school modalities include private schools, general schools, technical schools, and *telesecundarias* (televised classes). General and technical schools have distinctive curricula, while televised classes, aimed mainly at rural and marginalized urban zones, employ the technology needed to offer courses.

Researchers have found that over time a clear statistical relationship develops among the different educational modalities and that their hierarchical positions correspond to the students' social classes. A school's modality often determines, in decreasing order, grade averages in Primary Schools: 1) Private Schools, 2) Urban public schools, 3) Rural schools, 4) Community centers, and 5) Indigenous schools; in Junior High Schools: 1) Private schools, 2) General and technical schools, and 3) *Telesecundarias* (televised classes). Students attending private schools have the highest grade averages, while students attending Indigenous schools (in primary education) and *telesecundarias* (in Junior High Schools) have the lowest grade averages.

The National Institute for Educational Evaluation (INEE) has just published its fourth report about the quality of basic education in Mexico,[9] which contains the results of achievement in language and math tests administered in 2006 to randomly selected students registered in different primary and junior high schools. These results appear in Tables 7a and 7b. It is clear that the hierarchy for each type of school in both curriculum areas is the same as that reported by researchers over the years. The inequalities in achievement associated with students' socioeconomic backgrounds have not disappeared with time.

It is important to emphasize the less fortunate situation of students attending Indigenous schools and televised classes, because their schools serve a student population that belongs to the lowest social class of the modalities listed. These students live in geographically isolated areas or in marginalized urban zones.

To analyze the evolution of academic achievement over time, students would have had to take achievement tests on different dates to meet the psychometric conditions necessary to compare results from one period to the next. However, the SEP's Testing Center did not strictly meet these requirements when it made up tests to implement its *Estándares* project.[10]

Nevertheless, these tests yielded results coherent with diverse hypotheses, such as the relationship between achievement and marginalization levels of the cities where the corresponding studies took place. According to the SEP, the values of achievement test scores (expressed in the Rasch scale) "allow us to estimate comparable measurements of ability [italics added] within a determined time frame [since] the tests given to the students had similar levels of difficulty";[11] therefore, we decided to appraise the inter-temporal evolution of this phenomenon by comparing the standard deviations of the performances achieved in the same school grades on two different dates.[12]

What we really wanted was to find out from this analysis whether the disparity of academic performance by students in municipalities of different levels of marginalization would improve or diminish over time, assuming that a larger disparity implies more inequality and vice versa. To achieve this, we generated a sub-database of the schools that were evaluated from 1999 to 2002. We then compared the standard deviations of the 1999 third-grade students' grades to those of third graders in 2002.

Table 8 displays the results of this exercise, and an analysis of these results revealed, in general terms, a clear tendency towards a decrease in the standard deviations. In the majority of the thirty comparisons made, the signs of the differences among the deviations are negative. However— and most significantly—in the comparisons that refer to highly marginalized municipalities, the opposite occurred, which indicates that in these areas the inequality of academic achievement grew instead of diminishing during the dates under study.

It is, of course, difficult to explain this finding based on the information available. However, we may hypothesize that the expansion of school enrollment in highly marginalized municipalities (communities of families with low indices of human development and few resources whose economic incentives are channeled through programs such as *Oportunidades*) is creating greater inequality in student academic achievement, that is, is associated with an increase in enrollment. When they can, these programs enroll more children from more impoverished families. This could mean that the school system is not geared to helping children from impoverished families succeed in school. Thus, the generation, the evaluation, and the availability of a series of innovations designed to solve this problem continue to be necessary.

Direct Assessments of Program Outcomes

In order to analyze the effects of a program aimed at improving school inputs, we used the information about achievement from our sub-database on evaluated schools, and also utilized information gathered by a research team that began (in 1995) to evaluate PARE's educational impact.[13]

Since these two measurements used different measuring units, we had to make them match in order to establish the comparisons that we were trying to carry out. To this end, we described the grades from rural and indigenous schools as percentages that corresponded to those of urban schools in each of the stated measurements. As can be seen in Table 9, in 2006 there was a decrease in the difference between grades in rural and indigenous schools and those in urban schools. Rural school grades rose by 9.8 percent in Spanish and 2.9 percent in math.

Indigenous schools, on the other hand, advanced more slowly. In fact, the gap that separates their grades from those of urban schools declined by only 7.7 percent in the Spanish tests and 2.0 percent in the math tests. This result is significant, given that the improvement ceiling that these grades had in 1995 compared to urban school grades was higher than that of rural schools. This is consistent with the hypothesis that compensatory programs in effect are contributing less to satisfy the needs of the indigenous population than they do for the remaining rural population.

Nevertheless, the changes detected in this analysis (especially those referring to Spanish tests) make it possible to conclude that the academic achievement of students in rural and indigenous schools located in the four states we studied has been approaching that of students enrolled in urban public schools (provided that we eliminate other technical interferences in these observations, such as those that could be attributed to sample designs).

What we are reporting may very well be attributed to the simultaneous implementation, in approximately 85 percent of localities, of both the compensatory programs aimed at improving quality of school inputs and the programs that offer economic support to impoverished rural and indigenous families. From this finding, it is possible to deduce that the improvement in children's school attendance and their staying in school (as several research projects that we cite in the next part of this chapter have demonstrated) are being driven by the economic incentives that the *Oportunidades* program supplies. This is less apparent in indigenous schools than in urban and rural schools, which could mean that the educational model is less efficient—by being less pertinent—in indigenous schools than in others. Therefore, economically and culturally disadvantaged students who live in underdeveloped areas and who enter and stay in schools are contributing to the increase, in these areas, to disparities in the distribution of academic achievement.

While this analysis suggests that the incentives mentioned here are more beneficial to students who do not live in the poorest socioeconomic conditions, it is also possible that the school system is not able to ensure that these students from this sector receive a good education. This may especially be true of students who attend indigenous schools.

Effects of a Program Aimed at Strengthening Demand for Education

A program of this type, *Oportunidades* (Program of Human Development Opportunities), has undergone intense and rigorous evaluation. Several studies of this program's effects are available, thanks to the government's keen interest in seeing results in several areas (including those of the educational nature). It is important to note that these studies have been carried out with different databases, their geographical coverage has differed, and their authors have used different methodologies.

Shultz's studies (2000a and 2000b) referred to the *Progresa* program (the predecessor of the *Oportunidades* program) and used information from some states in Mexico. As he states:

> At the primary level.... statistical methods ... revealed that *PRO-GRESA* succeeds at increasing the enrollment rate of boys by 0.74 to 1.07 percentage points and of girls by 0.96 to 1.45 percentage points. At the secondary level ... the increase in enrollment effects for girls ranged from 7.2 to 9.3 percentage points and for boys from 3.5 to 5.8 percentage points. This represents a proportional increase of boys from 5 to 8 percent and of girls 11 to 14 percent.[14]

According to Shultz:

> If these effects could be sustained over the period in which a child is of school age, the accumulated effect on educational attainment for the average child from poor household would be the sum of the estimated change for each grade level. Summing these values for grades 1 to 9 suggests that the program can be expected to increase educational attainment of the poor of both sexes by 0.66 years of additional schooling. Girls in particular gain 0.72 years of additional schooling by the 9th grade while boys gain 0.64 years.

From another angle, Skoufias and McClafferty point out that "given that the average youth aged 18 achieved about 6.2 years of completed schooling prior to the program, these data are suggestive of an overall increase in educational attainment of about 10 percent." Shultz also found that "the impact of PROGRESA on enrollment rates is largest for children who have completed the 6th grade and are thus qualified to enroll in junior secondary school, increasing 11.1 percentage points for both sexes combined of 14.8 percentage points for girls and 6.5 percentage points for boys, representing percentage increases of over 20% for girls and about 10% for boys."

Parker (2004) updated these studies, widening their coverage to the national level. She sought to analyze the impact of *Oportunidades* in secondary schools and high schools, using information on dropouts and grade repetition rates in the cycle 1995–1996 to the cycle 2002–2003. Parker found that *Oportunidades* has had an important impact on student enrollment in rural secondary schools, and that the impact has grown over time. *Telesecundarias* and general secondary schools have seen increases of 24.0 percent in the cycle 2002–2003. In urban zones, the impact of *Oportunidades* is smaller, with an increase in student enrollment around 4.9 percent for the cycle 2002–2003, mainly in the female population. Likewise, Parker observed:

> The results at the high school level are astonishing. The estimated impacts are substantial, indicating that only two years after the implementation of the Program giving scholarships at this level, student enrollment in the first grade of high school has increased 84.7% in rural areas and 10.1% in urban areas, using the same student enrollment in the cycle 2001–2001 as a base.[15]

Regarding elementary schools, Parker mentions that "in preceding studies, it was shown that *Oportunidades* had not had an important impact on student enrollment (in this educational level)." She attributes this observation to the fact that "student enrollment at the elementary school level was very high even before that the program started." That is why she does not take into consideration the lag represented by the existing differences among the student ages and the grades in which they are registered. However, Parker affirms that her analysis on the effects of dropping out and repetition in elementary school shows that

> *Oportunidades* seems to have a positive effect. More than 17.4% of the male students who drop out from elementary school, stop doing so as a result of the program in rural areas (17,031 male students). Regarding grade level repetition in these same areas, the effects are lower but significant, implying that around 4.3% of the male students and 8.9% of the female students that would repeat

any grade in elementary school do not do so as a result of the implementation of *Oportunidades* (10,529 male students and 14,265 female students). In urban areas, significant effects are also observed in reducing repetition. The effects on the repetition rate are a little bit higher than the ones in rural areas, showing reductions from 7.9% in the percentage of male students who repeated grade and 12.9% in female students (16,988 male students and 18,673 female students). In elementary schools in urban areas, *Oportunidades* reduces the drop-out rate around 5.7% for female students and 3.5% for male students (6,001 male students and 8,378 female students).[16]

Parker also analyzed the impact *Oportunidades* has had on reducing the gap of student enrollment, grade repetition, and dropping out between male and female students. She found that

In rural secondary schools, *Oportunidades* seems to contribute to eliminating the gap between male and female students. Before the implementation of the program, there were 83 female students registered for every 100 male students. Considering only the impact of the program, this figure grew up to 96 female students for every 100 male students registered for the cycle 2002–2003. As a result of the program, in urban secondary schools the gap was reduced considerably in the first two grades (from 92 to 95 female students for every 100 male students in the first grade and from 95 to 99 female students for every 100 male students in second grade) and for the third grade, the trend even reversed.[17]

In high school, Parker observed that

While the gap in rural areas was not very wide before the implementation of the program (92 and 98 female students registered for every 100 male students in the first and second grades, respectively), *Oportunidades* has not helped to reduce the gender gap. Even though it is important to highlight that these gaps in practice have almost been eliminated, they may be due to other impacts in the enrollment of male and female students not associated with the *Oportunidades* program. In urban areas, where the enrollment of male and female students was very similar before the beginning of the program (98 and 109 female students for every 100 male students, respectively), *Oportunidades* had a bigger impact on the enrollment of female students, which would translate into figures of 100 female students for every 100 male students in the first grade (the gap is eliminated) and 111 female students for every 100 male students in the second grade, widening the inverted gap (that is, favoring female students).[18]

Lastly, in the elementary schools Parker detected that

The impact on repetition, where female students had much lower repetition rates than male students even before the implementation of *Oportunidades*, was to increase the gap. On the other hand, the drop-out rates, which before Oportunidades were greater for male students than female students, were reduced by the program in rural, but not in urban areas.[19]

Likewise, Escobar and González de la Rocha (2003) carried out a qualitative study to discover the social dynamics of the academic success or failure of the Oportunidades program. While looking for reasons why students who receive the scholarship attend school, they observed the following:

In the first place, there is a clear awareness that once the scholarship is granted, students can keep it only if they stay in school. In the second place, money devoted to school materials such as notebooks, pencils, uniforms, and shoes increased when households received the first two payments from the Program. Finally, students have breakfast more frequently than before. This is a decisive factor that in many families favors school attendance.[20]

On the other hand, they found that,

In most cases, children or youths who had already dropped out of school have not come back; this is attributed to three reasons: the first is that some young students had migrated, simply in search of better jobs in other cities (or in the United States), or because they had to satisfy the urgent needs of their families. The second reason is early pregnancy or the abandonment of their homes, in the case or female students. The third is that several of these young students (between 13 and 16 years old) were economic providers in their homes and could not quit that role.

Finally, as Escobar and González de la Rocha report, "a finding that emerged from the case studies and the focus groups is that *Oportunidades* raised parents' and students' educational goals and expectations."[21]

Effects on Achievement

The above studies analyze elements such as drop-out rates and retention. However, those variables may not reflect, in a reliable and objective way, actual student achievement. Student progress through grade levels and some achievement test scores depend on decisions made by individual teachers; these decisions reflect individual judgments and values. Sometimes the decision to pass or fail a given student depends on factors other than achievement, such as an attendance record; some teachers may believe that students who attend school regularly are the ones who acquired the knowledge and developed the skills necessary to satisfactorily complete the grade and advance to the next level. However, there is no evidence that this supposition is based on the learning that beneficiaries of the program have objectively acquired.

The impact of programs that are designed to strengthen demand for education and are based on actual student achievement has been objectively evaluated by Berhman, Sengupta, and Todd, in a research project carried out in 2000. (Although in the year in which this study took place its results refer to *Progresa*, its program strategies are similar to those embodied in *Oportunidades*.) Below is a transcription of some paragraphs from that study:

> To permit evaluation of the impact of *PROGRESA* on achievement test scores, *PROGRESA* arranged for the Secretary of Pubic Education (*Secretaría de Educación Pública*, SEP) to administer the same tests for students in schools attended by individuals in the *PROGRESA* Evaluation Sample as SEP administers annually to a national sample of schools. These tests were administered to students in about 500 primary and secondary schools in the localities in the *PROGRESA* Evaluation Sample plus schools close to these localities....
>
> The result of primary interest is that *after almost a school year and a half of exposure to PROGRESA, there is no significant positive impacts of PROGRESA on the achievement test scores.* There are somewhat more cases in which the control group tests scores exceed the treatment group scores than could be expected by chance, which to a very limited degree may be related to compositional

changes. *But, in any case, there is not evidence of significantly positive effects even when compositional effects are taken into account in so far as they can be with the available data.*[22] Possibly this may reflect the limitations in the data noted above, particularly regarding the evaluation of the effect after a little more than a year of exposure to the program, but also possibly caused by the relatively small sample sizes and the limited number of observations that could be merged with household survey data.[23]

The quoted evaluation clearly had some limitations. Besides those mentioned by the authors, additional limitations would include the fact that the tests had been applied after the original dates (this could have biased the test scores upward); or that

> [The tests] were given only to a sub sample of those in the Evaluation Sample who were enrolled in school, and this sub sample was not selected to be a random sample. A related point is that success in linking achievement test scores to children in the evaluation samples has been limited to fairly small proportions of the children in the Evaluation Sample households' surveys, which limits severely in practice controlling for possible selectivity in test taking.[24]

However, the finding that there are no statistically significant differences in achievement between those who participated in the program and those who did not raises serious doubts about the effectiveness of the educational model to which students participating in the study were exposed.[25] We should keep in mind that the program is improving students' attendance in school, which implies a greater contact of the students with the model. Therefore, the observation that a greater contact is not influencing positively students' learning can be interpreted as a signal that the processes taking place inside the classrooms are not relevant enough from the pedagogical point of view.

Determinant Factors in Achievement

By the end of the 1960s, the so-called Coleman Report focused intense attention on the importance of structural factors in student achievement. According to Coleman, social origin, family income, area of residence, and certain cultural family aspects were the factors that best explained the differences in achievement.

Several research projects soon confirmed the huge impact of these structural factors in academic achievement. This generated an enormous pessimism about the capacity of school to reduce the effect of the structural variables. The change that would foster improved achievement in the less favored social strata could only come from the transformation of the social structure.

However, other studies carried out later, using other analytical methods, proved that besides the structural factors, there are other variables relative to the school that affect students' achievement. These observations gave rise to the so-called school effectiveness movement, whose numerous followers have been attempting to clearly identify those variables, as well as the pedagogical and administrative processes through which they could have some effects on achievement.

Explanatory Model Developed by PISA

The model used in 2003 by the Program for International Student Assessment (PISA) to analyze the results of the assessment of academic achievement in 40 countries is probably one that has most accurately reflected the recent discoveries of the aforementioned research. This model considers diverse independent variables reflecting the family environment of students, the learning environment and the way in which learning is organized, policies and practices related to extracurricular activities, available resources in schools, the administration and financing of these resources, the characteristics of the learning process, and gender-related differences. These variables are as follows (OECD 2002 and 2003):

1. Variables related to the family environment: parents' working situation and education, family economic resources, communication regarding social and cultural issues, and family structure.

2. Variables related to the learning environment and the teaching organization: teachers' support of their students, and teacher and student-related factors that have an impact on the school environment.

3. Variables related to policies and practices regarding extracurricular activities: time devoted to school homework in language, math, and science, and teacher shortage.

4. Variables related to school resources: quality of physical school infrastructure and educational resources, and deficient equipment and facilities.

5. Variables related to school management and financing: school autonomy and teacher participation, and institutional type of control (public and private schools and private schools dependent on the government).

6. Variables related to learning characteristics: motivation and school dedication, learning strategies, and familiarity with the use of computers as learning tools.

7. Variables related to gender differences: aptitude gender differences, differences in gender regarding interest in specific subjects, dedication to reading, learning strategies, and the concept of self.

Available Knowledge on Educational Achievement in Mexico

At the end of the 20th century, few studies were available on this subject, probably because such studies are usually expensive, especially when researchers lack access to databases generated by government agencies or international organizations.

However, starting in 2003, the National Institute for Educational Evaluation (INEE) and the National Center for the Evaluation of Higher Education (CENEVAL) radically modified the situation that had prevailed up to that time. They offered to researchers the necessary support for the development of studies on this subject, and published the methodologies and the results of the studies sponsored by these institutions.

In general terms, it can be said that these researchers not only proved conclusively the validity of the models based upon the logic of the PISA model, but also shed some light on the interactions which exist between the different factors that determine academic achievement.

Rather than describe all of the research, we will summarize the principal conclusions of one study supported by the National Institute for Educational Assessment.[26]

The effect of external and internal factors on academic achievement in schools is more complex than is generally believed. In fact, some of the variables referring to the socioeconomic context of schools not only have a direct influence, but also an indirect influence on the academic achievement of students. This is because these characteristics are positively related to the variables referring to the quality of resources to which schools have access, and to the pedagogical processes carried out in the schools. In other words, schools located in poorer areas have access to resources of lower quality, and this prevents them from developing effective pedagogical processes. The opposite is true of schools in more favorable socioeconomic contexts.

There is a positive relationship between the number of students per teacher and academic achievement. This discovery, which contradicts the results of studies carried out in more developed countries, might be related to the fact that the student-teacher ratio is associated with the location of the schools. Thus rural schools, which from an academic point of view compare unfavorably to urban schools, have a lower student-teacher ratio because of the low population density of the communities where they are located.

With respect to the effects on academic achievement of the different variables related to the processes carried out within the schools, it is likely that learning can be enhanced by more frequent classroom visits by principals, improvements in the performance of teachers, and stronger support from families and from schools' technical boards. Since these actions can be carried out in the schools themselves, their implementation does not depend upon any other efforts to correct the inequalities observed in the academic achievement of students.

The assessment of the 2003 PISA model not only contains the results of the achievement tests applied to students in the countries participating in this program, but also the findings of analyses designed to identify the factors which determined these results. (These findings are detailed in Annex B1 of that report.)

When analyzing the situation in Mexico, PISA found that 39.4 percent of the variance of the mathematics performance—explained by the regression models that refer to the Mexican education system—comes from the differences in the operating conditions of schools participating in the study. At the same time, 16.6 percent of such variance might be explained by factors associated with the students' socioeconomic conditions. This means that schools have an important margin to operate (equivalent to almost 23 percent of the achievement variance) to improve their students' academic achievement.

Secondly, PISA estimated the influence that certain specific independent variables have on student achievement. Table 10 shows a summary of the findings that refer to the determining variables on Mexican student achievement in the mathematics test.

The first two columns of Table 10 show the values that the dependent variable assumes (math test scores) when the corresponding independent variable takes its lowest value (column 1) or it highest value (column 2). The third column shows how the dependent variable (expressed the same way) reacts when the value of the independent variable changes in one unit of measurement. This reaction may be considered as the "elasticity" for the math test scores with respect to the independent variable that is being considered. Finally, the fourth column shows the percentage that each independent variable provides to the variance of achievement on the math test that could be explained by the corresponding regression model.

The analysis of Table 10 brings a confirmation that the variables which better explain academic achievement are those that refer to the students' social, economic, and cultural background.[27] In fact, the model in which the students' backgrounds are expressed in a comprehensive way (by means of an index of economic, social, and cultural status) shows that they contribute to 17.1 percent of the variance that could be explained by the model in which the index is found. In other models, we were able to see that the "international socioeconomic index of parent's occupational status," the "index of possessions related to *classical* culture in the family home," and the "parent's years of schooling" have similar relative weights, which fluctuate between 8.9 and 9.5 percent.

Furthermore, there is evidence of three student attitudes that contribute to the variance regarding achievement, with proportions similar to the ones mentioned previously. These attitudes are the "index of self-efficacy in mathematics," the "index of anxiety in mathematics," and the "index of attitudes toward school." (The first one contributes 9.5%, the second 8.6%, and the third 7.6 %.)[28] However, as the OECD points out, these attitudes reflect student scores obtained in academic achievement—that is why the variables' behavior depends to some extent on the schools' functioning—and also influence academic achievement, helping students to get good scores on the tests.

Thirdly, we find (to a lesser extent, varying between 3.3% and 4.4%) that some variables relate to the schools' conditions. These variables are the "index of the quality of the school's educational resources," the "index of disciplinary climate in mathematics lessons," and the "index of the quality of the school's physical infrastructure." This finding likely reflects that the variation of such factors among Mexican schools is lower than the existing disparity in the socioeconomic factors, or that the corresponding measurement scales were not able to measure the existing variations in our society, or a combination of both arguments.

Finally, in the regression models estimated by PISA, other variables were included. These intended to measure the impact on student achievement of a particular process taking place inside the classrooms. These variables refer, on one hand, to student strategies to improve their learning processes, and on the other hand, to the common practice of periodically testing learning and using the results from the performed evaluations.

It is important to mention that although these variables had a secondary role in most of the participating educational systems in PISA, in the Mexican system the contribution of these variables to explain achievement was practically negligible. From this observation we derive two hypotheses: (a) Mexican students have not been sufficiently trained to use these learning strategies, or (b) the procedures used by their teachers to assess their students' academic achievement are uniform. In other words, they do not vary according to the school or to student characteristics.

The findings of these studies suggest a relationship between student achievement and compensatory programs. It is evident that the relative success which has been obtained in increasing school enrollment and reducing school dropouts may be attributed to the simultaneous implementation in many areas, especially rural areas, of the *Oportunidades* Program (oriented toward strengthening demand for education) and compensatory programs (oriented toward improving quality of school inputs).

Indeed, it is obvious that *Oportunidades* is helping to counteract the cost of opportunity implicit in school attendance and permanence. This cost, as many studies have shown, is one of the most important structural factors in determining academic achievement (since it is related to the standard of living of families, which in turn is related to the parents' occupations).

Likewise, the compensatory programs are contributing to the improvement of the resources available to schools in sparsely populated areas, as shown by the findings of the studies described here.

Therefore, the complementary nature of these two programs, as well as the interaction that (according to studies that we quoted here) exists between school factors and structural factors, seem to be helping to increase school enrollment and improve the efficiency of the educational system.

Furthermore, the evidence that these programs are not achieving the desired effect on academic achievement in some areas—especially in schools attending primarily to indigenous populations—suggests that the compensatory programs are not making use of outcomes from studies like the ones we have summarized here.

These programs are certainly improving the quality of the educational resources available to schools, especially those located in areas of low population density, as revealed by the studies.[29] However, as we pointed out earlier, this has not resulted in a substantial improvement in academic achievement.

It is very probable that this discrepancy between the expectations and the achievements of these programs can be attributed to two factors which are complementary to each other and which can be identified by reviewing the study findings.

First, both the geographical coverage and the volume of the resources distributed by the programs have been insufficient. This inference is based on the findings of PISA referring to the low proportion of variation in academic achievement that can be explained by the "index of school resources."

Second, it is probable that the above-mentioned resources are not being used to substantially improve the pedagogical and administrative processes in the schools.

This inference is based on the two studies reviewed in this section, which revealed, among other things, the need to increase the frequency of classroom visits by principals, to improve the performance of teachers, and to intensify the technical and family support of the educational process.

Finally, the PISA study detected—among other causes—that student attitudes, certain characteristics of classroom climate, and learning strategies used by students have little effect on academic achievement. From these results it can be inferred that a low number of students and teachers have been trained adequately enough to obtain satisfactory academic results.

Summary and Conclusions

Despite the programs that Mexico has implemented to satisfy the demand for basic education and to improve the quality of school inputs, the relationship that always existed between academic achievement and students' socioeconomic and cultural background has not disappeared. We found, in effect, that educational opportunities are still correlated with states' levels of economic development and with students' socioeconomic backgrounds. We also found an inverse correlation between municipalities' poverty levels and academic achievement in schools functioning in localities of the respective municipalities.

There is also tentative evidence (not a result of longitudinal observations corresponding to the same schools) that rural school student achievement is catching up with the achievement of students attending public urban schools. This tendency does not hold true, however, for predominantly indigenous school populations, which casts doubts on the effectiveness of the educational model implemented in the schools in which indigenous children are enrolled.

An analysis of the changes that have taken place over the past few years in the variation in achievement test scores reported by schools in municipalities with differing indexes of marginalization reveals that the most marginalized municipalities have the highest variation. The *Oportunidades* program in these areas is attracting and keeping in school students from families that are the most highly disadvantaged, both culturally and socioeconomically. The fact that the pre-existing disparities in academic achievement in these places are increasing could reinforce the previously stated hypothesis that refers to the ineffectiveness of the educational model implemented in these highly marginalized areas.

There is sufficient direct and indirect evidence to conclude that the *Oportunidades* program is instrumental in raising school enrollment and attendance levels as well as keeping students in school for longer stays.

This program is also contributing to a decrease in course failures. This decrease, however, does not reflect an effective improvement in achievement as measured by externally generated standardized tests. Although the program improves student attendance, at the same time it leads to longer periods of teacher exposure to students from lower social strata; this increased exposure is not producing tangible improvements in academic achievement. This observation reinforces the previously stated interpretation of the educational model's ineffectiveness in schools operating under highly precarious conditions.

The research into factors that determine academic achievement has consistently demonstrated that this variable does not depend only on the cost of opportunity, which is partially covered by the subsidies that the *Oportunidades* program distributes among needy families. It depends as well on the quality and use of the schools' human, material, and pedagogical resources, as well as on the learning that takes place inside the classrooms. The research has also demonstrated that variables inside the schools do not make up for the influence of external factors, which have direct or indirect bearing on academic achievement.

Because of this, Mexico has implemented a series of compensatory programs to improve the quality of the resources that are available to schools operating under precarious conditions. The country is confident that these programs will also improve the quality of teaching-learning processes.

Government authorities have not specifically aimed at assuring that compensatory programs are implemented in the same schools that receive beneficiaries of the *Oportunidades* program. However, since those in charge of both types of programs have the same goal of aiding the country's poorest communities (not precisely as a result of adequate planning), 85 percent of the cases of both types of programs are in fact in the same geographical areas.

In spite of this high convergence of both types of programs, exposure to the *Oportunidades* program has not produced positive results in academic achievement, suggesting that compensatory programs are not effective.

The next question (beyond that of fostering legitimacy) is: What sense is there in continuing to invest resources to keep children and teenagers in schools where academic performance is deficient and in compensatory programs that, according to the research findings presented here, fail to achieve their goals?

Research into factors that determine achievement (and more precisely research into the focus of efficient schools) has identified a variety of remedies to improve academic achievement in Mexico. It has also determined that Mexico possesses (from a technical point of view) a wide range of action to elevate its schools' academic test scores.[30] It is necessary to put these findings into use and conduct controlled and adequately evaluated experiments in order to detect the educational innovations and policies that are feasible, appropriate, and effective within the country's different regions and communities.

Tables

Table 1. Indicators of Educational Inequalities in the Most and Least Developed States in Mexico

Indicators	Most developed state*	Least developed state**
25–29-year-olds who were illiterate (in 2000)	1.0%	16.1%
25–29-year-olds who did not finish elementary education (in 2000)	3.6%	24.2%
25–29-year-olds who did not finish basic education (in 2000)	14.4%	25.8%
Probability of finishing elementary school in 6 years (2006)	0.86	0.58
Youngsters 13 years old who finished 6th grade (2006)	96.4%	81.4%
Youngsters 16 years old who finished 9th grade (2006)	74.0%	34.9%
Students who got high test scores in Spanish (2006)	16.2%	2.0%
Students who got high test scores in mathematics (2006)	14.8%	2.8%

* Federal District
** State of Chiapas
Source: Data obtained from INEE (2004, 2007).

Table 2. Time Frame and Financial Sources of Compensatory Programs

		Financing (Millions of U.S. dollars)			
Programs[a]	Time Frame	World Bank	Mexican Government	Others	Total
Program 1	1991–1996	250	102	—	352
Program 2	1993–1997	80	34	1[b]	115
Program 3	1994–1999	412	204.7	—	616.7
Program 4	1995–2000	-	260	390	650
Program 5	1998–2006	625	155	—	780

[a]1= PARE, 2=PRODEI, 3=PAREB, 4=PIARE, 5=PIARE 8
[b]UNICEF, UNESCO, and PNUD
Source: Data obtained from conafe.edu.mx.

Table 3. Students Participating Annually in Compensatory Programs

Years	Students
1992	1,018,671
1993	1,204,131
1994	1,286,047
1995	2,110,982
1996	3,735,490
1997	3,799,689
1998	4,014,215
1999	4,262,282
2000 (goals)	4,336,250

Source: SEP's Informes de Labores

Table 4. Course Repetition Rates in Communities with Compensatory Programs Compared with Communities without Programs

School year	Total	Communities served	Communities not served	Difference	Variation in communities not served	Variation in communities served
1991–1992	9.1	13.8	7.3	6.5		
1992–1993	8.7	13.2	7.0	6.2	0.6	0.3
1993–1994	7.2	10.5	6.0	4.5	2.7	1.0
1994–1995	7.0	10.2	5.8	4.4	0.3	0.2
1995–1996	6.8	10.0	5.5	4.5	0.2	0.3
1996–1997	6.9	9.6	5.9	3.7	0.4	-0.4
1997–1998	6.7	9.4	5.7	3.7	0.2	0.2
1998–1999	6.6	9.2	5.6	3.6	0.2	0.1

Source: CONAFE's, Memoria de la Gestión 1995–2000. México: CONAFE, 2000, pp. 202 and ff.

Table 5. Terminal Efficiency Levels in Communities with Compensatory Programs Compared with Levels in Communities without Programs

School year	Total	Communities served	Communities not served	Difference	Variation in communities not served	Variation in communities served
1991–1992	74.9	59.9	80.7	20.8		
1992–1993	75.8	60.8	81.7	20.9	0.9	1.0
1993–1994	78.5	64.9	83.9	19.0	4.1	2.2
1994–1995	79.3	69.0	83.2	14.2	4.1	−0.7
1995–1996	80.2	71.2	83.8	12.2	2.2	0.2
1996–1997	82.8	76.8	85.2	8.4	5.6	1.8
1997–1998	84.9	79.0	87.3	8.3	2.2	2.1
1998–1999	85.8	80.8	87.8	7.0	1.8	0.5

Source: CONAFE's, Memoria de la Gestión 1995–2000. México: CONAFE, 2000, pp. 202 and ff.

Table 6. Improvement of the Indexes in Each Segment of the School Population

Indices	Communities served	Communities not served	Total population
Improvement in the course repetition index	−4.6%	−1.7%	−2.5%
Improvement in the terminal efficiency index	+20.9%	+7.1%	+10.9%

Table 7a. Sixth-grade Students' Levels of Achievement in Spanish and Mathematics (in percentages, 2006)

Modality	Insufficient	Minimum	Intermediate	Advanced
Spanish				
Private	2.0%	25.4%	43.7%	29.0%
Urban public	13.2%	51.9%	28.4%	6.6%
Rural public	25.8%	56.0%	16.1%	2.2%
Community Centers	32.5%	56.3%	10.9%	0.4%
Indigenous Education	47.3%	46.0%	6.3%	0.5%
Mathematics				
Private	2.7%	31.2%	41.6%	24.5%
Urban public	13.6%	52.9%	26.2%	7.3%
Rural public	23.7%	56.9%	16.5%	2.9%
Community Centers	28.2%	57.9%	13.2%	0.7%
Indigenous Education	43.2%	48.8%	7.3%	0.6%

Table 7b. Ninth-grade Students' Levels of Achievement in Spanish and Mathematics (percentages, 2006)

Modality	Insufficient	Minimum	Intermediate	Advanced
Spanish				
Private	8.1%	27.4%	42.4%	22.2%
General education	29.7%	40.7%	25.0%	4.6%
Technical education	31.1%	39.8%	24.7%	4.5%
Telesecundarias				
(televised classes)	51.1%	35.6%	12.1%	1.2%
Mathematics				
Private	23.7%	31.0%	38.4%	7.0%
General education	50.5%	30.5%	17.9%	1.1%
Technical education	52.0%	30.2%	16.9%	0.9%
Telesecundarias				
(televised classes)	62.1%	26.0%	11.4%	0.5%

Table 8. Comparison of the Standard Deviations in Student Grades on Different Dates, Related to Marginalization of the Schools' Municipal Locations

Levels of marginalization and types of measurements used	Third grade			Sixth grade		
	Standard deviation 1999	Standard deviation 2001	Signs of differences (2001–1999)	Standard deviation 2000	Standard deviation 2002	Signs of differences (2000–2002)
Very high marginalization						
Overall measurement	50.37	64.36	Positive	48.99	53.21	Positive
Spanish tests	49.94	62.35	Positive	65.04	65.59	Ns
Math tests	68.06	80.37	Positive	55.37	56.93	Positive
High marginalization						
Overall measurement	82.93	69.42	Negative	61.45	59.33	Negative
Spanish tests	75.33	64.61	Negative	74.44	68.86	Negative
Math tests	103.11	92.3	Negative	65.97	61.05	Negative
Medium marginalization						
Overall measurement	60.33	61.5	Ns	71.02	50.22	Negative
Spanish tests	62.47	63.86	Ns	82.06	60.62	Negative
Math tests	76.41	80.2	Positive	77.47	54.67	Negative
Low marginalization						
Overall measurement	67.11	66.55	Ns	72.64	57.46	Negative
Spanish tests	65.31	62.68	Negative	85.26	69.91	Negative
Math tests	85.55	86.44	Ns	76.75	58.05	Negative
Very low marginalization						
Overall measurement	70.38	67.35	Negative	74.55	65.85	Negative
Spanish tests	71.02	68.71	Negative	90.15	76.98	Negative
Math tests	87.93	84.71	Negative	78.41	67.68	Negative

Table 9. Sixth-grade Spanish and Math Test Grades
in Rural and Indigenous Schools Described
as Percentages of the Corresponding Urban Schools

Schools compared	Spanish (6th grade)	Mathematics (6th grade)
Rural/Urban		
Measurements PARE (1995)	81.3%	89.5%
Measurements 2006	91.1%	92.4%
Differences	9.8%	2.9%
Indigenous/Urban		
Measurements PARE (1995)	73.7%	81.0%
Measurements 2006	81.4%	83.0%
Differences	7.7%	2.0%

Sources: Muñoz-Izquierdo, Carlos and Raquel Ahuja (2000); INEE (2006).

Table 10. Independent Variables Explaining Mexican Students'
Performance on the Mathematics Scale, According to PISA 2003

Variable	Performance at bottom of independent variable	Performance at top of independent variable	Change in performance per unit of independent variable	% of explained variance
Student attitudes				
Index of attitudes toward school	353	414	21.4	7.6
Index of student's sense of belonging to school	363	399	13.3	2.6
Index of self-concept in mathematics	373	419	24.1	5.4
Index of self-efficacy in mathematics	353	426	30.9	9.5
Index of anxiety in mathematics	422	359	−34.0	8.6
Student socio-economic status				
International socio-economic index of parents' occupational status	357	424	23.5[a]	9.5
Index of "classical" culture in the family home	367	424	31.5	9.0
Mother's education	371	411		
Father's education	366	415		
Index of economic, social and cultural status	342	433	29.3	17.1
Parents' years of schooling			5.1	8.9
School factors				
Index of principal's perception of student-related factors affecting school climate	370	398	9.9	1.4
Index of disciplinary climate in mathematics lessons	365	411	18.9	4.1
Index of the quality of the school's physical infrastructure	375	419	14.9	3.3

Index of the quality of the school's educational resources	369	406	15.1	4.4

Source: OECD, Programme for International Student Assessment. Learning for Tomorrow's World. First Results from PISA 2003. Annex B1.

[a]Change in the mathematics score per 16.4 units of the index.

Values that are statistically significant are indicated in bold.

Definitions of student's attitudes:

Student's sense of belonging to school.

Students were asked to express their perceptions about whether their school was a place where they felt like an outsider, felt that they belonged, felt out of place, or felt lonely.

Student's self concept in mathematics.

Students were asked about their belief in their own mathematical competence.

Student's self-efficacy in mathematics.

Students were asked to what extent they believe in their own ability to handle learning situations in mathematics effectively.

Anxiety in mathematics.

Students were asked whether and to what extent they feared trying to do work in mathematics.

Notes

1   See, for example, Muñoz-Izquierdo, C. et al. (1979).

2   The most economically developed state is the Distrito Federal, and the most disadvantaged is the state of Chiapas.

3   In Mexico, basic (or compulsory) education ends at 9th grade.

4   In Mexico, primary (or elementary) education ends at 6th grade.

5   Estimates based on figures in INEE (2007).

6   Cf. Cited Secretary's web page.

7   Cf. CONAFE (2000), p. 156 and ff.

8   The use of this concept indicates that the categories described have already been defined regarding where the schools are located. There is, however, a clear correlation between a school's location and the social status of its students.

9   Cf. Instituto Nacional para la Evaluación de la Educación (2006).

10 This affirmation is supported by various studies on this topic undertaken by the National Institute for Educational Evaluation (INEE). See *Memorias de las Jornadas de Evaluación Educativa*, which, under INEE's auspices, took place in Mexico City in July, 2004.

11 This quotation is from General Directorship of Educational Evaluation (2003).

12 It is important to point out that the "National Standards Project" (which in 2002 was turned over to the National Institute for Educational Evaluation) produced the database that allowed us to estimate differences in test scores and standard deviations over time, controlling for marginalization indexes of municipalities.

13 Cf. Muñoz-Izquierdo, Carlos y Raquel Ahuja (2000).

14 In Mexico, the term "secondary level" refers to junior high school.

15 Cf. Parker, Susan W (2004): Executive Summary.

16 Ibid.

17 Ibid.

18 Ibid.

19 Ibid.

20 Escobar, Agustín and Mercedes González de la Rocha (2003, 32).

21 Ibid.

22 Italics added by authors.

23 Behrman, Jere R., Piyali Sengupta, and Petra Todd (2000, chapter 5).

24 Ibid.

25 From our point of view, the educational model is composed of all the elements included in the school system, such as the curriculum, the teaching method, student-teacher interaction, teacher training, teacher's, principal's, and supervisor's behavior, school resources and facilities, and so on.

26 Cf. Muñoz- Izquierdo, C and A. Márquez-Jiménez (2003).

27 It is important to mention that percentages are not additive, since they were obtained through different regression models in which the mentioned variables were expressed in different ways.

28 A brief definition of these variables appears at the end of Table 10.

29 See, for example, Muñoz-Izquierdo, C. and R. Ahuja (2000).

30 Cf. Muñoz Izquierdo, C. (2005).

References

Behrman, Jere R., Piyali Sengupta, and Petra Todd. 2000. *The Impact of Progresa on Achievement Test Scores in the First Year: Final report.* Washington, D.C.: International Food Policy Research Institute, September 20.

CONAFE. 2000. *Memoria de la gestión 1995–2000.* México.

Escobar, Agustín, and Mercedes González de la Rocha, 2003. *Evaluación cualitativa del programa de desarrollo humano Oportunidades: Serie documentos de investigación.* Mexico: Secretaría de Desarrollo Social (SEP), 3.

General Directorship of Educational Evaluation. 2003. *Aplicación de los instrumentos de los Estándares Nacionales 1998–2002. Descripción del aprovechamiento escolar.* Mexico: SEP, Dirección General de Evaluación (Mimeo).

Instituto Nacional para la Evaluación de la Educación. 2004. *Panorama Educativo de México, 2004.* Mexico: INEE.

————. 2006. *El Aprendizaje del Español y las Matemáticas en la Educación Básica en México.*

————. 2007. *Panorama Educativo de México, 2007.*

Muñoz-Izquierdo, Carlos, 2005. "Análisis de los resultados de México en el PISA-2003: Una oportunidad para las políticas públicas." *Perfiles Latinoamericanos* 26: 83–107.

Muñoz-Izquierdo, Carlos, et al. 1979. "El síndrome del atraso escolar y el abandono del sistema educativo." *Revista Latinoamericana de Estudios Educativos* XIX (3).

Muñoz-Izquierdo, Carlos, and Raquel Ahuja. 2000. "Function and Evaluation of a Compensatory Program Directed at the Poorest Mexican States: Chiapas, Guerrero, Hidalgo, and Oaxaca." In *Unequal Schools, Unequal Chances: The Challenges to Equal Opportunity in the Americas*, ed. Fernando Reimers. Cambridge: Harvard University Press.

Muñoz-Izquierdo, Carlos, and A. Márquez-Jiménez. 2003. *Factores internos y externos que determinan el aprovechamiento escolar en la educación primaria.* México: INEE.

Parker, Susan W. 2004. Evaluación del impacto de Oportunidades sobre la inscripción, reprobación y abandono escolar. In Instituto Nacional de Salud Pública y CIESAS. *Resultados de la Evaluación Externa del Programa de Desarrollo Humano Oportunidades 2003.* Documentos finales.

Schultz, T. P. 2000a. *The Impact of PROGRESA on School Enrollments.* Washington, D.C.: International Food Policy Research Institute.

————. 2000b. *The Impact of PROGRESA on School Attendance Rates in the Sampled Population.* Washington, D.C.: International Food Policy Research Institute.

Skoufias, Emmanuel, and Bonnie McClafferty. 2001. *Is PROGRESA Working? Summary of the Results of an Evaluation by IFPRI.* Washington, D.C.: International Food Policy Research Institute, Food Consumption, and Nutrition Division.

6

School Improvement and the Reduction of Poverty

Richard F. Elmore

Most social scientists, most policy makers, and most citizens believe that education matters in reducing poverty. However, education has proven to be a fickle and unreliable ally in this quest. Investments in education seem to work best as a poverty-reduction measure when the "treatment" is some schooling versus no schooling—that is, in situations where large segments of the population gain access to schooling for the first time. As access to schooling increases in the population at large, education seems to reinforce, or at the very least mirror, the broader economic and social inequalities in the population at large. The more developed the economy, it seems, the more troublesome and problematic becomes the relationship between education, economic well-being, and the reduction of poverty.

In the United States, education policy has been preoccupied, some would say obsessed, with what we call the achievement gap—the gap between the lowest- and highest-performing students, which is highly correlated with income, race, and ethnicity, and which is among the largest of any industrialized country in the world.[1] Policy makers and educators across a broad ideological spectrum espouse the belief that education should close the achievement gap, yet despite forty-plus years of various types of policy interventions, the results seem, at best, to reflect an unstable and small rate of progress. At the aggregate level, there have been modest positive changes in the level and distribution of school performance, but these changes have not been robust or consistent over time, nor have they been of a magnitude that would come close to closing the gap between the highest- and lowest-performing students in any reasonable period of time.[2] In addition, at the aggregate level, the relation between educational expenditures and measured student performance seems weak to non-existent.

This kind of inscrutable and unreliable relationship between policy and performance breeds disillusionment among those who believe in the education sector but have no specialized expertise in it—a population that includes most policy makers. Something seems not quite right about investing large amounts of resources in a system that cannot deliver on its most basic purpose. Alternatively, realists or cynics argue that the education system is working precisely the way it was designed to work—it rewards the privileged and legitimates an essentially inequitable social order by deliberately confounding educational performance with merit. In this view, those who advocate using education to combat poverty are either hypocrites, espousing policies for symbolic reasons that they know will not work, or hopelessly naïve, working against at least forty years of accumulated evidence.

The debate about education as a poverty-reduction measure, then, is a debate both about the effectiveness of the education sector and about its social authority and legitimacy. To the degree that the education sector purports to remedy social and economic inequalities, but in reality seems to be engaged in the reproduction of these inequalities, it loses whatever social and political legitimacy it has as a sphere of specialized knowledge. To the degree that policy makers espouse education as a poverty-reduction measure, while the system itself seems powerless to reduce poverty, policy makers begin to question the purpose of the enterprise. The education sector seems an unreliable and feckless partner in this effort.

In a broader context, the social authority of the education sector in the United States is already quite tenuous; perhaps more so than in any other industrialized country. Teaching, in this country, is still a relative low-status occupation. Careers in education are not regarded as the most highly desirable in a society preoccupied with material accomplishment. Policy makers manifest no particular willingness to defer to the professional judgment of educators on matters of education policy, in fact, quite the opposite.[3] Most policy makers regard education as a matter of "common sense,"[4] amenable to the simplest kinds of ad hoc judgments and rules of thumb, not requiring any particular expertise. As the social authority and legitimacy of the education sector decline, so too does its capacity to respond to social and political signals about what it should be doing. Performance failure breeds loss of authority, which in turn leads to less capacity to perform. And so it goes.

Within this largely negative scenario, at the aggregate level, a few positive patterns emerge when the picture becomes more fine-grained. First, we know that school attainment matters in the United States. That is, there are substantial returns to the number of years of schooling one completes. Income differentials between those who fail to complete high school, those who complete high school but fail to advance to post-secondary education, and those who complete some post-secondary education are significant.[5] We know that certain types of knowledge and skill are differentially rewarded in the labor market, and that most of them can be taught—whether they are or not is another matter.[6] We know that, other things being equal, better-educated teachers—measured in the grossest terms: years of schooling, undergraduate major, courses taken, and so forth—have a significantly positive effect on students' academic performance, measured by standardized tests.[7] Consistent with this finding, we know that the largest proportion of variance in measured student performance is explained by differences among teachers within schools, not, as one would expect, by differences among schools.[8] We know that schools seem to respond to incentives—parental choice, competition with neighboring schools and districts, performance-based accountability systems, to name the main ones—although the magnitude, variability, and clarity of these responses are never as great as ideologues, policy makers, and academic researchers would like.[9] We know that in the total distribution of schools, some significant, but small, proportion of high-poverty schools out-perform others with similar demographics, although our knowledge of why this is true is sketchy and anecdotal at best. We know increasingly how to measure attributes of school organization and instructional practice that can be linked to differences among schools in student performance. And perhaps most importantly, we know enough about how to teach children to read to be able to say that there is no reason why all but a small fraction of children can't be reading fluently by their third year of school; we know a significant amount, but not as much, about the teaching of mathematics and writing; however, we do not know nearly as much about the teaching of everything else.[10]

An acute reader might discern a pattern here. At the aggregate level, education looks unpromising and unresponsive as a poverty-reduction measure. As the grain size gets smaller, the evidence points to a more positive, if considerably more complex picture. It is this problem I would like to address. However, before I do, let me digress a bit on the topic of policy and policy research.

The Discourse of Policy-making and Policy Research[11]

First, let me be candid about my own professional biases and bona fides. I am a product, although not a particularly orthodox or well-bred product, of the U.S. policy analysis enterprise. I have been a policy analyst in the federal government; I have taught in a public policy school; I have done policy research; I have been an officer of the association of public policy schools in the United States; and I have been called upon to consult with local, state, and federal agencies as a researcher and policy analyst. Why it is necessary for me to say this will become clear in a moment.

I have, over the past ten years or so, shifted my focus from relatively large-scale issues of policy analysis—school finance, the politics of school reform, school choice, accountability, and so forth—to a somewhat finer-grained set of issues: how do schools, as organizations, improve their performance and what are the conditions in the broader environment that enable or constrain their improvement? As I have shifted my focus, I have become increasingly aware of how limited and counterproductive the discourse, the mindsets, and the culture of policy analysis and of policy-making are to the solution of the problems that are entailed in school improvement. I have also become aware of how much the discourse of policy analysis reinforces and encourages some of the most counterproductive tendencies of policy makers—counterproductive in the sense of working against the objectives that policy makers themselves claim to espouse.

The first of these counterproductive tendencies is what I call the fallacy of main effects. Policy makers and policy analysts are programmed to ask the question "does it work?" The "it" here is a policy intervention—a change in the institutional structure, a change in incentives, a change in the nature of the treatment that clients receive, and so forth. The premise underneath the question is that if the intervention is "successful," its effect emerges from the noise of uncontrolled variation; statistically significant effects produce promising evidence that the policy intervention is successful. The problem with this view is, as everyone who has ever done research on a policy intervention knows, that it is almost never true that interventions worth doing produce unequivocal evidence of main effects. In education in particular, the main effects are often small in a cross-sectional sense, and the variations in effects among different schools or sites implementing a given intervention are often larger than the differences in main effects among competing interventions. Policy analysts do their best to interpret these results in a responsible way: speaking judiciously about how to understand and interpret effect sizes, explaining the difference between statistical significance and policy relevance, and making sense of why an intervention might have large effects in one place and no effect, or a negative effect, in another, wiping out or reducing the main effect.

I have seen policy analysts and policy makers repeatedly ignore evidence of variability in effects from one setting to another in the interest of focusing on main effects. The only thing that matters is how "robust" the effects of an intervention are across settings, because, of course, any policy worth its salt has to work consistently everywhere. Policy analysts are usu- ally mute on the subject of what could explain variability, because their methods are mostly attuned to analyzing main effects, or partitioning variability among "explained" and "unexplained" categories. When policy analysts do focus on variability, they tend to say patently silly things like, "context matters," or "there are unmeasured sources of variability that deserve further research" (which, of course, never gets done).

I am not making a claim here about research or analytic methods per se, but about the use of research for policy purposes. There are methods that are capable of giving a much more nuanced picture of how policy interventions work. There are no particularly powerful theories, at pres- ent, to give meaning and direction to these methods, but the methods exist and they are widely used. My claim is about how the discourse of policy- making affects the way evidence is interpreted; that discourse drives policy analysis in the direction of main effects.

Policy analysts focus on main effects because that's what they think pol- icy makers want to hear about, and because they—policy analysts—notice that when the discourse around effects gets too complicated and nuanced, policy makers' eyes glaze over and they start looking at their wristwatches. Policy makers are impatient with nuanced explanations because they live in a world where political credit, stature, and influence accrue on the basis of simple claims of success and failure, keyed to politically driven timelines— electoral cycles, budget cycles, planning cycles, and so forth. The discourse of main effects is as close as policy analysts can get (or at least as close as they think they can get) to bridging the gap between the world of political credit and the messy world of evidence on large-scale interventions.

As will become more clear later, I am inclined to assert a counter- proposition to the main effects fallacy: all important effects are interaction effects. By this I do not mean to restate the vapid truism that "context mat- ters." I mean, instead, that the work of explaining variability in the effects of policy requires more powerful theories about what actually happens when people and organizations respond to policies, how policy interven- tions fit into the range of factors to which people and organizations respond, and what the prerequisites are, in terms of knowledge, skill, and organizational capacity, that determine how people and organizations will respond. There is, in other words, no main effect worth knowing about, except in the most superficial sense; what determines the "effect" of a pol- icy, particularly policies that are designed to influence the work of people in complex institutional and organizational settings, is an array of factors resident in the individuals and their settings about which we have to have theories in order to understand them.

A corollary of the fallacy of main effects is the fallacy of attractive nuisances. Abraham Kaplan, the eminent philosopher of science, once coined what he called "the first law of instruments." It was: "Give a child a hammer and suddenly everything in the world needs pounding." Let me give an American example of this fallacy: the United States has, for last the last decade or so, embarked on an ambitious experiment in performance-based accountability in schools. It started as a largely state and local reform movement led by entrepreneurial governors, mainly from southern states, trying to harness education to their ambitious strategies of economic development. It has since been turned into a federally mandated reform with the passage in 2001 of the No Child Left Behind (NCLB) Act. Performance-based accountability in schools is, as one might expect, quite a complex matter. It is actually a made-to-order demonstration of why the main effects model does not say much about the impact of a policy intervention. The centerpiece of performance-based accountability is, or course, testing. Now, any responsible social scientist would be able to repeat the litany of caveats that should accompany the use of tests for policy purposes: that tests do not measure learning, they only create an imperfect construct that represents learning; that any test is a fallible measure and it is more fallible (less reliable) at the individual level, and as a cross-sectional measure, than at higher levels of aggregation, accumulated over time; and that tests of academic achievement are only one measure—albeit an important one—of the quality of academic work in a given school. Despite these caveats, and despite powerful critiques not just by anti-testing zealots, but also by eminent psychometricians and testing experts, NCLB has turned performance-based accountability into test-based accountability. Why? Because testing is a relatively cheap, highly visible policy instrument. Because testing is highly efficient—it is both the policy variable and the instrument by which we measure the main effect of it (a classic circular, rationalist trope). Moreover, whatever the complexities of the underlying processes the tests are trying to measure, tests can be given on a timeline that is consistent with the institutional cycles within which policy makers operate. That is, testing tends to crowd out other elements of performance-based accountability—standards, professional development, investments in infrastructure to support teachers and schools, the introduction of new, more complex materials and practices, research and development on new instructional methods, and so on—because it is an attractive nuisance: a simple, seemingly understandable intervention that is consistent with the fallacy of main effects. One could generalize the fallacy of attractive nuisances to say that all policy interventions—no matter how sophisticated they are in initial design—are likely to degrade over time in the direction of their most simplistic elements. Policy makers are often intolerant of things that are complicated, difficult to explain, and require time to unfold. The institutional structure of policy-making creates its own logic, and that logic has nothing to do with the logic by which organizations on the ground respond to external demands and integrate them into internal operations.

Finally, I think the fallacy of attractive nuisances leads to what I would call the fallacy of inverse relations: those things over which policy can assert the greatest direct, short-term effect are likely to be the least important factors in producing what policy makers claim to value over the longer term; those things over which policy asserts the least direct, short-term effect are likely to be the most important factors in producing what policy makers claim to value. The logic of policy-making pushes policies toward less complex, more immediate, more visible solutions that obey the timing of institutional cycles of elections, budgets, plans, and the like. These kinds of policies, as we shall see later, operate on the edges of organizations, and they constitute relatively weak treatments for what policy makers are trying to fix. There are, of course, policies that address more directly the factors that determine what policy makers claim to want to fix, but because they operate at the core of organizations, not at the edges, because they produce, at least initially, highly variable effects, and because the timing of the processes by which they produce these effects is inconsistent with the timing of political cycles, these policies are not likely to be favored by policy makers. The institutional logic of policy-making is, other things being equal, incompatible with the demands of large-scale improvement in the quality of work in complex organizational settings.

It should not surprise us, then, that our "best" policy interventions produce weak, highly variable, disappointingly complex effects. Nor should it surprise us when our best attempts to bring policy research and analysis into a powerful relationship with policy-making result in odd, inconclusive, and disappointing results. To the degree that policy analysis and research focus on main effects, they come into a closer relationship with the institutional imperatives of policy-making, but widen the distance between them and the actual processes that operate in the organizations they try to influence. To the degree that policy analysis follows the path created by the logic of policy-making, it will become increasingly focused on policy instruments that have the most superficial and perverse effects.

Moreover, to the degree that policy analysis focuses on main effects and attractive nuisances, it will undermine the very processes in organizations that would produce the outcomes that policy makers claim to value most.

The Organizational Logic of School Improvement

If what I have argued thus far has any merit, one would expect the actual processes by which schools undergo improvement over time to be significantly at odds with the "best intentions" of policy makers who claim to be interested in school improvement. I am, as the above analysis suggests, a pessimist about the possibility of any long-term rapprochement among policy makers and practitioners around issues of school improvement—a kind of peaceable kingdom. I have learned a great deal from Michel Foucault's analysis of knowledge and power about how to understand this fractious and difficult relationship.[12] The ideology of policy analysis embodies a naive rationalist optimism that is not borne out in fact—if we just get the "right" information in the hands of the "right" people at the "right" time, then we will get "better" decisions. Policy makers do not make "bad" decisions because they are somehow misinformed; they make decisions they believe are good, which have perverse consequences because they operate in an institutional sphere that rewards such decisions. They will not respond favorably, at least in the short run, to "good" decisions made by practitioners, even if those decisions correspond to their espoused beliefs, because those decisions are often in direct conflict with the institutional rewards that influence their behavior. The bottom line is that we should expect success in school improvement to create political conflict even when both policy makers and practitioners think they are working toward the same purposes.

I also want to stress that what I have to say about school improvement is highly provisional. The research base, while promising, is still quite weak. Most of the powerful knowledge about sustained improvement in schools over time is embodied in practice, not research, and it is, from the point of view of practitioners, a-theoretical. This knowledge needs to be understood for what it is and to be put into a more powerful theoretical understanding in order to be usable beyond the settings in which it currently resides. I hope to be appropriately provisional in what I have to say.

First, let me stipulate a simple definition of improvement. Put performance and quality on the vertical, time on the horizontal. Improvement is moving the herd roughly northeast.

Second, improvement requires an element of scale. For improvement to occur, we must see increases in quality and performance across classrooms within schools, across schools within systems, and across systems within larger governance structures. Random acts of performance and quality are not improvement; we may learn something from them about what is involved in improvement, but they do not add up to it.

This simple model, at the first iteration, provides the parameters within which improvement occurs. I stress both performance and quality on the vertical axis because I have learned the hard way from watching skilled practitioners that improvements in quality usually precede improvements in performance, and that improvements in performance usually lag significantly behind improvements in quality. (We will see in a moment what performance and quality mean in the world of practice.) This relationship between quality and performance involves some serious risk and uncertainty. Within the space defined by the vertical and horizontal axes, one can make judgments about, for example, what constitutes an adequate and fair standard of performance, given what we know about the demands of improvements in quality and performance, and what constitutes a fair expectation about the amount of time required to meet this standard.

In the analysis that follows, I talk about the form of the function that we might expect schools to follow if they are engaged in improvement, and the factors that might determine both the rate at which improvement will occur and the shape of the path that schools are likely to follow. Then, in keeping with my prior critique of main effects logic, I will suggest some ways in which the rate and the shape of the path might differ for schools under different initial conditions and different conditions of intervention and support.

As we move beyond the analysis of schools as organizations and into the problem of systemic improvement, it becomes important to see the improvement function not simply as a function describing the path of a single school, but as a distribution of schools around that curve. Imagine a cloud of points describing the path of schools over time. We should be looking both at the main effect of the mean path and at what is happening to the distribution of movement around the path.

The next piece of the model focuses on the instructional core.[13] (See Figure 1.) The instructional core is that irreducible place in the organization of schools where learning occurs. I define the instructional core as the relationship between teachers and students in the presence of content. Schools do not "improve" by some mystical process of levitation; they get better at what they are doing by increasing the level of cognitive demand under which students work, by motivating students and teachers to engage in higher levels of work, and by introducing the resources required to make it possible for students and teacher to do higher levels of work. The instructional core tells us that, no matter what the policy intervention is, if you cannot see its presence ultimately in the instructional process, it is unlikely to have any impact on student performance. The instructional core also tells us that ultimately there are only three possible points of intervention if one is interested in improvements in performance: you can intervene by increasing the level of content, you can intervene by changing the knowledge and skill that teachers bring to instruction, or you can intervene by changing the role that students play in the instructional process and/or the knowledge and skill they bring as students. The model also suggests that intervening on any one point in the instructional core has consequences for the other two: Changing the level of content requires alterations in the level of knowledge and skill that teachers bring to the instructional process and requires a different level of initial knowledge on the part of students; changing teachers' knowledge and skill requires changes in the level of the content and the role of students; changing the role of students in the instructional process requires changing the content they are exposed to and the level of knowledge and skill of teachers in managing instruction.

At the second level of iteration, then, instructional improvement is the deliberate change of the instructional core to produce increases in quality and performance over time. Understanding how these improvements in the instructional core occur, the conditions under which they are more likely to occur, and the entailments of those conditions in terms of organizational and individual actions is central to any theory of school improvement. Most policy interventions in education have a quality of "and then a miracle happens." That is, they assume that certain changes in conditions external to schools—a change in the incentive structure under which schools work, the introduction of a new curriculum or a new set of curriculum standards, the introduction of a new teacher training regime—will translate somehow into changes in school performance. What this model of improvement suggests is that these external changes by themselves do not affect school performance. They affect it only insofar as they change the instructional core and the organizational conditions under which instructional practice occurs. All important effects are interaction effects.

The next element of the school improvement model is accountability. The policy discourse around accountability is quite confused. Policy makers seem to think that when they pass laws related to education, they are introducing something called "accountability" to schools for the first time.

The reality on the ground, as any student of organizations knows, is that schools operate in a dense field of interaction with parents, communities, local public officials and school administrators, neighboring school districts, state agencies, textbook publishers, voluntary accreditation agencies, post-secondary institutions, to name the main ones. Schools define their relationships with these parties in various ways, but they have to manage these relationships in some way—in this sense, schools are "accountable" if they exist at all. When policy makers introduce accountability measures, then, what they are actually doing is intervening in an existing network of accountability relationships that antedates their intervention and is very likely much stronger and more immediate than anything policy makers can devise. What policy makers define as accountability, then, is actually a set of accountability measures that operate on the margins of the existing network of relationships that surround schools.

In thinking about accountability, we distinguish between internal accountability, which describes the level of agreement and coherence among members of a school on expectations of what will occur in the instructional core, and external accountability, which describes the array of external relationships, including formal accountability policies, which shape a school's response to its environment. At the simplest level, the theory suggests that (a) the level of internal accountability, and (b) the degree of alignment between internal and external accountability determine how "successful" a school will appear to be in terms of formal accountability systems. The theory also suggests that internal accountability may be a much stronger predictor of how well a school performs than the degree of alignment between internal and external accountability. In other words, highly coherent schools tend to do relatively well in external accountability systems, no matter how well their beliefs, values, and instructional practices are aligned with the external accountability systems in which they operate.[14]

The final element of the school improvement model is capacity.[15] Capacity essentially defines the level of individual and organizational resources in a school relative to the external demands or expectations under which the school is operating. There are two important elements of this definition. Resources should be defined broadly to include not just material resources—physical plant, textbooks, people, instructional expenditures—but more importantly, as we shall see, the less tangible resources that determine quality in the instructional core—knowledge and skill of teachers and administrators, access to networks outside the school, and the work environment inside the school. It is also important to define capacity in terms relative to external demands. Schools that operate in settings where only a small fraction of school-aged population attend school, where literacy rates are low, and where the number of years of schooling in the population at large are relatively low operate at very different capacity levels than schools in settings where everyone completes basic education, where the population is literate, and where attainment is relatively high. Capacity is also a relative concept in the sense that, as schools improve their performance, their capacity requirements to reach the next level of performance increase. As with any organization, schools do not reach higher levels of performance simply by "spending" or "using" their existing capacity; they often reach points where their existing capacities simply won't permit them to reach higher levels of performance, and in order to improve they have to increase their capacity.

These, then, are the basic elements of a theory of school improvement: a definition of improvement as increases in quality and performance over time; a definition of the instructional core as the teacher and the student in the presence of content, which provides points of entry for the improvement of quality and performance; a definition of accountability as both internal coherence and external demand, which provides a way of thinking systematically about how schools as organizations respond to their environments; and a definition of capacity as the material and intangible resources that individuals and the school bring to bear on the instructional core relative to the external demands under which they operate.

What do schools actually look like when they are improving? Here my language will become considerably more provisional because we know a great deal less about what school improvement looks like, at the classroom level, at the school level, and at the aggregate level, than we should know. In large part, this lack of knowledge is a consequence of the strength of the main effects fallacy in policy analysis and policy-making. Researchers have been so preoccupied with trying to figure out whether policies "work" that they have been uninterested in the complex interaction effects of policies on the ground that can teach us about the conditions that determine how organizations respond to policies. Unlike many policy areas, this knowledge gap does not exist because we do not know how to do the research. In fact, the data exist to do much of this work, and the data collection instruments for mapping school improvement over time also exist. The work does not exist because the demand for the knowledge on the part of policy makers does not exist. The demand does not exist because policy makers and policy analysts are asking the wrong questions.

There is another reason why knowledge is weak in this area; most of the knowledge that exists is in the domain of practice. Most social scientists who study policy and most policy makers—at least in the United States—do not believe that practitioners possess useful knowledge, or if they do, they do not believe that that knowledge can be codified in any systematic way. Knowledge of practice is, in the language of the ultimate social science putdown, "anecdotal." The authority and legitimacy of knowledge derived from practice in education is weak because, as a political matter, education is believed to be low-status work, and educators are believed to be the main source of the problem that policy makers are trying to solve. Educators, and the organizations they work in, are blame objects in the discourse of reform, not sources of knowledge or potential allies.

In my work with schools and school administrators on system-wide problems of school improvement, we have noticed some interesting patterns both in the data at the school level and in the practices that present at the classroom and school levels. One very prominent pattern is that improvement in school performance, when it occurs, seems rarely, if ever, to occur in a straightforward linear pattern over time. (See Figure 2.) The most common pattern is relatively steep increases in performance in specific subject-matter domains—reading or math, for example—followed by periods in which performance goes flat or even in some instances declines. If schools stay engaged in improvement, these flat spaces usually turn into successive gains in improvement, followed again by flat spaces, or declines.

Looking at the data from a distance, this pattern seems mysterious and aggravating, no less to practitioners than to researchers. There is usually no discernible reason why performance should go flat. The teachers are working as hard as, or harder than, they have previously worked. There is usually no influx of new students with background characteristics that would predict lower achievement, and when there is, it is clear where they are in the school and what effect they are having. Usually, there has been no change in the resources that the school is bringing to bear on the instructional core: professional development continues as it has previously; monitoring, supervision, coaching of teachers proceeds as before, and so forth. Any morale problems that occur are typically of the "good" kind; that is, teachers and administrators are worried about their own performance and trying to figure out what to do next, rather than blaming the students or their parents for the school's lack of success.

From the classroom level, however, the pattern is considerably less mysterious. What one sees in schools that have leveled off is precisely that they are doing what they have previously done, often quite well, but the work that is required to achieve the next level of performance is considerably harder and more complex than what was needed for the level of work they are currently performing. In other words, they have reached the level of performance that exactly matches the current level of capacity in the individuals and the organization; in order to achieve higher levels of performance, they first have to invest in higher levels of capacity.

This realization often comes as a shock to teachers, school administrators, and policy makers, when they choose to acknowledge it. The implicit assumption behind education reform policy, especially performance-based accountability policies, is that people in schools know what they need to do in order the produce better results. If they do not, then they need to get better people, and those better people will know what to do. Yet relatively competent people run out of knowledge fairly quickly when confronted with new problems of instructional practice; in fact, even the best minds in educational research run out of new ideas when confronted with the kind of problems people in schools face when they want to improve performance under challenging conditions. Schools hit flat spots in the improvement process and do not know what to do next because there is no reason why they should know, never having previously confronted the problem they are now facing. In order to continue to improve their performance they have to learn how to do new things, and by definition, this new knowledge is not resident in the organizations where they work. Therefore, they have to search the environment for new solutions and often the environment is not very helpful either in producing solutions, or in providing access to the solutions that already exist.

So what seems mysterious and puzzling at the aggregate level seems reasonable and understandable at the classroom and school levels. It also seems reasonable at a more global theoretical level. If school improvement is a developmental process at the individual and school level, we know that there is a common pattern in virtually all developmental processes. This pattern is variously called "punctuated equilibrium" or "stage-wise" development. It happens to human beings as they age. It happens to corporations as they grow and expand. It happens to countries as they develop economically. Periods of growth are typically followed by periods of stagnation, decline, or consolidation, which are in turn followed by periods of growth. Successful individuals, organizations, and societies use these periods of stasis or decline to marshal new resources, ideas, and capacities in the service of solving new, as yet undefined, problems. Sometimes the flat spots are periods where nothing much occurs because the individual or organization has run out of capacity, but sometimes these periods are actually powerfully important stages of growth in the developmental process. The organization is not stagnating but is actually building capacity that will be deployed to achieve future gains in performance. You can see this happening if you look carefully at what people in the organization are doing; it is not evident if you look only at the organization's performance.

In schools that are improving, one can see this pattern vividly. One of two things is typically happening in improving schools that hit flat spots: they are either diagnosing the next level of problem they are facing in the instructional core and searching for the next level of knowledge and skill necessary to address it, or they are investing heavily in the development of new knowledge and skill that they haven't yet been able to deploy successfully in the classroom. From the perspective of policy makers, these schools are "doing nothing," because there is no visible evidence from their performance that they are improving. Also, from their perspective, it is impossible to distinguish between schools that have hit flat spots because they are "doing nothing" and those that have hit flat spots but are engaged in building capacity for the next level of performance. In this way, performance-based accountability can become an extremely blunt and counterproductive policy instrument. Policy makers are not known for their capacity to discern what they do not know; in this case, what they do not know can have very large and destructive consequences.

School Improvement: Two Case Studies[16]

Two actual cases illustrate what improvement looks like. The Extend School is a K–8 school in a major urban school system. It is a relatively large school for its district, about 900 students, with a history of being one of the lowest-performing schools in the district. Its population represents the student population of the city at large: more than 70 percent of its students meet the income criteria for free and reduced lunch, which is the standard measure of poverty in U.S. schools. More than 40 percent of its students are African Americans, about 25 percent are recent Asian immigrants (many from families that are not literate in their home language), about 10 percent are Hispanic (mostly from families where English is not spoken at home), and the remaining students are white (virtually all from nearby public housing; virtually all poor). In 1998, almost 90 percent of Extend's students scored in the lowest two categories of the state accountability test, putting the school at the bottom of the distribution of schools in its district. In that year, Extend's new principal—a veteran in the system with a track record for turning around failing schools—came into the school and immediately started a full-bore push for improvement. Her strategy was to focus virtually all her energy, and that of the teaching staff, on reading and math. She used the district's external coaching and professional development resources to bring assistance for teachers directly into the classroom. In addition, she used her own time and the time of her assistant principals (two, whom she recruited) to monitor the progress of teachers in incorporating the curriculum into their practice. A few teachers transferred to other schools, but most stayed. (See Table 1.)

At the same time, the school district in which Extend is located had adopted high-level curricula in reading, writing, and math. The reading and writing curriculum was developed by the district itself from a composite of the most challenging curricula they could find in other districts. This decision by the district meant that it ran afoul of state and federal authorities, making the district ineligible for supplemental support for literacy, because the state and federal governments concluded that the curriculum was not "scientifically based." The math curriculum that the district adopted was a well-known, but controversial, program that stressed higher levels of mathematical understanding and an integration of content across traditional mathematical topics. The curriculum was criticized by traditionalists for paying insufficient attention to computational and procedural knowledge (a criticism that supporters strenuously rejected) and for blurring the boundaries between traditional mathematical subjects (students would, for example, study statistics and probability as early as the fourth grade and would develop simple geometric models of equations around the same time—all in the interest of increasing mathematical understanding).

These changes in curriculum at the system level were also accompanied by significant investments in professional development for teachers and administrators. Content coaches were assigned to schools to work with teachers on the new curricula and the instructional practices accompanying them. In addition, the structure of the school day and school week was changed to provide time for teachers to work individually and collectively on instructional issues. Extend's principal was particularly skillful at manipulating these resources to the school's advantage, positioning herself to acquire the best coaches and closely managing how professional development time was used.

For the first two years of the new principal's tenure, from 1998 to 2000, Extend's test scores did not change dramatically. To an outside observer, it would have continued to look like a failing school. The only discernible change was a steady decline in the number of students scoring in the lowest category of the state test on reading and writing, and a modest increase in the proportion of students in the next-lowest category. The proportion of students scoring in the highest two categories stayed about the same—

almost none in the highest category and fewer than 20 percent in the next highest. In math, there were steady reductions in the numbers of students scoring in the lowest category, and corresponding increases in the next-lowest category.

In the context of the state and federal accountability system, these modest gains were not especially significant, as the school's performance was evaluated according to the proportion of students in the "proficient" and "advanced" categories, not the movement of students out of the lowest into the next category. It should also be said that this particular state test is among the most challenging among the fifty state accountability systems in the United States. Scoring at the proficient and advanced levels requires students not just to answer multiple-choice questions and demonstrate content knowledge, but also to demonstrate, through explanations and writing samples, their explicit understandings of their responses.

During the period when the principal and her staff were making maximum changes in instructional practice in the school, Extend looked like a modestly improving, but still failing school. Most of the changes in performance were taking place at the lowest possible levels, with little or no discernible movement of students into the higher categories.

The 2001 school year was not good for Extend. Its performance actually declined significantly. The proportion of students scoring in the lowest category increased by a few percentage points in both reading and math, putting the school back further into the category of a failing school. This decline caused serious morale problems for teachers. In the words of one teacher, "we had given it everything we had. The results weren't great, but we started to believe that we could do it. Then, boom, it looked like we were back where we started." Interestingly, the principal did not share this view. A veteran of school improvement efforts, her diagnosis was that the investments in new knowledge and skill for teachers had not really began to pay off yet. The improvements in the lowest-performing categories, she argued, were simply attributable to teachers paying more attention to the amount of instruction students were getting in reading and math, not to the quality or intensity of that instruction. Teachers were still struggling with the demands of higher-level work required by the new curricula and were not actually teaching at a high enough level yet to get the results that should come with a more challenging curriculum and more intensive professional development. The decline in performance, the principal argued, was unfortunate, but not unexpected. The school was going through a difficult period of internal change, and that was bound to be reflected to some degree in its overall performance. Patience, courage, she advised.

In 2002, things changed dramatically at Extend. The proportion of students scoring in the lowest category of the state test in reading and writing, which had been as high as 37 percent in 1998, dropped from 23 percent to 11 percent to 8 percent, between 2001 and 2003. In math, there was a similarly dramatic shift, from 29 to 15 to 12 percent. More importantly, there was a general upward shift in the distribution of scores in both reading and math. Whereas in 1998 about 12 percent of Extend's students had scored in the top two categories in reading and writing, and about 20 percent in math, by 2004 about 60 percent were scoring in the top two categories in reading and writing and about 50 percent in math. The distribution of performance on the state test at Extend, with its predominantly poor and minority population, had begun to resemble the distribution of scores in neighboring middle- and working-class communities with many fewer poor and minority children.

Teachers were gratified by the scores. One teacher said: "Look, we weren't really doing anything differently than we had been doing for the previous two years, we just got better at doing it. We had started to feel like all the effort we had put into changing the curriculum and teaching was going nowhere. We felt like we were doing what we were supposed to do, but nothing was happening. And then. . . we got this major shift in scores, and suddenly everyone is coming in here trying to figure out what we're eating for breakfast. Actually, we're just doing what we set out to do; only we're doing it a lot better."

The principal of Extend was more measured in her assessment. "It takes a very high level of instruction to get students into the 'Advanced' category on the state test. We are facing issues around higher-level instruction for our students that no other schools are facing. No one knows exactly how to do what we are doing. We're operating on the outer edge of everything we know about instruction. So I expect that this trend isn't going to continue. We got a lot more work to do to get the proportion of students scoring in the Advanced category up to the level of the very best schools in the state. We also have to focus on eliminating students scoring in the lowest two categories. We're in range of doing that, but you have to consider that we've got serious mobility in this school, so some of the students being tested haven't been with us very long." Extend has been in the process of introducing a detailed assessment and monitoring system for its students, using interim, teacher-administered assessments to check on individual student progress and developing diagnostic strategies for helping students who seem not to be responding to the existing curriculum and instructional strategies. "We hope," the principal says, "that by focusing more on the problems of individual students, we can learn what we need to learn to get more students into the Advanced category. We know these kids can do this work now. We just have to figure out how make it happen for everyone."

The Stable School is similar in its demographic composition to the Extend School. It is in another urban school system not far from where Extend is. The principal of Stable is also a veteran who has a reputation as a "good" administrator in the school system where he worked his entire career. He thinks of Stable as a remarkably successful school, "considering what we have to work with in the way of families and kids." Indeed, within its school system, Stable is regarded as an exemplary school.

Over the 1998–2003 period, the proportion of the school's students scoring in the lowest category of the state test has declined from 56 percent in reading and writing to 2 percent, with a major glitch in the 2000 school year, when the proportion jumped from 26 to 40 percent and then dropped dramatically to 10 percent the next year. In math, the proportion of students scoring in the lowest category dropped over the same period from 49 to 18 percent, in a more or less steady gradient.

What's interesting about the Stable School, however, is its pronounced pattern of moving many students out of the lowest category into the next lowest, and fewer students out of the next lowest into the proficient category, and very few proficient students into the advanced category. In other words, Stable's success is at the very lowest level of performance; its success with moving students into higher levels is modest, at best. In the state accountability system, unfortunately, this kind of improvement does not count for much, since the system evaluates performance based on the proportion of students scoring in the top two categories.

The principal of Stable has a clear philosophy about this matter. "We have a particular population of teachers here and a particular population of families and students. These are good teachers, but they get demoralized when you put them in a situation where they are likely to fail. Our students need a lot of work on basic skills because they come to us from family backgrounds where there is really no emphasis on academic success. So we chose a curriculum that focuses mainly on strengthening the foundation for reading and math; it was the district's idea, and we endorsed it. We have had a lot of success with it, I think, in part, because it is well adapted to the skill levels of our teachers and students."

The curriculum that the principal refers to is a well-known, nationally validated reading and math program that has a dedicated and loyal following among its users. It has a heavy remedial focus—that is, it purports to focus on the basic skills required for mastery of reading and math through heavy emphasis on drill and practice and relatively low-level content. And, perhaps most importantly, the curriculum materials and the professional development that accompany the program are tailored to provide the maximum amount of guidance to teachers with the minimum challenge to existing patterns of practice. Teachers at Stable find the curriculum to be quite congenial: "At first we had some difficulty adapting to the fact we were all expected to use the same curriculum. We had been pretty loose about teaching in the past. But once we got into it, it seemed pretty reasonable and pretty well-adapted to our particular population of kids. The challenge is about right for our kids."

Because the curriculum adopted by Stable met the federal and state governments' criteria for "scientific validation," it was eligible for supplementary federal funding, which the district and the school used to purchase additional materials and training sessions for teachers. Most of the training for the program occurred away from the school site, either at a district center or at a training center in another city. Representatives of the curriculum developers visited the school only in the initial stages of its adoption, and not at all thereafter.

This point of view among the staff at Stable is reflected in district-wide policy in the school system in which Stable resides. The superintendent of the district has adopted an explicit strategy of letting schools choose their own instructional strategies from a list of district-approved curricula, or, alternatively, developing their own instructional programs. A number of schools have adopted the curriculum that Stable adopted because it was readily accessible, easily adapted to the existing skills and knowledge of teachers, and widely endorsed as a remedial program for schools with high proportions of poor and minority students. The extent of administrative oversight from the district level and the amount of professional development schools received were a function of the particular instructional approach that the schools adopted. At its highest, however, professional development activity was relatively low compared to Extend's school system. Some schools received almost no external support and were essentially on their own to develop their own instructional approaches. The superintendent, the principal at Stable, and the teachers in the school all seemed to think that this approach to improvement was consistent with the culture of the district and the community. "People here," the superintendent said, "don't respond well to a lot of control."

Extend and Stable represent just two data points in a virtual blizzard of school-level examples of accountability and improvement. In what sense are these two schools improving? There is a *prima facie* case that Extend is an improving school, and it is the kind of school that we would like to think would become the model for others. The case for Stable is more complex. In Figure 2, Extend looks more like School A, moving upward in a succession of gains and plateaus toward a performance standard (AYP, or Adequate Yearly Progress in the language of the accountability system), while Stable is moving at a slower rate, with little hope of closing the gap with the standard. It is important to understand, however, that in terms of current federal policy both Extend and Stable are failing schools. The accountability system does not distinguish between the two of them, and both would be treated in the same way, subject to the same sanctions, and put under the same regulatory controls.

In addition, Extend is, at the end of our story, embarked on a far more difficult challenge—a challenge that is at the far edges of practical knowledge and research—and it is likely that during the period in which it is engaging this challenge it will, once again, nominally look, from the perspective of the policy system, as either not making progress at all or losing ground. It takes grit and courage to operate under these circumstances, and it often feels as if the environment is downright hostile to the work one is doing.

Stable presents another problem. Stable is, in fact, improving in the sense that it is doing what it is expected to do—adopting and implementing a new curriculum and instructional program—and it is showing some progress in moving students out of the lowest category into the next highest category. However, when we look at the level of challenge that the principal, the teachers, and the students have taken on, it is very clear that they are not going to get anywhere near where they need to get with the path they have chosen. It is also clear that they don't know what they don't know. These are the circumstances in which outside observers often conclude that, despite our best efforts, some students simply cannot learn past a certain level, and some schools cannot improve beyond a certain level. Yet what is interesting and compelling about the case of Stable is that we can see that the limits on its further growth are self-inflicted and are deeply embedded in the instructional core—the level of demand that teachers are willing to put on themselves and their students is calibrated against a different set of expectations than at Extend. Simply put, Stable will probably never get to the level of performance it has to get to, given the instructional strategy it has adopted. Yet the accountability system is giving it signals that reinforce what it is doing. Given the self-sealing nature of the attitudes and expectations among the district and school-level personnel, it is unlikely, other things being equal, that Stable will ever become anything like Extend.

We can also see in Extend and Stable the unmistakable footprints of the predictable elements and processes of school improvement. The external accountability system plays a large role, at both the system and school level, in the improvement process, but not the role that advocates of performance-based accountability would necessarily predict. In both cases, external accountability works not by causing people in schools to do what they were already doing more effectively, but by focusing and galvanizing capacities at the school and system levels around problems that involve a high degree of uncertainty and risk. Essentially, you can't get to a higher level of performance in either school by doing what you were previously doing more effectively, and the external accountability system does not tell schools what to do; it simply tells them whether they are delivering what the system expects. For schools and systems that operate at relatively low levels of capacity this game can seem Kafkaesque: bad stuff happens to you, and when you try to adjust to the stuff that is happening to you, more bad stuff happens. Notice that in the case of Stable, the bad stuff that is happening to the school reinforces the school's image of itself as a low-performing school. It also reinforces society's image of schools like Stable as beyond repair.

In schools and systems with higher levels of capacity, the effect of external pressure on performance can be quite different. Extend is always in a precarious position, always on the brink of failing to meet its own and society's expectations as expressed through the external accountability system, always operating in an accountability environment that is, at best, indifferent, and, at worst, downright hostile to what it is doing. However, Extend, which also operates in a relatively high-capacity system, has developed its own capacities to function in that system: high-level curricula in literacy and math, targeted external support to help teachers meet the challenges of a new, more demanding curriculum, increasingly specific diagnostic and instructional capabilities internal to the school, and, probably most importantly, an internal accountability system that supports teachers in the face of daunting problems. The effect of external accountability pressure on Extend, and on the system in which Extend resides, is to mobilize and focus capacity, but the external accountability system does nothing whatsoever to create or nurture the capacity that has to be mobilized. In fact, the federal and state accountability systems are downright hostile to the capacity issue, making it more difficult for Extend and its school system to garner support for the literacy program that is producing substantial gains because the program does not meet federal and state standards of "scientific validity." Meanwhile, the same policy is supporting a curriculum in Stable that is virtually guaranteed not to produce the results that Extend has achieved, because it does meet state and federal standards of "scientific validity." These sorts of things happen when the people who are in control don't know what they don't know.

Extend also reveals something I described earlier about the relationship between quality and performance (see Figure 2, 'p' and 'q' on the vertical axis). Improvements in quality—that is, increases in the level of content, the skills and knowledge of teachers and administrators, and the active role of students in the instructional process—precede improvements in performance; and improvements in performance lag behind improvements in quality. The teachers at Extend were learning how to teach in more powerful ways and were using these practices in their classrooms well before the results showed up in their test scores. Anyone familiar with the nitty-gritty side of change in complex, knowledge-based organizations knows this phenomenon, but it is usually not apparent to researchers, policy analysts, or, least of all, policy makers. It takes time for improvements in practice to become reliably seated in the individual and collective routines of an organization, and it takes time for these routines to become mature enough to produce results.

One of the domains in which our knowledge is extremely weak is understanding the relationship between changes in quality and changes in performance. The stakes are potentially high here. If you intervene in a school that has made major changes in quality but has not yet seen the pay-off in performance, you are likely to disrupt and derail the very processes that are leading to improvement. Conversely, Stable's problem is that it is responding to signals about its performance, without paying sufficient attention to quality. Consequently, if you intervene, without understanding something about the complex relationship between performance and quality, you are likely to reinforce the patterns that got Stable into its current situation.

Extend is one school in a system of several dozen schools. Extend is on the far end of a distribution of schools in that system in terms of its capacity to respond to external accountability pressure and to capitalize on the capacity-building strategies of the district. Schools in Extend's district are currently quite dispersed, although there is less variability in school performance now than there was six or seven years ago. The general trend in reading, writing, and math scores in the system at large has been positive, with all the usual caveats about flat spots and unexpected dips. While Extend is at the far end of the distribution in its district, it is not alone in that place. There are other schools in the system that have made similar gains, with similar populations, in very diverse settings. One school in particular that I visited several years ago in another research project was, at that time, a case study in total chaos—teachers screaming at students, noise and confusion in the hallways, huge variability in student engagement and level of work from classroom to classroom, and extreme passivity and negativity among teachers about students' capabilities. This school is now among the highest performing schools in the city. The principal is the same principal who was there when I visited it before—a tough, cagey, persistent, unpolished woman with an underlying confidence in her own knowledge and an appreciation of the limits of what she knows. The teaching staff in the school has turned over remarkably little. The attitude of the teachers toward their work has changed dramatically. And most people in the school still think of the external accountability system as an extremely dangerous and unreliable partner in their work. Other schools in the system are struggling to make sense of their work in ways that are way behind Extend. The demands of the new curriculum are still daunting to many teachers, the principals in these schools are still uncertain about their role in the instructional process, and the external accountability system is still seen as a collection of random, catastrophic events that occur at periodic, unexplained intervals. From the system's perspective, large-scale improvement becomes an exercise only slightly more systematic than herding cats. The superintendent and four deputy superintendents supervise a portfolio of schools at various levels of performance and capacity. The senior managers of the system try to orchestrate the scarce resources they have around curriculum and professional development support in a way that speaks to the variations among schools. In addition, the performance of schools in each portfolio wobbles and jumps in predictably unpredictable ways. In all this modestly controlled chaos, the external accountability system continues to deliver stern, inscrutable messages about the "progress" of individual schools and the district as a whole.

Another clear theme in the cases is the centrality of the instructional core. Schools and school systems improve by managing their technical core. As the framework suggests, there is only a limited number of points of entry for managing the core, which makes the practice of managing the core simpler in the sense that it limits the scope for intervention, yet more complex in the sense that it exposes what we do not know about how to do the central work of the organization. The schools in the case studies improved their performance by introducing more cognitively challenging content, provoking a gap between what teachers currently know and what they need to know about content and pedagogy in order to meet the new demands; the teachers and students alike then have to engage in work that produces higher levels of understanding. Extend operates in a high-challenge, high-support environment; Stable operates in a low-challenge, low-support environment. It is important to see, after the dust settles, that the performance profile of Extend and Stable closely matches the level of cognitive demand embedded in the curricula they are implementing. You cannot produce high-level performance with a low-level curriculum—no matter how well implemented or how "scientifically validated" it is—any more than you can produce good research with bad data. Having a high-level curriculum, however, poses greater challenges on the capacity front and greater risks and uncertainty to a performance gradient than a low-level curriculum. By minimizing risk and uncertainty, Stable is effectively putting a ceiling on its performance, and attributing its lack of success to the attributes of its clients.

The existing accountability system in the United States treats improving schools that are mobilizing capacity the same as schools that are not improving and not mobilizing capacity. Any school that fails to meet its annual performance target, no matter what the cause, is subject to sanctions under the existing accountability policy. If the timing of its improvement process had lagged by a couple of years, Extend would have been subject to extensive harassment under the existing accountability system that would have made it more difficult to achieve what it has. The school will probably be subject to future harassment under the accountability system, because the requirements are that schools not only have to meet overall performance targets but also specific performance targets for each population of students each year. The likelihood that any school can meet these standards in any given year if it is engaged in serious improvement is quite remote.

What creates this gap between the accountability system and the practice of improvement on the ground? Simply put, policy makers are themselves not accountable for improving schools. They are accountable to the electorate for initiating policies that address the problem of school improvement. If these initiatives fail, they shift the responsibility for their failure onto people in schools and even claim credit for the blame. The primary incentives that operate on policy makers reward the initiation of policy, not its results. Results are someone else's responsibility. The institutional processes and cycles that determine credit and visibility—electoral, budget, and planning cycles—do not correspond, except in the most coincidental ways, to the actual requirements of school improvement processes on the ground. So we easily arrive at a situation where both

Extend and Stable are viewed as failing schools despite the fact that Extend is operating at the far edge of existing knowledge about school improvement, and Stable is operating at the center of the lower end. This is, I think, the operating definition of a perverse incentive.

Elected officials and their appointed executives are not rewarded for making long-term investments in the capacity of systems to deliver performance, because the results that those investments deliver are beyond the timelines that drive their behavior. The resulting political dynamic is that public officials initiate reforms, take credit for their short-term effects if they exist, and blame people in schools for their failures when they happen.

The important point here is that neither the quantity nor the content of policy initiatives has any rationale other than the amount of electoral credit they generate for policy makers. Hence, there is no way of controlling and focusing the demands of policy makers through the electoral structure in ways that actually comport with what we know about school improvement.

From the ground, this incentive structure looks bizarre and Kafkaesque. Ironically, the more alert and thoughtful people are about the process of school improvement, the more bizarre the incentive structure looks. Educators are doing what policy makers say they want them to do but somehow they look like they are not. The more clueless people are in schools, the more it simply looks like the weather—"stuff happens, we have learned to expect that it will be bad stuff, maybe it will go away."

Consider the way this process works in other sectors. When Congress or state legislatures set the regulatory structure for air pollution control, and when regulatory agencies set emission standards for specific pollutants, they do so in highly institutionalized and politically charged settings. There are explicit limits on the amount of pollution abatement that can feasibly occur within a given set of cost constraints, and these limits are a function of the existing design parameters of the internal combustion engine and the relative skill of various parties to the regulatory process in using data to push the limits in one direction or another. The result is a set of standards that define a temporary equilibrium in a longer-term political and technical battle over what constitutes a good result and what the technology can deliver. This process is disciplined both by the technical knowledge necessary to set "good" standards, and by the relative influence of various political interests in the process.

Now consider educational accountability. There is no model of the feasible limits on gains in performance, given the state of knowledge and capacity in schools. Nor is there any particular interest among policy makers in finding one, because to do so would unduly complicate the process of accumulating credit for education reform. Neither, in the current structure of political interest groups around educational policy, is there an array of interests that can articulate what is feasible to expect in school improvement and use their influence in political debates to push standards in one direction or another. This has occurred both because educators have not developed the expertise necessary to make this case, and because politicians have progressively worked to exclude educational professionals and researchers from decisions about education policy because they are considered ill informed and "self-interested." (As if the decision makers were not themselves self-interested, but who's keeping score here?) So in the domain of educational accountability we are, as it were, trying to make policy about auto emission control without a working model of the internal combustion engine. Not a promising scenario.

In this sense, the problem of school improvement is essentially a political problem. If there is no discipline or control over the content or frequency of educational reform at the legislative or executive level, then the gap between policy and practice will continue to widen. There is no "peaceable kingdom" solution to this problem, where policy makers and educators lie down together in a pasture and make reasonable solutions to pressing problems. Electoral incentives drive both what is attractive for policy makers to focus on and what the feasible domain of action is. Policy analysis abets this process by focusing attention on main effects rather than on the complex processes and interaction effects that actually drive organizational responses. The only solution to this problem is to introduce countervailing political interests that discipline policy makers and drive policy in a less destructive direction. The only political interest that has the incentives to do this is that of professional educators, and they are, at the moment, the least well equipped institutionally or politically to do the work.

We know some powerful things about the process of school improvement at the level of practice. Nevertheless, inherent in that knowledge is a very large domain where we lack knowledge altogether, or we only possess knowledge with a high degree of uncertainty. The Extend school has figured out how to introduce high-level academic work systematically to students who have traditionally not had access to it. Consequently, because of their success, they have opened up a new set of problems about what happens with students who do not presently respond to this high-level teaching. Given Extend's track record, we expect—with time and support and continued pressure to achieve—that the school will break through this frontier and immediately find another one. We do not yet know enough about how to bring the strategic and tactical lessons of Extend to a larger population of schools working at lower levels of knowledge and practice. Nor do we know how to intervene in the Stable school and its district in order to shift instructional practice and performance expectations dramatically upward. Least of all do we know how to design and build accountability systems that are more responsive to the actual problems of improvement, that limit perverse incentives, and that engage schools at the level required for large-scale improvement. Much of this knowledge is technical and practice-based, but a large part of it is political.

A Return to Education and Poverty

If the path out of poverty for poor and minority children has anything to do with schooling, then reduction of poverty depends to some large degree on our capacity to provide access to high levels of instruction for large numbers of children in schools that are currently failing in the most basic sense. There are many other ways to address the issue of children in poverty—better preschool programs, child health and nutrition, drop-out prevention programs, school-to-work programs, and so forth. However, a basic feature of post-industrial society is that young people spend a very large fraction of their time in schools; those who do better economically tend to spend more time in school than those who do less well. It is possible that if we dramatically raised the level of academic performance of children in schools—if, for example, Extend became the modal urban public school—that people of privilege would still find a way to sustain the position relative to others, given that American society is so fundamentally racist and predatory in its culture and attitudes. Nevertheless, however risky, this is at least an experiment worth running.

I have tried to suggest that school improvement, against ambitious standards, at scale, is a function of three closely related, interlocking domains. At the center is the technical/organizational domain. Whatever policy makers intend, if the knowledge and skill of teachers and school administrators in the instructional core does not improve dramatically and if the capacity of schools and school systems to work on the improvement of knowledge and skill does not increase systemically over time, then children in poverty will not have access to high-level knowledge. Teaching produces learning. If you want to affect learning, you have to affect teaching. As instructional practice develops, increasingly difficult problems surface. The people who are going to solve these problems are, for the most part, the people who are currently working in schools, and the generation of people who are—or are not—considering education as a career. To the degree that we make blame objects of these people we are, in effect, under-mining our future. To the degree that we address problems of capacity, in tandem with tougher, more exacting expectations for performance, we will create a culture in schools that reinforces norms of access to high-level academic work for all students.

The second domain is policy. I have, as is obvious from my analysis, developed a deep and abiding distrust of policy and policy analysis, in the conventional sense, as either benign or positive forces in the improvement of schools. The search for main effects—recruiting "better" teachers, put-ting "tough" principals in failing schools, turning every school into a char-ter school, cashing out the system and turning it into vouchers, insisting that every student salute the flag and study phonics three hours a day, and so forth—has had a profoundly destructive effect on the efforts of serious professionals who are doing the actual work of learning how to improve schools. Most simple reform proposals have nothing to do with the actual process by which teachers teach and students learn. Charter schools pro-duce vague and inconsistent results largely because the people who found and run them know so little about instructional practice that they are busily reinventing all the pathologies of the existing system without know-ing it. Vouchers produce weak and inconsistent effects because, for the most part, people who advocate vouchers put most of their energy into proselytizing about the virtues of competition, rather than trying to find out what the state of knowledge is in the teaching of reading and math. "Good" teachers entering dysfunctional schools quickly adopt the atti-tudes and behaviors of their peers in those schools, or they leave and go to business school. Most reform proposals that are attractive to lay "experts," to elected officials, and to foundation officers are attractive nuisances. They work around the edges of the problems that need solving, and they usually do not reach the people who are actually accumulating the knowl-edge and skill that is required to achieve school improvement. Right now, policy is seriously over-invested in attractive nuisances and seriously underinvested in building the infrastructure to support the accumulation of knowledge about instructional practice and the skills necessary to bring it into schools and school systems.

Whether, and in what ways, schools respond to the blizzard of signals being sent through policy depends, ultimately, on their internal capacities. The kinds of investments that are necessary to build capacity are the kinds that policy makers are usually either oblivious to or find trivial and unat-tractive. The issues that high-performing schools and school systems are working on, largely without support and often in opposition to the prevailing interests represented by policy makers, include, for example, taking a generation of teachers who have had largely negative experiences in their own educational careers with mathematics and turning them into experts on how children come to understand and apply complex mathematical ideas; taking our basic knowledge of how children, starting from vastly different points, come to understand written language and learn to use it powerfully in their communication with others and in their writing, and making it part of the practice of every teacher from pre-school through high school graduation; removing the current structural constraints in schools to student access to higher-level content, which have developed largely because of teachers' unwillingness to teach students who are more challenging and to parents' manipulation of the system to secure advantages for their children; and working at the outer edges of what we know about teaching children who don't, for whatever reason, respond to our best ideas about instructional practice, to find out how to think about instruction differently.

I think the implications of my argument for educational systems that are less far along or less fully invested in accountability as a school reform mechanism are relatively clear. Accountability instruments work, as policies, primarily to the degree that they mobilize capacity in schools, and to the degree that they provide incentives for schools to search for, capture, learn, and internalize in practice progressively more ambitious ideas about what students can learn. The chief constraints on this process of improvement are the beliefs, expectations, and instructional practices of adults in schools, not the characteristics of the students or their families. The process of mobilizing capacity around instruction is not linear; it is developmental. The challenge for education systems looking for large-scale improvements as a way of addressing poverty is how to find the right combination of investments in human capital in the education system and accountability measures—the right combination of challenge and support—that will, in effect, teach the adults who work in schools about the enormous potential of the children who go to school.

The problems with policy are mostly attributable to the problems in the third domain, politics. There is currently a widening gap between the demands of school improvement, on the one hand, and the politics of educational reform, on the other. The problem lies in the lack of institutional incentives to discipline and focus policy makers on issues that matter at the ground level. Policy makers construct accountability systems without the knowledge required to engage schools in improvement; they do not have this knowledge because they are not required to gain it as a condition of their success. The incentive structure under which policy makers' work is disconnected from the processes they are trying to improve, and they have little or no incentive, in their own work, to connect the two. This problem is, at base, a problem of political legitimacy and authority. Educators do not carry sufficient professional or political authority to influence conditions fundamental to their own work. Policy makers have no incentive to rectify this situation, since they are, at least in the short term, beneficiaries of it. They operate as "experts" with relative impunity and lack of discipline in a policy area where expertise is largely undefined. Educators have largely done this to themselves. The solutions to these problems are rarely attractive. They involve conflict, the mobilization of countervailing interests, and the use of knowledge and power in highly manipulative ways.

There is, I have noticed, in the community of people who worry about poverty, a visceral suspicion of educators and especially of the pretensions of educators to "professional" knowledge. I think this suspicion is, in an historical context, well founded. Schools have been a major force, although not the only one, in the reproduction of inequality in society. However, I also think that if schools figure in future attempts to reduce poverty and inequality, we are going to have to acknowledge that there is such a thing as professional expertise in education and build an infrastructure to support it. We will also have to build a structure to discipline and focus this expertise on problems worth solving and to hold education professionals accountable for their impact on inequality in ways we traditionally have not done.

Tables and Figures

Table 1. "Extend" School at a Glance

Year	Advanced	Proficient	Needs improvement	Warning
4th Grade ELA				
98	1	12	56	37
99	0	11	62	27
00	0	18	67	15
01	5	35	37	23
02	9	46	34	11
03	11	48	33	8
4th Grade Math				
98	8	12	26	54
99	9	17	44	30
00	9	21	43	27
01	13	16	42	29
02	15	27	42	15
03	17	29	42	12

Demographics

Size: 850 students; Afr. Am. 43.4%; Asian 24.9%; Hispanic 5.2%; Limited Engl. 20%; Free & Reduced Lunch 71.5%; Spec. Ed. 15.6%

Table 2. "Stable" School at a Glance

Year	Advanced	Proficient	Needs improvement	Warning
4th Grade ELA				
98	0	2	43	56
99	0	5	69	26
00	0	0	60	40
01	0	25	65	10
02	2	37	52	10
03	2	34	63	2
4th Grade Math				
98	0	9	42	49
99	0	11	44	45
00	0	19	49	32
01	0	14	60	26
02	0	19	55	19
03	0	13	70	18

Demographics

Size: 900 students; Afr. Am. 17.9%; Asian 0%; Hispanic 43%; White 36.1%; Limited Engl. 15.4%; Free & Reduced Lunch 83.5%; Spec. Ed. 20.2%

Figure 1. The Instructional Core

Content

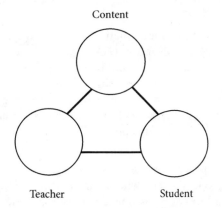

- Knowledge, skill of teachers, principals
- The students' role in instruction
- The level of curriculum content
- The conditions of instructional work
- Norms, values, expectations for the level of the work

Teacher   Student

Figure 2. What School Improvement Looks Like

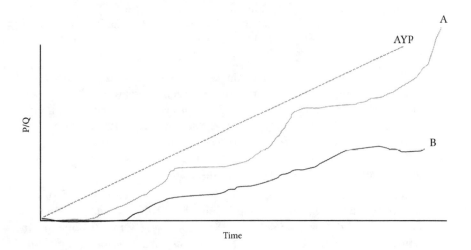

Time

Notes

1   See Paul Barton, *Parsing the Achievement Gap: Baselines for Tracking Progress* (Princeton, NJ: Educational Testing Service, Policy Information Center, 2003), which reports basic data on the gap between poor and middle-class children in academic opportunity (rigor of curriculum, teacher quality, school safety, etc.) and social conditions (parent participation, student mobility, access to academic support at home, etc.). See also Christopher Jencks and Meredith Phillips, eds., *The Black-White Test Score Gap* (Washington, D.C.: The

Brookings Institution, 1998); and John Chubb and Tom Loveless, eds., *Bridging the Achievement Gap* (Washington, D.C.: The Brookings Institution, 2002).

2 Between 1990 and 2003, for example, mathematics scores on the grade 4 National Assessment of Educational Progress (NAEP) showed a modest decline in the gap between whites and blacks and between whites and Hispanic students, but a modest increase, and then a slight decline, on the grade 8 test. Patterns were similar, although less variable for reading. See: http://nces.ed.gov/nationsreportcard/mathematics/results2003/scale-ethnic-compare.asp and http://nces.ed.gov/nationsreportcard/reading/results2003/scale-ethnic-compare.asp.

3 Elizabeth Debray describes the process of executive and legislative decision making at the federal level in No Child Left Behind, the groundbreaking federal intervention in accountability policy, as one that largely excluded both traditional education interest groups and research on the prior effects of accountability policies at the state and local levels. See Debray, *Politics, Ideology and Congress: The Formation of Federal Education Policy During the Clinton and Bush Administrations* (New York: Teachers College Press, forthcoming). See also Paul Manna, "Federalism, Agenda Setting, and the Development of Federal Education Policy, 1965–2001" (Madison, WI: Dissertation, Department of Political Science, University of Wisconsin-Madison, 2003).

4 As Frederick Hess argues, for example, "School reform is the province of utopians, apologists, and well-intentioned practitioners who inhabit a cloistered world where conviction long ago displaced competence." Hess, *Common Sense School Reform* (New York: Macmillan, 2004). Diane Ravitch similarly argues for a return to a simpler view of schooling that antedates the period reform beginning in the 1960s; Ravitch, *Left Back: A Century of Battles Over School Reform* (New York: Touchstone, 2001).

5 See Philip Trostel, Ian Walker, and Paul Wooley, "Estimates of the Economic Returns to Schooling in Twenty-Eight Countries," *Labour Economics: An International Journal*, Vol. 9, no. 1 (2002), 1–16; David Card, "Estimating the Return to Schooling: Progress on Some Persistent Econometric Problems," *Econometrica*, Vol. 69, No. 5 (2001), 1127–1160; Orley Ashenfelter and Cecelia Rouse, "Income, Schooling, and Ability: Evidence from a New Sample of Identical Twins," *Quarterly Journal of Economics*, Vol. 113, No. 1 (1998), 253–284.

6 Richard Murnane and Frank Levy, *The New Division of Labor: How Computers Are Creating the Next Job Market* (Princeton, NJ: Princeton University Press, 2004).

7 See Jennifer King Rice, *Teacher Quality: Understanding the Effectiveness of Teacher Attributes* (Washington, D.C.: Economic Policy Institute, 2003), which reviews all major studies of teacher effectiveness.

8 See Brian Rowan, Richard Correnti, and Robert Miller, "What Large-Scale Survey Research Tells About on Student Achievement: Insights from the Prospects Study of Elementary Schools," Report RR-051, Consortium for Policy Research in Education, University of Pennsylvania, 2002.

9 See Martin Carnoy, Richard Elmore, and Leslie Siskin, eds., *The New Accountability: High Schools and High Stakes Testing* (New York: Falmer, 2003); Martin Carnoy and Susanna Loeb, "Does External Accountability Affect Student Outcomes: A Cross-State Analysis," *Education Evaluation and Policy Analysis* (2003), and Caroline Hoxby, "Does Competition Among Public Schools Benefit Students and Taxpayers," *American Economic Review*, Vol. 90, No. 5 (2000), 1209–38.

10 See Catherine Snow, et al., *Preventing Reading Difficulties in Young Children* (Washington, D.C.: National Research Council, National Academy of Science, 1998).

11 My thinking here has been heavily influenced by Ann Norton's irascible, argumentative, and powerful critique of social science methods, *95 Theses on Politics, Culture, and Method* (New Haven, CT: Yale University Press, 2004), which should, I think, be required reading for every entering graduate student in the social sciences.

12 See especially, Michel Foucault, "Truth and Power," "Power and Strategies," and "The Eye of Power." In *Power/Knowledge: Selected Interviews and Other Writings, 1972–1977*, by Michel Foucault, ed. Colin Gordon (New York: Pantheon, 1980); also, Michel Foucault, *The Archeology of Knowledge and the Discourse on Language* (New York: Pantheon, 1972).

13 See also David Cohen and Deborah Ball, "Instruction, Capacity, and Improvement," Research Report RR-43, Consortium for Policy Research in Education, University of Pennsylvania, 1999.

14 This model is developed further in Charles Abelmann, Richard Elmore, et al., "When Accountability Knocks Will Anyone Answer?" in Richard Elmore, *School Reform from the Inside Out* (Cambridge, MA: Harvard Education Press, 2004).

15 See also Cohen and Ball, above, note 13.

16 The schools in this section are real schools; their names have been changed to protect their confidentiality.

PART

IV

SAFETY NETS

Introduction

Even countries with both strong and growing economies and high-quality educational systems cannot assume that poverty will no longer be a problem. Inevitably, some families will not be able to prosper even in a very good economy. They will face temporary or permanent poverty because of conditions that limit the adults' ability to work or that lead to losses of assets, either physical or human. Because of the ubiquitous risks of human existence, countries develop safety nets as part of their anti-poverty strategy. They include social insurance systems, in-kind and income supports for the chronically poor, and various kinds of temporary assistance for those afflicted by hard times.

The challenge in designing safety nets is to structure them in ways that enhance and complement a country's economic and human-capital development strategies. They must encourage and support work, savings, and investment, rather than provide incentives for recipients to avoid or delay work, or to neglect investment opportunities. They must also be designed in ways that support families and other informal support networks. Countries tackle these design problems in different ways, more and less successfully.

This section of the book includes chapters on safety nets in the United States and in Mexico, and illustrates the different approaches that the two countries have taken and the different challenges that each faces. Mexico has put substantial resources into the *Oportunidades* Program, which is by far the most important safety-net program for poor families with school-age children. *Oportunidades* was ostensibly designed as a human-capital program with the goal of encouraging families to keep children in school and obtain health care for them. A great deal of progress has been made on the school enrollment goal. Meanwhile, *Oportunidades* has become an important financial safety net for poor families, raising the question of what will happen to them when they no longer have school-age children. Escobar's chapter raises the question of whether *Oportunidades* ought to become a more self-conscious income-support program, with eligibility criteria and administrative procedures explicitly designed to tailor benefits to the level of financial hardship of the recipients.

Sheldon and Sandra Danzinger's analysis of safety-net programs in the United States shows how the country has developed a safety net which focuses on supporting and providing incentives for work, even by single-parent families. The social safety-net system in the United States is comprised of a number of programs, each directed at a different segment of the poor. It includes, for example, a Food Stamp program for very low-income people, a means-tested program (SSI) to supplement social security for the elderly and disabled, a tax-credit program for the working poor, and short-term cash assistance conditioned on work for poor families with children. But mainly because of the concern in the United States for supporting work, the Earned Income Tax Credit, which supplements the earnings of working poor families, has become the largest means-tested cash program in this country.

The two chapters show how different sets of worries and approaches can lead to very different safety-net designs. But they also show the weaknesses of each approach: troublingly high post-transfer poverty rates in the United States, and coverage problems in Mexico. The chapters raise important questions about safety nets in both countries and suggest approaches that each can learn from.

7

Mexico's *Progresa–Oportunidades* Programs: Where Do We Go from Here?

Agustín Escobar Latapí

The *Oportunidades* program (created in 2002 as a reformed version of *Progresa*, of 1997) was designed to build human capital (an objective towards which it can show significant accomplishments), but its relative additional success as a social-assistance, income-supplementing program forces it to face a fundamental dilemma. In its original formulation, it can enhance the employment opportunities and empower the next generation, or, instead, it can provide a minimum guaranteed income to the poor. Furthering the achievements in its human capital dimension would require the program to maximize its impact on children's nutrition, health, education, and occupational attainment. To do this, it would need to ensure that schooling improvements are *dynamic*, not merely in the sense that they add a given number of school years to the average among poor families, but that improvements keep taking place. This may require developing new components for the households currently lagging behind average to increase completion rates at the levels of *secundaria* (junior high) and EMS (Educación Media Superior, or grades ten to twelve), and considerably re-tune incentives for schooling beyond grade 12. Another necessary enhancement lies in an area already identified as a priority by the program: current food supplements are not sufficient to guarantee both sufficiency and balance of its caloric, protein and micronutrient make-up, especially iron and zinc, and this leads to anemia and long-term disadvantage.[1] Finally, a third area that would require priority attention lies in the school/work nexus. Today, participating students achieve higher schooling levels, but most observers recognize that the skill and knowledge contents of that additional schooling may not prepare students to perform significantly better as independent rural or urban producers or as employees. Rural and marginal schools require significant reforms to close the gap with the rest of the school system. In addition, labor demand *has* to improve for the program to succeed in this respect.

For *Oportunidades* to succeed as a social safety net in the making, it would need to be developed along different lines in order to come as close as possible to guaranteeing that households chronically or temporarily in need of assistance receive it.[2] The main change would consist of either a permanent transfer mechanism to families that are unable to compete successfully in the labor market (or in small-scale farming), *whether they fulfill the program's human development goals or not*, or of a temporary mechanism that provides transfers subject to the family's acquisition of whatever it needs to enable it to earn a sustainable income above the poverty level (a "bridging" program for families earning an income below a given threshold, such as Chile's *Puente*). This second emphasis would also require improving the health coverage—in terms of both population and the range of illnesses covered—in marginal communities, to restore the well-being of families affected by ill health and catastrophic events and expenditures.[3] Because *Progresa–Oportunidades* was originally designed as a human capital program, transfers are independent of the family's initial income and well-being;[4] to perfect the program as a social safety net, it would need to be tailored to that income gap, possibly with special co-responsibilities for families in need of extra transfer income, to avoid eliminating incentives for self-reliance. Short-term income shortfalls would also need to be considered, something that is out of the question with the program's current design, which is unable to detect them. Finally, the program would need to attend to the elderly.[5] Mexico's demographic transition is advancing rapidly, and labor emigration to urban Mexico and the United States is accelerating and transforming this transition in the countryside,[6] with hundreds of thousands of households consisting only of senior citizens or senior citizens and small children. Close to 50% of all children aged 5 to 9 years old who resided in rural communities in 1995 had left rural areas by 2005.[7] Households consisting exclusively of elderly persons will rapidly increase in the near future, and their well-being will require special actions. Although successes have been achieved simultaneously in both its human capital and social safety-net dimensions, the actions and new components needed for each would differ substantially and, at times, be contradictory.

The general frameworks of the program and our evaluations are described in the first section of this chapter. In the second, the accuracy of its targeting methods is discussed. In the third, the most recent changes in educational enrollment are described, followed by the first occupational outcomes of the program. Finally, I outline my suggestion for an appropriate context for the definition of the future nature of the program.

Oportunidades: Program Objectives and Evaluations

Oportunidades came out of a targeted program called *Progresa* begun in 1997. It provides cash transfers, food supplements, school supplies, subsidies, and health and education services to families below a certain socioeconomic level, after a selection and verification process. In order to remain in the program, mothers and individual beneficiaries must comply with specified minima of school attendance, health check-ups, and attendance at health and nutrition talks. Very often, there are also additional community tasks that they must perform. The minimum transfer is equivalent to $17 dollars per month, for a family with no school-age children. The maximum is $145 for families with one or more students up to grade 9, and $191 for families with children in grades 10–12. Individual scholarships range from $12 per month for a third grader, to approximately $73 for a young woman in grade 12.[8] Scholarships are intended as individual benefits, and mothers are repeatedly told to use that money for the food, clothes, shoes and school costs of those specific children. In early 2005, there were 5 million households and approximately 24 million individuals enrolled in the program.

Originally, the main aim of *Progresa* was to *break the cycle of poverty* among the rural poor. Thus, once the program had been designed and approved, its first objectives were:

- To achieve substantial improvement in the education, health, and nutrition of poor families, particularly of schoolchildren and their mothers.

- To do this with a comprehensive approach in order to avoid the obstacles that poor health and nutrition pose for educational attainment.

- To help households avail themselves of the means and resources necessary to allow their children to complete their basic education.

- To stimulate responsibility and the active participation of parents and all family members in the education, health, and nutrition of children and youths.

- To promote community participation in and support of *Progresa*'s actions, so that educational and health services would benefit all families in those communities; and to participate in and

promote actions that complement or further the program's goals
(*Progresa*, 1997).

The aims outlined above favor the well-being and attainment of girls
and boys (through their mothers), and interpret the improvements in
household economies as mostly (but not exclusively) instrumental to that
end. Short-term impacts on poverty alleviation were also part of the
design, but the principal aim was to enable the offspring of these households to compete on an equal footing in the labor market. It was therefore
meant as a long-term effort. The prevalence of this long-term objective
over other possible positive outcomes could be observed in the emphasis
placed on its various components: transfers were linked to co-responsibilities;
in other words, beneficiaries had to carry out certain individual, family,
and pro-community activities to receive the transfers. Among co-responsibilities, children's school attendance was pushed forward whereas adult
literacy,[9] skill acquisition, or other training programs were not. Food supplements for infants during their first six months of life, or later if they
were diagnosed as malnourished, were mandated, but mothers received
food supplements only when they were pregnant or breastfeeding, and
adult men were never candidates for food supplements. Mothers were
trained to use transfers to improve the general quality of food and drink-
ing water in their households, and to buy children's clothes, shoes, and
school supplies; the adult men's role as income providers was irrelevant to
the household's commitments regarding co-responsibility. Scholarships
were designed to encourage girls' schooling more than boys' schooling;
however, there was no attempt to empower homemakers, with the exception of their decision-making power in household management, which
was estimated to yield substantial benefits to the children.

The emphases on co-responsibility and the second generation defined
two significant social and territorial limitations of the program. Households with low incomes but no children (a low dependency ratio) were,
until 2000, likely to be excluded. Households that failed to comply for
whatever reason were dropped first temporarily and then permanently,
and these households might be better off or much worse off than households that complied, thus weakening the program's impact as a social protection net.[10] Finally, households in communities lacking access to health
or education services were excluded, because they had no way to fulfill
their co-responsibilities. The argument, from 1997 to 2000, was that the
gap in coverage of the target population (the rural poor without access to
health and educational services) was less than 5%. This gap is being
addressed today through a new program (Food Support Program).

The ultimate outcome is meant to be improved labor-market performance for the second generation, and the short- and medium-term impacts
should consist of an improved diet and overall health, longer schooling,
and increased cognitive performance among children.

The program was not created in a void. Mexico had significant experiences in a number of fields relevant to the program. Its designers relied on
these previous experiences to design a successful and relatively comprehensive policy. If these experiences had not been incorporated, *Progresa–Oportunidades* would be far less successful. The government's main
nutrition program (LICONSA) was already considered very successful in
a number of ways: it served a targeted population to which it provided
enriched milk at production prices; its production and distribution network were highly efficient; and it was virtually self-financing. Programs
were in place to provide incentives to teachers to help them remain in
highly marginal communities.[11] The Health Ministry had programs to set
up and equip clinics in very poor and marginal communities and to
extend coverage by means, among others, of Itinerant Health Teams. The
cash-transfer mechanism had been tried two years earlier in the state of
Campeche. All of these programs, however, had significant shortcomings.
LICONSA reached households in deciles 3 to 8 and virtually none below
that, because it was overwhelmingly urban. This meant that the most seriously malnourished (in indigenous rural communities) were beyond federal reach.[12] Incentives to teachers in marginal communities had unknown
impacts, because supervision was virtually non-existent and many of these
teachers had two jobs. The cash transfer mechanism in Campeche had several problems, due partly to imperfect targeting. Moreover, Mexico's
largest ever program for poverty reduction, *Solidaridad*, operating from
1989 to 1994, was considered very seriously flawed: it was biased in favor
of politically sensitive states, it tended toward metropolitan rather than
marginal areas, there was widespread corruption, and it provided much
less per-capita funding to states with the highest marginality and poverty
rates (Dresser 1991; Molinar and Weldon 1994; Chávez, Navarro, and
Hernández 1994; Roberts and Escobar 1997). Its specific impact on
poverty remained unknown: access was denied to 31 of its 32 state-by-
state evaluations. In sum, although certain programs functioned well, they
were heir to a time when *economic* policy was the cornerstone for the
improvement among Mexico's poor (Escobar and Roberts 1991; Roberts
and Escobar 1997). What was needed was a program that could show real
improvements in well-being, with *or without* considerable economic
development.

Policy makers began working on *Progresa* at the outset of Ernesto Zedillo's presidency, in 1995. The goal was to operate a program that could be shown to be effective, free from the electoral and social biases tarnishing previous efforts, and as transparent in its achievements as possible. The cumulative experience, technological skills, and analysis of a weighty group of policy makers were fundamental. Santiago Levy (2004) provides a detailed account of his participation in the design of *Progresa*. He reviews the discussions behind the inclusion of key policy components, and other members of that design group have also highlighted significant improvements. These include:

1. Targeting. *Progresa* for the first time was able to target highly marginal communities, not just municipalities, thanks to CONAPO's[13] (National Population Council) information and analysis.[14]

2. Within these communities, a census allowed the program to pick only poor households.

3. Households were assessed for incorporation not on declared income, but on the basis of a complex function which included, as its salient elements, the number, quality, and diversity of its assets, foremost housing. Occupations and dependency rates were also important.

4. After discussions, the program opted to rely upon Mexico's public health system rather than devise an alternative private service in the targeted communities. This entailed subsequent moderate but visible improvements in these services.

5. *Progresa* was viewed as the main form of public intervention in these communities and households, and its benefits and services were defined as non-overlapping: households forfeited other similar federal benefits when they joined the program (except for agricultural subsidies).

6. Demographers in the group stressed that households should not receive an incentive for additional fertility, and so children's transfers were strictly linked to school attendance and started at 3rd grade.

7. Transfers were not intended to close the poverty gap because this would remove the incentive to work. Instead, they were tailored to provide the adequate stimulus to change behavior.

8. A currently controversial provision states that the program provides temporary support to a household. Households should

"graduate," but no clear link has been established between the household's participation in the program and the means by which it should overcome poverty, except for the accumulation of transfers.

9. Finally, another socio-demographic emphasis resides in the program's gender component, which defines higher scholarship amounts for girls, to promote more rapid improvements in their school achievement.[15]

To show the extent to which it achieved short-term results in nutrition, health, and education, *Progresa–Oportunidades* commissioned a number of evaluations and studies. On the Mexican public policy scene, it is probably the most carefully studied program ever,[16] with quasi-experimental evaluations launched at the same time as the program. It has also implemented internal performance assessment mechanisms, which work through continuous monitoring, and external evaluations, performed by a number of institutions. In 2004, for the first time, the program carried out medium-term achievement evaluations, including an exploratory analysis of labor-market performance, in accordance to its original design priorities (briefly discussed in the fourth section).

From 1998 until 2000, the International Food Policy Research Institute (IFPRI) performed the main external evaluation;[17] in addition, a growing number of Mexican and other academics have to date analyzed the databases produced for this evaluation. This evaluation, and the corresponding database, took the form of an experimental or quasi-experimental[18] representative panel sample of similar communities and households, some excluded and others included in the program. The samples were large (around 20,000 households); households were interviewed six times; and, in addition to constant basic performance variables, a number of topical modules were rotated in each successive interview.

This evaluation arrived at significant positive results. Individuals participating in the program lengthened their educational careers, attended school more regularly, and were less subject to illnesses. Pregnant women, mothers, and infants were better nourished and there were some indications that households not only had higher incomes (as a result of cash transfers) but that the consumption levels of fundamental goods and services improved considerably, resulting in greater well-being. This last finding points at a reduction of poverty not just in terms of income, but also in the more direct, real sense of an improvement in the satisfaction of needs.[19] More recent analyses and updates of this database found a small but significant increase in the percentage of households investing in productive assets.

No re-analysis of this panel has found significant flaws in those results. The evaluation has, however, been the object of criticism regarding its experimental nature (i.e., the possibility that some highly marginal communities, which required priority attention, were excluded from the program's benefits) and the non-independent nature of the database. Basic preparation of the database was carried out in-house by program authorities, which meant IFPRI did not have access to the data as they arrived from the field. This has a potential impact on the reliability of the analysis, but also on the actual cost of the evaluation, which was extremely significant for any Mexican social program. There is some justification for in-house processing, in the sense that individual record-matching among the various panels was extremely difficult because of deaths, migration, exits from the program, and changes in household composition, all of which can better be controlled by program authorities who rely on administrative databases to track these changes. Since 2001, the large-scale evaluation of the program has been carried out by the INSP (National Institute of Public Health), with similar research designs, although the evaluation is today of a clearly non-experimental nature.[20]

At the same time, the program commissioned CIESAS to perform a qualitative evaluation of its performance (Escobar and González de la Rocha 2000; 2003[21]). While this project was also termed an *impact* evaluation, ethnographic approaches allowed us to observe the *processes* at work in the communities in both beneficiary and non-beneficiary households. In other words, our main interest was to observe the behavior, forms of organization, attitudes, norms, and values of the actors involved, and to relate them to varying impacts. This in turn would serve to point at areas of concern or in need of specific intervention by program authorities. A *process* approach, in our view, served to break down the causal mechanisms defining higher or lower impact levels. We were particularly concerned with establishing how and whether differences in (a) community (levels of marginality; ethnic, political, and economic organization); (b) household composition and organization; and (c) local, municipal, and state governments could affect impact levels. Our second area of interest was the process of selection and incorporation. We assessed whether the method and organization of the selection census and the process of incorporation were accurate. We were also interested in assessing the way in which the program interacted with social and economic changes taking place at that time: the demise of subsistence agriculture, weak local and regional labor markets, and international migration (for an elaboration of these interactions, see González de la Rocha in this volume). Our approach was complemented in two ways in the research design. First, we defined a "type matrix" of communities defined by a small number of independent (in this case intervening) variables. This was aimed at ensuring that we had an analytical sample comprising the breadth of variability in the program, according to this limited set of intervening variables. Second, in each community we looked at similar beneficiary and non-beneficiary households, to attempt to control local intervening factors.

Our first evaluation was initially planned as an external evaluation commissioned by the Mexican Congress. After a breakup in the negotiations for the evaluation, a political party offered to finance the project. We decided not to carry it out under this institutional arrangement, and instead relied on mostly private funding (Escobar 2000; 2003). The study consisted of six "first phase,"[22] highly marginal, rural, indigenous, and non-indigenous communities, in which we looked at both beneficiary and non-beneficiary households.

Since 2000, we have carried out yearly qualitative evaluations of different aspects of the program.[23] We have contracted the job directly with the program authorities, and the results are received and reviewed by Congress. In 2001, we performed a baseline study of small urban communities and households immediately before their incorporation into the program, which included control communities and households,[24] and in 2002 we carried out a follow-up of those communities and households (Escobar and González de la Rocha 2002; 2003).[25] The program was just expanding to these small urban centers. In 2002, the program started incorporating households in larger cities with a new method, partly relying on application to the program by the households themselves. In 2003, we performed an analysis of these new methods of incorporation and first impacts of the program in small areas in these cities (Escobar and González de la Rocha 2004). Most recently, in 2004, we returned to four of the highly marginal, rural communities we had studied in 1999 and 2000, and examined two others we had not visited previously. Although this last study was not designed as a baseline and follow-up study from its inception in 2000, we found that the comparison of our results in 1999–2000 to 2004 was extremely useful.[26]

Although we have concentrated our attention on the changes in the generation of the offspring, we have also argued that the program's transfers significantly reduce households' vulnerability while they remain in the program. We have shown how they improve their asset base, and the ways in which a higher, more stable income improves their lives in general. We have also documented, analyzed, and interpreted the reactions of the communities, households, and individuals: their adaptation, resistance, and responses to the program, and what we have termed the rise of an *Oportunidades* culture. Both the program and Mexican society are changing. Neither is what it was in 1997. Men, for example, are today far more willing to accept women's increasing autonomy. As a process, *Oportunidades* is enmeshed in a number of other changes. In the following section we assess the program's impact on education and health and then discuss the program's first impacts on labor-market performance.

The focus of evaluations has been, until 2004, on the changes that may lead or hinder progress towards much higher human capital levels among the young. Some attention has been paid to short-term impacts on poverty levels, but the evaluations have in general responded to the program's initial aim: to break the cycle of poverty among the poor.

Targeting

Initially, observers dismissed *Progresa* as just another presidential, one-term program, like COPLAMAR (1978–1982), *Solidaridad* (1989–994) and many others. But thanks to its proven impact (in which the design and implementation of evaluations played a key role), *Progresa* survived the Zedillo *Sexenio* (six-year presidential term) and was transformed into *Oportunidades*. In addition to its impact, *Progresa* was highly efficient (over 90% of its operational budget reached beneficiary households), its selection procedures were by far the best Mexico had ever seen, and it was virtually corruption-proof.[27] And not only did it circumvent the sectoral, state, and local government realms of power that biased, fed from, and bogged down many other programs, but on the contrary, it ensured (at very low financial cost) the cooperation of other government agencies in order to enhance its objectives. These unusual traits have helped it earn the consistent support of both the executive and legislative branches of government, and grow to twice its 2000 size.

Since the year 2000, the program has expanded its coverage of poor households from 2.6 million to its stated objective of 5 million by the end of 2004. This has been hailed by the government as achieving coverage of over 80% of households designated as being in capability[28] poverty.[29] This assertion calls for some detailed discussion. First, *Oportunidades'* criteria for eligibility differ from those used to define capability poverty. Second, self-selection into the program is extremely limited: households that consider themselves extremely poor are actively able to claim incorporation only in some places and during specific short periods.[30] Finally, *Oportunidades* only updates its payroll in any one specific settlement once every three years, which means new poor households or households falling into poverty have to wait for a time before they are interviewed for selection purposes.[31] Given the dynamic nature of poverty levels, this entails a certain permanent mismatch of the poor and the beneficiary populations.

The sheer size of the program in fact now allows assessments of the accurateness of selection, of the correlation between household income and transfer payments, and of its impact upon poor households based on general-purpose national surveys, which now include individual government transfers. Fernando Cortés has performed a number of analyses of this kind.[32] According to his analysis of the 2002 Household Income and Expenditure Survey (ENIGH), 87.7% of the transfers reached households in the five lower income deciles.[33] Capability poverty was estimated at the time to be 25%, but since the highest endowment poverty threshold was set at 45%, this would suggest a relatively good match. At that time, the program had barely begun to incorporate urban households, so they are excluded from the analysis. However, most households in the two lowest deciles are rural, which calls for a closer look.

From the distribution of transfers in the income distribution structure, it is possible to approximate the extent to which the program excludes poor households or includes non-poor households. If we assume equal average transfers to households regardless of their position in the income distribution structure,[34] then in 2002 the program provided transfers to 48% of all households in the poorest decile, 43% in the second, 39% in the third, 25% in the fourth, and 21% in the fifth.

This may be further elaborated in terms of inclusion and exclusion mismatches. If income and eligibility[35] criteria were the same, the program should benefit 100% of the two first income deciles, since there were 21 million households at the time in Mexico and the program covered 4.2 million, or 20%. However, according to these estimates, 52% of all households in the first decile and 57% of those in the second did not participate in the program. In addition, 54.5% of all beneficiaries belonged to the eight higher-income deciles.[36]

Again, eligibility criteria do not match criteria for income stratification. Mismatches between income stratification and program incorporation need not be considered errors: one defines poverty according to income, the other by a mix of asset quality, employment, services, and dependency. The above estimate of exclusion and inclusion nevertheless suggests that if the program intends to target poor households according to officially recognized criteria defining poverty, it still must fine-tune its methods. Mexican law has set guidelines for a new multidimensional method for the measurement of poverty. Results are expected for 2009, and the program should adjust its eligibility criteria accordingly.

In addition to the figures presented above, a state-by-state breakdown of *Oportunidades* transfers shows that in the poorest states over 80% of all households participate in the program, while in the most prosperous the figure falls below 8%. Overall, *Oportunidades* shows much better targeting of poor households than other current and past programs. *Solidaridad*, for example, failed to target the poorest, most marginal states (Roberts and Escobar 1997). LICONSA, the subsidized milk program, benefits households in deciles 3 to 8. PROCAMPO, a cash subsidy to farmers, distributes only 48.2% of its total transfers to households in the lower 5 deciles, and transfers 23.9% of all its resources to the highest decile.[37]

Based on our work we have suggested that targeting can be improved by the following means.

1. Develop a large-scale re-interviewing process of households in small urban centers. These households were incorporated mostly in 2001 and early 2002, and the method used to define high-intensity interview areas was too coarse to locate the specific city blocks where poor households concentrate. The method used in the area of influence of larger urban centers since 2002 overcame these problems. The program complied with this recommendation in 2004, when the program returned to small urban centers to re-select households with the newer method.

2. Develop national, permanent, or yearly self-selection processes. The program only re-interviews households in any one specific settlement once every three years.[38] The radical alternative is to carry out yearly national selection processes, for households residing in all qualifying settlements, allowing households to come forth to apply for inclusion. A non-generalized form of this method is currently being used in large cities. This radical alternative poses a serious problem arising from the intervention of local leaders, and is bound to privilege households with better information, political connections, or both. Care must therefore be taken to verify the information provided, and to guarantee that all poor households receive accurate and timely information.

3. Items 1 and 2 are only feasible if, simultaneously, communities are surveyed to detect households whose incomes have improved

beyond the eligibility threshold. The program has already excluded households above the eligibility threshold in communities joining the program in 1997 and 1998. This is always a delicate task.

4. Deal with obstacles to incorporation and permanence.

  a. Diminish census and incorporation bias. The method first used by the program was biased against the incorporation of households distant from the center of the community, of dubious community classification, or where all members over age 15 worked regular hours (interviewers' schedules did not allow for interviews at other times). The new "module" system partly overcomes these problems, but still has a certain bias against women-headed households, especially if they have small children or if they work long hours away from home. These women often cannot devote an entire morning or day to the application process and they may be absent from home for the "verification" interview.

  b. Facilitate permanence. The program places a heavy burden on women. They must manage the transfers, attend health information lectures, take their children for periodic check-ups (more frequent if they are malnourished), prepare and distribute food supplements, participate in community improvement efforts, and in fact ensure that all family members fulfill their commitments to the program.[39] Some women, especially in female-headed households, cannot do all of this, and their households are excluded from the program. A few women face the choice of remaining in full-time employment or joining the program. This choice is almost inescapable for beneficiary representatives who perform additional tasks. There is an uneven burden on household members: adult men's only commitment is to attend health check-ups twice a year.[40] However, if they are not allowed to be absent from work, or if the check-up appointment system is not working properly, they may miss their appointments, which can lead to exclusion when added to other co-responsibility failures by other members of the household. Paradoxically, households with one or more chronically ill members can miss their appointments for health reasons, a problem which, if not properly managed, can lead to being dropped from the program.

The program has dealt with some of these difficulties; current targeting is much more accurate than early efforts, although it must still improve. Some changes would entail higher costs for the program, the ministries, or the municipalities (for example, increasing the frequency and coverage of selection or certification surveys; on the other hand, in some areas, efforts have been made to open health clinics and interview modules outside working hours). Other changes could lead to significant selection bias based on education, political affiliation, or information. Any strategy will lead to some level of error, and the added cost of a more sophisticated identification, selection, incorporation, and retention strategy must be weighed against the drop in the number of eligible households that would be excluded for lack of funding.

Education: Achievements and Challenges

The *Oportunidades* program has undoubtedly helped raise the schooling levels of poor Mexicans. Parker, Behrman, and Todd (2005), using a matched sample of old, recent, and non-beneficiaries, estimate the program's impact on both schooling and cognitive performance based on different lengths of exposure to the program. They find youths with 1.5 years more exposure lengthened their school attendance by approximately one year. Comparison of those in the program for over 5 years with those never in the program yields a gain for beneficiaries of approximately 14%, on average, on the duration of their school careers. The longest-exposure cohorts also show gains in the percentage, advancing smoothly from one schooling grade to the next. Improvements in cognitive performance are significant only for cohorts profiting from the longest exposure to the program. This includes an improvement of 7% in math, 8.1% in reading, and 10.4% in writing (Parker, Behrman, and Todd 2005, p. 18).

In our qualitative evaluation, the schooling levels we found in 2004 were significantly higher than those we found in 1999–2000 in the same communities. I believe the program is the main factor accounting for this change. Our life history analyses have shown that living with both parents, and living with two parents with above-average schooling account for above-average schooling levels. However, they do not explain the changes observed during these four years.

Studying the communities where the program was first implemented in 1997 may provide a very good idea of the extent and limits of the program's ability to trigger social change. The program comprised 500,000 families by the end of 1997. From that point, it has gradually grown to include larger, less marginal communities and since 2002, large cities. Conditions differ in communities incorporated at later dates: they are generally less poor, the proportion of poor households is lower, the poverty levels are less extreme, and the dispersion levels are much higher (from the perspective of the program's eligibility thresholds, the poor in these larger settlements show low levels of segregation, which means finding them requires new methods for location and selection). This means that extrapolating the findings from the very first communities to those incorporated later must be done carefully.

Nevertheless, the achievements and limits of *Progresa–Oportunidades* in these pioneering communities may be those of the program as a whole. Enrollment at the primary, secondary, and EMS (grades 10 through 12) levels is analyzed, in order to establish the extent to which change has taken place and whether or not it may progress much further.

During our recent work, we have found that primary school enrollment is very close to 100%, and that the population in the corresponding age group is stable or falling, due both to the demographic transition and emigration. Secondary schooling still shows room for improvement, since initial enrollment stood at roughly 70%. The level which shows both spectacular growth and much further possible growth is EMS, with increases in total enrollment close to 100% in 2 years, total age group enrollment of less than 30%, and approximately 3 scholarship receivers[41] for every 4 students in the smaller (most marginal) settlements. The following paragraphs explore these findings in some detail.

The above coverage has been reached in extremely marginal communities that have participated in the program for five to seven years. These communities have been the object of processes which have both excluded better-off households and included a higher proportion of poor households. These processes have improved targeting to such an extent that we found it difficult to identify poor, non-beneficiary households in most communities.

Two main questions suggest themselves: what further improvements in enrollment can be expected among these "first-phase" communities and families; and how likely is it that this process will be extended and its achievements equaled or surpassed among communities and families entering the program at later dates?

In the first-phase communities that are highly marginal and very poor, and where almost all the families joined the program, the potential for improvement is as follows.

Primary school enrollment is unlikely to improve further. Almost the entire age group is enrolled, and the obstacles for those not attending are very specific: it may be that the children themselves are physically or mentally disadvantaged, that the families are extremely poor and thus unable to afford shoes and clothes and provide them with spending money for school, or that the composition of the household is such that it could not do without the domestic labor of children (caring for smaller children, the elderly or the ill, or performing household chores), or that one or more of the adults is unfit to work and the children must help provide an income. A few teenagers would like to return to primary school to complete it, but they are too old or lack the necessary paperwork. All of the above tend to worsen if severe alcoholism is present. These children, in summary, will not attend school unless specific attention is provided to these households. This means that, aside from monitoring the performance of future enrollment, evaluations should assign a lower priority to this issue in the future. There will be no further impacts.

Secondary enrollment, conversely, is far from that position. First-year enrollment levels are about 70%, but they drop to approximately 50%. We also saw roughly equal registration levels for boys and for girls, although aggregate measurements point at the persistence of a small preference for the enrollment of boys. Depending on the generalized poverty level of the community, from just under half to over 80% of students receive scholarships. In the less poor communities, the proportion of beneficiary households is lower, and non-beneficiary households are better able to send their children to school (in the poorest communities, non-beneficiary households can be just as poor).

There are two other significant findings in secondary schools. First, total enrollment, and the enrollment of *Oportunidades* scholarship holders, have been roughly constant for the past two or three years. Second, some families were recently excluded from the program because it was detected they were not eligible (they were significantly above the eligibility threshold). In a number of these cases, more often applying to girls, parents stated they would stop sending them to school. Teachers disagree with the parents who made this decision, and tend to think that these families can afford to keep them there. In their opinion, *Oportunidades* scholarships led them to value their children's education mostly in terms of the additional income, not for education itself. When the money stopped, education was of no further value to them.

Even though coverage is not complete, we saw no evidence of enrollment drives for children completing primary school. It may be that, since enrollment did increase rapidly until 2002, program officials see no need to expand their student body (some teachers in fact thought it had been extremely difficult to cope with this past increase: in many schools, classes had to be added and infrastructure was insufficient). Likewise, there is a possibility that secondary enrollment at roughly 70% of the age group is the current, structural ceiling of the program in these communities. While teachers are being moved out of some primary schools because of falling enrollment,[42] we did not see evidence of an equivalent movement to hire teachers at the secondary level.[43] It seems that out-selection by the families (and the students), plus slow expansion of supply will keep enrollment constant, and a significant part of the age group will stay out of school.

At the EMS level, enrollment is between one quarter and one fifth of enrollment in primary school. There is tremendous recent growth here. Roughly three out of four youths attending from the communities we studied had scholarships. Some institutions are attempting to recruit from poor communities. Teachers visit secondary schools, where they show videos advertising the quality of their education and the employment prospects for their graduates. Social workers resort to a number of programs to aid poor students: scholarships, part-time employment, or low-cost lodging. Other EMS institutes, however, are not attempting to further recruit, mostly because their funding is not likely to grow (in one, the principal said they would have to eliminate 150 students the next academic year because of budget cuts).

Oportunidades extended its scholarship program to EMS education in 2001. At the time, we observed that information had not been provided in a timely way[44] for most candidates to profit from this extension during that academic year. However, since 2002, enrollment of *Oportunidades* grant receivers has increased continually. Today, most families know about these scholarships and make well-informed decisions. The recent availability of EMS scholarships and diffusion of information concerning their much higher amounts ($73 per month for girls and $60 per month for boys attending the third year of EMS education), are likely to have further impacts in the coming years. A less-than dynamic labor market is another factor pushing youths towards school.

Unlike what we found at secondary level, at the EMS level there is no question that the vast majority of students from beneficiary families need financial support. In other words, even if these families were just above the eligibility threshold, they would be unlikely to be able to support their children in school because of higher direct and indirect costs, which typically involve paying for 10 to 40 km transport daily, providing spending money, about $100 dollars in registration fees per semester, no less than $15 a week on materials, computer use and related expenses, and a much higher dress standard, related to the much higher economic level of other students. This is in addition to their children's opportunity income.

When some families were excluded from the program for the same reason as discussed above (i.e., because they were classified as errors of inclusion), they visited the school as a group, and teachers were actively involved in finding out exactly why the families were excluded and what were the chances of re-incorporating them. When it became clear the families would be excluded indefinitely, the teachers found some resources for a few students (mostly transport scholarships and part-time jobs as teachers in adult literacy programs), but they agreed the rest would quite simply be unable to continue their studies.

There are three main questions. One question considers the extent to which households are committed to education, or whether their main motivation is the scholarships. We have observed repeatedly that households are significant co-funders of their children's education. While households make an obvious effort to diminish expenses as much as possible (in many instances, mothers cook a meal which they take to their children during school breaks, and they arrange transportation with friends and relatives when possible), the typical scholarship covers less than half the expenses of secondary education, and considerably less than half of EMS education. The fact that families co-fund their children's education signals that they don't, as a rule, view scholarships as an income source, but as an aid to education.

This is not to say that parents view just any education as good. Falling registrations at primary levels have led many schools to admit students not living in their district, and something similar is happening in secondary schools. Parents choose schools when they can, and they do so on the basis of a school's or teacher's reputation, their ability to afford transport, and the convenience of the school, including the risk of having their daughters travel longer distances alone. Most parents know who the better teachers are.[45] Since school performance ratings are barely beginning to work in Mexico, parents look at higher-level schools' admittance preferences, or they compare the abilities of children attending different schools. It is true that Mexican education is substantially authoritarian, and that the performance of rural schools is far below average. Nevertheless, parents exert these choices when they can, and they will make additional efforts to secure a better education for their children. Finally, our most recent work suggests that there are demonstrated effects in the communities where the program has been in operation for a number of years. Educational expectations of parents participating in the program have risen, but they are rising among non-participant parents too, who often go to remarkable lengths (to intensify their money-earning strategies) to be able to afford their children's schooling.

The second question considers whether the program enhances school performance or not. Teachers' opinions vary. Most teachers believe performance has not changed as a result of the program. A number of them, however, point out that overall class performance has fallen because classes have become less selective than previously. Today, they note, almost every child attends in order to secure scholarship payments, while a few years ago schools served students who were self-motivated and keen to learn. Some teachers in this group state that their schools are now earning fewer distinctions and awards because of the "downgrading" of the student population. These teachers would like the program to link scholarships to the achievement of minimum grades. However, teachers also remark on the opposite phenomenon: because children must attend regularly, and because the transfers are tied to attendance and the fulfillment of families' responsibilities towards their children's education, children now comply with their obligations far more dutifully than before, and their interest in education has grown. A few teachers have succeeded in communicating with the parents and stressing that attendance is not the key to success, and that they must make sure their children are in fact learning. Children will not get ahead in life because they have a certificate of primary or secondary education, but because they know and can do things. These teachers organize contests and participate in state student tournaments, which significantly incentivize their students.

Parents' understanding of this kind of value of education for their children is normally the product of two phenomena. The first is teachers' efforts to show that capable people do better in life. The second is families who have sufficient social capital that allows them to sketch or plan ways in which their children could gain access to better occupations and know of students who have succeeded because of higher levels of education.

This leads to the third question, which considers the relevance of occupational perspectives as priority factors for families when granting a formal education. Occupational advancement is not the only reason why an education is valued. Both youths and adults often point out that they do not want to be trodden on and abused, and that having an education is the only way they can avoid it. Whether they find themselves facing local authorities, store owners, money-lenders, husbands, foremen, or labor contractors in the United States, being able to understand math calculations, read contracts or instructions, file complaints, or fill in voting ballots will improve their lives.

Yet the prospect of moving into an occupation is the prevailing factor in the definition of the importance of education. The next section details the changing opportunities for the children of laborers and poor peasants. However, in terms of parents' perspectives, the nature and dynamism of local and regional labor markets serve to define the level of effort families are likely to undertake. While this seems obvious, it works in unexpected ways. Until recently, for example, one community was relatively prosperous and dynamic on the basis of a fishing economy. Education was not highly valued, because unskilled jobs abounded. Now the fishing economy is declining substantially, but the labor market in the state is relatively prosperous. Parents now assert that secondary and EMS education will allow youths to leave the village and earn a higher income. Something similar is happening to a community in Guerrero: the maize crops are failing but the village has well-established social networks in two nearby cities, and families now place a much greater emphasis on education. In another city, a secondary school certificate will secure a manual, stable job with social security, and an EMS certificate will secure a non-manual, stable, formal job. Families and students set their goals accordingly. In another village, however, the regional labor market is stagnant, EMS graduates work as day laborers, and families see no use for education. At times, families' horizons go beyond the regional economy. Longer-distance social networks in dynamic Mexican cities can be important. While migration to the United States has usually weighed against education, internal migration to cities can enhance education because school credentials are recognized there. This was the case in several villages and small towns. And in one village in 2004, families thought education was important for international migrants too (this is the first time we have found this opinion).

In sum, these villages may show high levels of improvement because they were among the first to enter the program, and that in turn means that they were among Mexico's most marginal, with extremely low schooling levels and significant room for improvement. A full primary schooling was difficult to attain for most children, and it is now very close to 100%. But stagnation in secondary school enrollment may mean the program is close to its limits at this level in these communities, although it is far from reaching full coverage. The remarkable growth of EMS enrollment, however, suggests more scope for change. In settings where the initial levels were high, improvements are likely to be lower at the primary school level but higher at the secondary and EMS levels. However, whether or not these communities will reach full coverage at secondary or EMS levels is something that will have to be tested later. In the extremely poor communities studied in 2000 and 2004, the local and regional labor markets are of no help. A "culture of achievement" relating more or better schooling to occupational success is virtually absent. Conversely, its presence in non-marginal and urban settings is likely to affect outcomes in a positive way.

Social Mobility and First Labor-Market Impacts

Mexico's period of rapid growth, modernization, and urbanization came to a halt in 1982, and since that time, economic growth has been low, unstable, and highly uneven. The occupational structure has also changed direction. From a period in which middle- and higher-level, non-manual, formal occupations were growing rapidly, the labor market has since experienced growth mainly in informal occupations, with few exceptions.

It would therefore seem that the students achieving higher levels of education by means of *Oportunidades* scholarships would face tough competition in the labor market. In other words, the program's ultimate test (the ability of the younger generation to break the cycle of poverty) is getting a start in particularly unfavorable circumstances.

Their opportunities, however, are defined not simply by their credentials and the slow growth of non-manual employment, but also by changing levels of achievement inequality. Until recently, there were no assessments of changing patterns of social mobility after the Mexican crisis. Today there are at least two. One is based on a 1994 survey of six Mexican cities, and the other on a 2000 nationally representative survey.

Escobar (2001) and Cortés and Escobar (2005) have performed an analysis of the first survey. They found that (a) the probability and the general odds of upward social mobility have fallen; (b) the class-of-origin inequality of achievement has increased (but not homogeneously), which means that (c) levels of ascription rigidity have risen; and (d) gender inequality of achievement has fallen (again, not homogeneously).

For *Oportunidades*, the most relevant aspect of social mobility is the one corresponding to the children of farmers and day laborers. Cortés and Escobar analyze three age groups. The first entered the labor market up to 1982, the second between 1983 and 1987, and the youngest between 1988 and 1994. According to this analysis, the children of farmers and day laborers saw their odds of achieving professional, managerial, and entrepreneurial occupations (the top occupations) in their first full-time job fall from 0.011 before 1982 to 0.010 between 1983 and 1987, to 0.002 after 1988, for a drop of 80%. In addition, their odds relative to the children of the highest class fell from 1/20 to 1/40 during the same period. In other words, inequality relative to offspring of the top level rose by 100%.

At the same time, extremely few children of farmers and laborers can be expected to climb the occupational structure as rapidly as this. A much more likely upward movement for them is to technical and clerical non-manual occupations. This includes teachers, nurses, office workers, store clerks, and other similar occupations. This movement is far more frequent. The odds of farmers' and laborers' children of reaching or not reaching this stratum start at 0.230 for those entering the labor market until 1982; they rise to 0.445 for those entering between 1983 and 1987; and finally to 0.460 for those entering the labor market in 1988 or later.[46] This is remarkable, because these job sectors have not expanded visibly since the early eighties.

The above analysis of these two kinds of social mobility suggests that, although it is highly improbable for the graduates of *Oportunidades* to reach professional and managerial occupations, the program might in fact have a significant impact on their chances of entering formal, non-manual (and sometimes technical) occupations, thanks to their additional education. The recent, not-infrequent movement to these jobs may mean that some of these families possess the networks that may link them to those opportunities.

Zenteno and Solís (2008) analyze the 2000 EDER (Retrospective Demographic Survey). While they deal with the social mobility of cohorts over a longer span of time, their results are also useful because the survey is quite recent. They conclude that education is still, in Mexico, the single most important asset for social mobility, more so than class of origin. Persons may exit the lower strata if they possess the right education levels.

During our most recent evaluation, we looked at the labor-market performance of *Oportunidades* graduates, that is, youths who had completed their EMS education in 2003 and 2004. They come from Mexico's poorest, most marginal, and isolated communities, some of which are mostly indigenous, with a large part of the population, including some primary school students, speaking indigenous languages. In addition, these scholarship recipients did not receive the full benefits of the program. They did not receive nutritional supplements as infants, and they and their families did not participate in the program before they entered sixth grade. Based on 130 seven-year life trajectory analyses, Janssen (2004) concluded that there was a very modest improvement in their labor-market performance, relative to non-scholarship recipients. While a few had managed to enter university, others were still seeking employment. This medium-term impact should increase during the next few years. In addition, this kind of impact should be larger in communities joining the program more recently, because they are less poor and less physically—and socially—isolated.

In summary, although current labor-market impacts among the second generation are still incipient, both existing social mobility analyses and first-phase community studies suggest that the program may achieve its original main objective in terms of improved employment opportunities, and lower achievement inequality.

Final Remarks

Whether the program directors decide to stress its capacity-building impact among the second generation or its safety-net aspects, it seems that they still need to perfect its targeting methods. These have improved since 2002, but the program's payroll has not been substantially modified for the past two years. A dangerous temptation would be to expand the program based on existing surveys and known settlements, a move that would be low-cost and would improve the program's overall financial efficiency. In all likelihood, the program needs a significant push for either continuous or periodic updating of its household and settlement databases. Schools and clinics are built, small settlements change quickly, and the target population moves and changes considerably. The ministries of health and education need to work with *Oportunidades* to update this registry. The program has been relatively successful at dropping no longer poor households. However, the next effort lies in devising a system that keeps track of these changes.

In order to further its original objectives of enhancing labor-market performance and lowering achievement inequality, efforts which would ensure that youths graduating from *Oportunidades* would break the cycle of continuing poverty, the program has improved its nutritional intervention. The nutritional composition of its supplements has been modified, and a change in the nutritional education component is underway. In addition, it is advisable to provide more support to youths by offering more substantial help for their university-level studies, by facilitating their entry into career-type employment, and by intervening at the *secundaria* and EMS levels to more accurately prepare them for suitable work. And although the transition rates of primary to secondary and secondary to EMS have improved markedly, some additional efforts may be required to ensure that more rural poor children achieve these transitions. The stagnation of secondary enrollment rates in highly marginal communities may require more study and attention.

If, however, the government decides to stress the second nature of *Oportunidades* as a social assistance program, then it is highly advisable that the program design

1. Methods that detect or respond to the applications of households suddenly facing income losses or catastrophic expenditures.

2. Incentives to help existing households achieve higher and sustainable incomes in the medium term and then to "graduate" these households to other forms of social assistance. This should include better coordination with the payroll of other assistance programs, such as the cash transfer programs aimed at rural producers. We have found many who have not been able to benefit from them.

3. An improved coordination with health facilities for the poor that will provide care for chronic or catastrophic illnesses, and development of successful educational and care initiatives for alcoholism and drug addiction.

4. A well-targeted program for the elderly. The elderly often cannot fulfill the program's co-responsibilities, and their poverty is the opposite of younger households: their assets have improved after a lifetime of effort, but their incomes may be very low. They are thus dropped from *Oportunidades* or simply not incorporated. (In 2005, the program devised a new component specifically for the elderly, which would allow them to maintain or increase their cash transfers.)

5. Coordination with the agencies developing risk maps, to monitor them especially carefully.

6. Assistance to households suffering severe income drops or catastrophic expenditures should demand significant co-responsibilities by able men. Currently, women bear the entire burden.

The impact of *Oportunidades*' transfers on the income-provision efforts of households needs to be debated further. Moreover, the program did not plan for any improvements in the abilities of households to generate independent income.

Finally, all of the above needs to be decided within a *narrow*, or *specialized*, understanding of social policy. If the economy were itself able to provide the incentives for households to intensify their income-generating strategies, dependence on social transfers would be a far less significant problem than it is likely to be if poor households perceive these transfers as their main source of social and economic progress. Even a relatively defective education system can prepare youths for skilled manual or non-manual work if the economy demands workers in these sectors. However, it is not currently doing so. Whether in its human capital or safety net guises, *Oportunidades* can improve its impacts on the poor and restore them to a more equal footing with other Mexicans, provided they do not multiply as a consequence of economic stagnation. Social policy should not and cannot deliver national development. The economy needs to do its part.

Notes

1   Neufeld *et al.*, 2005. The program started distributing improved food supplements in the fall of 2005.

2   The World Bank defines safety nets as the provision of transfers, services, subsidies or micro-credit to families at risk of falling below poverty. It distinguishes formal and informal actions and differentiates formal programs according to their target population: the chronic poor, the transient poor, and persons in special circumstances (World Bank 2005).

3   This is the objective of *Seguro Popular,* or Popular Insurance, to which *Oportunidades* beneficiaries have recently been granted access under a subsidized scheme. The performance of this program has not yet been sufficiently assessed.

4   This avoids incentives to poverty. Households receive the same amount regardless of improvements in their autonomous income, unless their aggregate eligibility score surpasses a certain level, above which they are dropped from the program.

5   As of 2006, the program incorporated a new component that provides a stable monthly income to adults 70 years of age and older in rural communities. Coverage is still short of the estimated population qualifying for this subsidy, however.

6   And also, albeit to a lesser extent, in poor areas in the cities.

7   Author's estimates, based on the 1995 and 2005 population counts.

8   All these figures correspond to "traditional" beneficiaries, who comprise over 90% of the payroll. There is another kind of beneficiary household. Benefits may extend to high school graduates attending college, but that component functions differently and many candidates are not familiar with it.

9   In some states, special agreements ensure that illiterate mothers attend adult education workshops. This is not generally required throughout the country, however.

10 Since 2002 there is a more clearly defined way for these households to re-join the program.

11 These programs (PARE, Programa de Atención al Rezago Escolar; PAREB, Programa de Atención al Rezago Escolar Básico; and PAC, Programa de Ampliación de Cobertura en Salud) were strengthened after *Progresa* evaluations showed teacher and doctor absenteeism was a major problem in poor, marginal communities.

12 This bias in coverage worsened after December 1997, when a large part of the social development budget was decentralized, and *municipalities* became free to administer most of these resources according to their own priorities.

13 The National Population Council is an inter-ministerial body coordinating population policy. It possesses a highly developed capacity to diagnose population related issues.

14 Since 2002, the program is able to target recruitment interviews to the level of city blocks.

15 In the author's views, these are improvements. They have nevertheless been criticized.

16 This does not mean public policy is not evaluated. Social and public policy paradigms (as entire sets of policy measures and programs) have been assessed in the past in terms of poverty alleviation, inequality, social mobility, and other impact variables.

17 IFPRI (2002), and Skoufias (2005).

18 There are at least two contrasting accounts of the research design for this evaluation. According to one, a number of communities were randomly excluded from the program in order to perform the evaluation. According to the other, some communities had to be excluded for budgetary reasons, and they were then chosen for the evaluation (Cortés, personal communication).

19 D'Amato worked with the IFPRI team to carry out qualitative and focus group interviews with participants. Her findings were published together with our work in 2000 (Progresa 2000, Vol. 8). Among other things, she concluded that inclusion and exclusion created new divisions in communities.

20 In order to approximate an experimental design, current evaluations perform *post-hoc* elaborate beneficiary and non-beneficiary matching of eligible, threshold and non-poor households.

21 Salomón Nahmad directed the first evaluation performed by CIESAS in 1999. In this text, however, I refer mainly to the evaluations directed by the author and Mercedes González de la Rocha since 2000.

22 In the program's vocabulary, its gradual expansion is referred to in terms of phases. First phase communities were therefore the first to participate in the program, in 1997.

23 Since 2006, González de la Rocha is the sole director of the qualitative evaluation.

24 This included a critical review of the method of incorporation used in 2001, which was used only once and immediately replaced by a third, partly self-ascriptive method.

25 Except for the control communities, which were incorporated before the follow-up study.

26 The executive summaries of these studies can all be found at http://www.Oportunidades.gob.mx, under "publications," some under the CIESAS and some under the INSP headings. The 2004 evaluation is due for release in March, 2005.

27 During our 7 years as evaluators, we have had direct knowledge of extremely few instances of corruption. There are also some questionable practices, such as beneficiary representatives charging beneficiaries for their services, or doctors charging patients who are eligible for free care under program rules.

28 Capability poverty stood at 25.3% in 2000, and seems to have fallen slightly in 2002. I interpret the meaning of capability, as used by the Mexican government, as related to, but different from, the meaning attached to the word by Amartya Sen. It refers basically to households' ability to afford food, education and health care.

29 According to an external panel of experts convened by the Social Development Ministry (SEDESOL) (Comité Técnico para la Medición de la Pobreza 2005), extreme poverty, in rural areas especially, has been significantly reduced from 2000 to 2004, which would mean that "virtual" coverage of the program is closer to 90% of its target population. Further, some argue social policy as a whole, and *Oportunidades* specifically, are responsible for this reduction.

30 Admittedly, the program has increased the opportunities of households to apply for inclusion, and there are plans to open the range even further, which might have significant drawbacks (bias towards the information-privileged, politically connected and institutionally savvy).

31 There are, on the contrary, clearly specified ways to incorporate new scholarship recipients in households already participating in the program.

32 The tables on which this paragraph is based were prepared by Fernando Cortés, but the estimates were prepared by the author.

33 And 95% reached the lowest 6 deciles.

34 A household's cash transfer varies according to its number of school-going children, their sex, and the level they attend.

35 Initially, the program did not have the means to translate its eligibility formula into per capita income levels in a given household, which produced a mismatch between the poor as defined by their income and the eligible population. It developed that ability in 2004.

36 Similar analyses, based on 2006 databases, showed targeting had improved: the percentage of beneficiary households in the lower deciles increased, while it decreased in the higher deciles.

37 PROCAMPO was not designed to benefit poor farmers especially, but it is often referred to both by officials and analysts as a social program.

38 Households twice classified as poor are not re-scheduled for evaluation (this is likely to change soon).

39 In some highly marginal, isolated communities, taking a child to a health check-up appointment can take an entire day and cost more than 15% of the total monthly cash transfer (in transport and food).

40 Except male single heads of household, who must perform the same tasks as the housewives.

41 Most of these receive *Oportunidades* scholarships, but there are other programs at this level.

42 Average class sizes in primary schools have fallen consistently since approximately 1994.

43 In some states, age limits seem highly restrictive. Boys and girls aged 16 and above are not allowed to register in secondary school. Since in highly marginal communities it is not uncommon for students to finish primary school at age 14, this age limit may in fact exclude a significant group from secondary education.

44 Information did not reach either EMS institutions or families in time to affect their decisions for the 2001 school year.

45 Although we have also found that parents evaluate teachers on the basis of their respect for their students.

46 Calculated for this paper on the basis of the transition matrices in Cortés and Escobar (2005).

References

Chávez, Ana María, David Moctezuma Navarro, and Francisco Rodríguez Hernández. 1994. *El combate a la pobreza en Morelos: Aciertos y desaciertos de solidaridad.* Cuernavaca: CRIM (Centro Regional de Investigación Multidisciplinaria).

Comité Técnico para la Medición de la Pobreza en México. 2005. *Medición de la pobreza 2002–2004.* Mexico City: Author.

Cortés, Fernando, and Agustín Escobar. 2005. "Movilidad social intergeneracional en el México urbano." *Revista de la CEPAL* 85 (April): 149–167.

Dresser, Denise. 1991. *Neopopulist Solutions to Neoliberal Dilemmas.* La Jolla: Center for U.S.–Mexican Studies, UCSD.

Escobar Latapí, Agustín. 2000. "El programa Progresa y el cambio social en el México rural." In Enrique Valencia, Mónica Gendreau, and Ana María Tepichín, eds. *Los dilemas de la política social. ¿Cómo combatir la pobreza?* Guadalajara: ITESO.

———. 2001. "Nuevos modelos económicos: ¿nuevos sistemas de movilidad social?" *Serie Políticas Sociales* (50) Santiago: CEPAL.

———. 2003. "The Progresa Programme and Social Change in Rural Mexico." In Louise Haagh and Camilla Helgo, eds. *Social Policy Reform and Market Governance in Latin America.* London: Macmillan.

Escobar Latapí, Agustín, and Bryan Roberts. 1991. "Urban Stratification, the Middle Classes, and Economic Change in México." In Mercedes González de la

Rocha and Agustín Escobar Latapí, eds. *Social Responses to Mexico's Economic Crisis*. La Jolla: Center for U.S.–Mexican Studies, UCSD.

Escobar Latapí, Agustín, and Mercedes González de la Rocha. 2000. "Logros y retos: una evaluación cualitativa del Progresa en México." In *Progresa: más oportunidades para las familias pobres*. México City: Author. http://evaloportunidades.insp.mx/441c7c1a3d30adf64e0e724174a9d527/impacto/2000/ifpri_2000_impacto_comunitario.pdf Accessed: September 13, 2006.

————. 2002. *Evaluación cualitativa del Programa de Desarrollo Humano Oportunidades: Estudio basal de Comunidades de 2,500 a 50,000 habitantes*. Mexico DF: CIESAS.

————. 2003. *Evaluación cualitativa del Programa de Desarrollo Humano Oportunidades: Seguimiento de impacto 2001–2002. Comunidades de 2,500 a 50,000 habitantes*. Mexico DF: CIESAS: http://www.oportunidades.gob.mx/e_oportunidades/evaluacion_impacto/2002/Evaluaci%F3n%20Cualitativa%20Final%20-%20dic02.pdf

————. 2004. "Evaluación cualitativa del Programa de Desarrollo Humano Oportunidades en zonas urbanas, 2003." In Bernardo Hernández and Mauricio Hernández, eds. *Evaluación externa de impacto del Programa Oportunidades 2003, Chapter IV*. Cuernavaca: INSP–CIESAS. http://www.oportunidades.gob.mx/e_oportunidades/evaluacion_impacto/2003/julio/tomo%202003%20oport.pdf

IFPRI (International Food Policy Research Institute). 2002. "Mexico: Evaluation of PROGRESA, 1997–1999." (Dataset) Washington, D.C.: Author.

Levy, Santiago. 2004. "El programa educación, salud y alimentación." In Santiago Levy, ed. *Ensayos sobre el desarrollo económico y social de México*. Mexico DF: Fondo de Cultura Económica.

Molinar, Juan, and Jeffrey Weldon. 1994. "Programa nacional de solidaridad: determinantes partidistas y consecuencias electorales." *Estudios Sociológicos* 12 (enero-abril): 155–181.

Neufeld, Lynnette, Daniela Sotres Alvarez, Paul Gertler, Lizbeth Tolentino Mayo, Jorge Jiménez Ruiz, Lia Fernald, Salvador Villalpando, Teresa Shamah, and Juan Rivera Dommarco. 2005. "Impacto de Oportunidades en el crecimiento y estado nutricional de niños en zonas rurales." In Bernardo Hernández and Mauricio Hernández, eds. *Evaluación externa de impacto del Programa Oportunidades 2004*, Vol. III, Chapter 1. Cuernavaca: INSP–CIESAS.

Parker, Susan W., Jere R. Behrman, and Petra E. Todd. 2005. "Impacto de mediano plazo del Programa Oportunidades sobre la educación y el trabajo de jóvenes del medio rural que tenían de 9 a 15 años de edad en 1997." In Hernández, Bernardo and Mauricio Hernández, eds. *Evaluación externa de impacto del Programa Oportunidades 2004*. Vol. I. Cuernavaca: INSP–CIESAS.

Progresa (Programa Educación, Salud y Alimentación). 1997. *Programa Educación, Salud y Alimentación*. Mexico DF: Author.

————. 2000. *Progresa: Más Oportunidades para las familias pobres*. Vol. VIII (*Aspectos Comunitarios*). Mexico DF: Author.

Roberts, Bryan, and Agustín Escobar Latapi. 1997. "Mexican Social and Economic Policy and Emigration." In Frank D. Bean, Rodolfo O. de la Garza, Bryan Roberts, and Sidney Weintraub, *At the Crossroads: Mexico and U.S. Immigration Policy*. Baltimore: Rowman and Littlefield.

Skoufias, Emmanuel. 2005. "PROGRESA and Its Impacts on the Welfare of Rural Households in Mexico." Research Report. Washington, D.C.: International Food Policy Research Institute (IFPRI).

Zenteno, René, and Patricio Solís. (2008) "Movilidad estructural e inequidad de oportunidades laborales en México." In Cortés, Fernando, Agustín Escobar Latapí, and Patricio Solís, eds. *Cambio estructural y movilidad social en México*. Mexico DF: El Colegio de México.

8

The U.S. Social Safety Net and Poverty

Sheldon Danziger, Sandra K. Danziger

Following World War II, the American economy experienced a long period of sustained economic growth, rising real wages, and low unemployment rates. The benefits of prosperity were widely shared among most of the poor, the middle class, and the wealthy. Even though poverty had fallen rapidly from the late 1940s to the early 1960s, concerns were raised by both popular authors and economic policy analysts that many families, especially those headed by less educated workers, minorities, and women, were not benefiting much from the prosperous economy (Galbraith 1958; Harrington 1962; Lampman 1959). These authors and analysts called for government to target policies and programs at those being left behind.

Some writers emphasized the "paradox of poverty amidst plenty," arguing for anti-poverty policies on moral grounds. For example, Michael Harrington (1962), in his influential *The Other America*, wrote:

> It is an ethical proposition, and it can be simply stated: In a nation with a technology that could provide every citizen with a decent life, it is an outrage and a scandal that there should be such social misery.... We must perceive passionately, if this blindness is to be lifted from us. A fact can be rationalized and explained away; an indignity cannot.... I want to tell every well-fed and optimistic American that it is intolerable that so many millions should be maimed in body and in spirit when it is not necessary that they should be. (p.19)

Others, particularly economists, viewed an anti-poverty initiative as the next logical step in the evolution of economic policy. Just as monetary and fiscal policies were being used to dampen the effects of the business cycle, economic policies could be adopted to raise the incomes of the poor.

Robert Lampman (1971) completed a study that showed that the anti-poverty impact of economic growth was lower in the late 1950s than it had been a decade earlier. He argued that economic growth, on its own, would not be sufficient to eliminate poverty within a generation, and that government should intervene to raise the employment and earnings prospects of the poorest workers. To Lampman, the anti-poverty goal was similar to the full employment goal: "Ending income poverty does not require and will not achieve a transformation of society. It is a modest goal" (p.167).

Responding to both the moral and economic arguments, President Johnson declared War on Poverty in January 1964. In his transmittal letter to Congress for the 1964 *Economic Report of the President*, he declared,

> We cannot and need not wait for the gradual growth of the economy to lift this forgotten fifth of our nation above the Poverty line. *We know what must be done, and this Nation of abundance can surely afford to do it.* Today, as in the past, higher employment and speedier economic growth are the cornerstones of a concerted attack on poverty.... But general prosperity and growth leave untouched many of the roots of human poverty. (p.15)

This Economic Report discussed many strategies for reducing poverty. Some were restatements of long-standing policy goals; others were new. They included maintaining high employment, accelerating economic growth, fighting discrimination, improving labor market prospects for less-educated workers, expanding educational opportunities, improving health, and assisting the aged and disabled.

The conventional wisdom among the President's advisers was that stable economic growth would continue for the subsequent two decades much as it had for the prior two decades. As a result, the income poverty goal could be achieved by macroeconomic policies that could keep the economy growing and by devoting modest additional resources to new anti-poverty initiatives. Poverty was thought to be high in the "affluent society" because the poor could not find enough work or because their skills left them with low earnings even if they worked full-time, full-year. Lagging economic growth in some regions, such as Appalachia, insufficient labor market skills of the working poor and labor market discrimination were also considered problems that could be resolved by public policies. Government actions could improve economic performance, raise the productivity of the poor, and remove discriminatory barriers to economic participation.

Poverty in America was not eliminated in the next generation. Indeed, two generations later, the vision of President Johnson and the War on Poverty planners remains unfulfilled, primarily because the optimistic economic forecasts of the 1960s were wrong. The era of rising real wage rates for most workers and the steady economic growth that raised living standards for most families came to an abrupt end in the mid-1970s.

Economic forces since the mid-1970s have caused rising economic hardships for many workers and their families and overwhelmed the ability of anti-poverty policies to reduce market-generated poverty. These forces include labor-saving technological changes, the globalization of markets, and contemporaneous weakening in labor market institutions (for example, declines in the inflation-adjusted minimum wage and declines in the percentage of workers covered by union contracts). From the early 1970s to the early 1990s, unemployment rates were high, growth in real median earnings was slow, and wages and access to employer-provided health insurance and pensions fell for workers on average. Even though the economy boomed in both the late 1980s and the mid- to late 1990s, the average inflation-adjusted weekly earnings of production workers were 9 percent lower in January 2008 than they were in January 1973 (www.bls.gov).

In the 45 years since the declaration of the War on Poverty, progress in reducing poverty, except for the elderly, has been slow. Poverty among the elderly declined dramatically because of the safety net that was developed for them in the aftermath of the Johnson initiative. The living standards of the elderly became more secure than the living standards of the non-elderly in the mid-1970s, just as the economy entered a long period of high inflation, high unemployment rates, and declining real wages.

Fighting poverty is no longer a national priority in the United States. Nonetheless, there are lessons that can be learned from its four decades of anti-poverty policy experience. We begin with a brief review of the scope of anti-poverty programs. We then emphasize the evolution of welfare policies for families with children, as this demonstrates how the top policy priority shifted away from raising the incomes of the poor toward raising their work effort.

Although it appears unlikely that the United States will launch a comprehensive anti-poverty effort in the near term, its experiences with anti-poverty policies suggests some promising approaches that might be adopted by nations that choose to make fighting poverty a top priority. In fact, the United Kingdom launched a major anti-poverty initiative in the late 1990s that borrows heavily from U.S. programs and policies. We conclude with a few suggestions for choices in anti-poverty policies that might be relevant for Mexico.

The Scope of Anti-poverty Policy: Spending on Income-tested Programs

Government spending for social welfare is large in the United States, though not as large a percentage of GDP as it is in other countries. The Social Security Administration (2002) defines "public social welfare expenditures" as "cash benefits, services, and administrative costs for all programs operating under public law that are of direct benefit to individuals and families. Included are programs providing for income maintenance through social insurance and public aid, and those providing public support of health, education, housing, and other welfare services."

Social welfare expenditures increased rapidly following the declaration of War on Poverty, rising from 11.0 to 18.2 percent of GDP between 1965 and 1975. In 1995, they comprised 20.9 percent of GDP. However, if spending on health and medical care are excluded, then spending on the remaining programs increased from 9.8 to 15 percent of GDP between 1965 and 1975 and was 14.8 percent in 1995 (Social Security Bulletin 2002). As we show below, the anti-poverty effects of government income transfers follow this same pattern—an increase between the mid-1960s and the mid-1970s, then a leveling off over the next three decades.

Income maintenance programs are the primary levers of anti-poverty policy for dealing with market-generated poverty. These programs may be divided into two categories—social insurance and income-tested (public assistance) programs. Spending on social insurance programs such as social security benefits for the elderly far exceeds spending on income-tested programs such as cash assistance for single mothers and the working poor (Scholz, Moffitt and Cowan 2008).

Eligibility and benefit levels for social insurance programs depend on past contributions (usually paid via payroll taxes on the employer and/or worker) and some identifiable problem, such as old age, death of a spouse or parent of a child, work-related disability, or unemployment. Social insurance programs include social security retirement, disability and survivors' benefits, unemployment insurance, workers' compensation, and veterans' benefits. One generally does not have to prove financial need to claim benefits, but these programs do substantially reduce poverty. Although retirees qualify for social security benefits based on their employment history and not their current incomes, many would be poor in the absence of their social security benefits.

Income-tested programs provide benefits only to those whose incomes (and for some programs, whose assets) from other sources fall below a specified eligibility threshold. The Congressional Research Service (Burke 2003) reports more than 80 such programs that provide cash or other benefits to persons with limited income. These programs include cash assistance, the Earned Income Tax Credit, Food Stamps, school nutrition aid, Medicaid, and programs that fund education, employment and training, housing, and social services.

In this chapter, we describe the evolution of income-tested cash assistance programs, as they have been a source of great political controversy in the United States. The largest cash assistance programs today are Temporary Assistance to Needy Families (TANF) which targets families with children, the Supplemental Security Income program (SSI) for the aged, blind, and disabled, and the Earned Income Tax Credit (EITC) for working poor and near poor families with children.

Cash assistance grew dramatically in the aftermath of the War on Poverty, but has grown slowly after the mid-1970s. For example, in fiscal year 1978, cash benefits were 29 percent of all income-tested benefits, equal in size to the share spent on medical benefits. Food programs comprised 11 percent, work/training programs, 11 percent, with the remainder spent on housing, education, and other services. By fiscal year 2002, in-kind medical benefits (primarily payments to hospitals, nursing homes, and physicians) comprised 54 percent of all expenditures for income-tested programs; the share for cash benefits had dropped to 20 percent and that for work/training programs to 1.5 percent (Burke 2003).

We compare spending on income-tested cash transfers to estimates of the number of pretransfer poor persons. The pretransfer poor are those whose incomes from wages, property income, and other private sources, before the receipt of government benefits, falls below poverty lines. Such a comparison provides a rough estimate of the scope of cash programs targeted on the poor (all figures are in constant 2002 dollars) because some income-tested programs, such as the EITC, provide benefits to families that have incomes up to about twice the poverty line. This indicator demonstrates rapid growth in cash assistance in the decade after the War on Poverty—spending increased by 57 percent, from $681 to $1,067 per pretransfer poor person between 1968 and 1976. Spending per poor person did not change much over the next decade, averaging $987 in 1989. With the rapid rise in the EITC in the 1990s (discussed below), spending per poor person then increased by 47 percent to $1,454 per pretransfer poor person in 2002. To put these amounts in context, the poverty line for a family of four persons was $18,392 in 2002.

The anti-poverty effects of all cash transfers (social insurance and public assistance) on the official poverty rate follow a similar pattern. (The official poverty rate does not value non-cash transfers, such as Food Stamps, housing assistance, or the EITC.) Danziger and Plotnick (1986) find that cash transfers raised the incomes of 37 percent of all pretransfer poor persons above their poverty lines in 1965, rising to 68 percent in 1976. This anti-poverty effect fell to 46 percent in 1983. We estimate that the anti-poverty effect has been relatively constant over the past two decades—it was 47 percent in 2006.[1]

These data foreshadow one of our key conclusions. Most of the increase in the anti-poverty effectiveness of the social safety net occurred in the decade following the War on Poverty, when spending on all social programs increased dramatically. Income-tested spending on cash and near-cash programs for the poor has increased since the mid-1970s mainly because of the emergence of the EITC and its expansion (without political controversy) in the mid-1990s as an anti-poverty policy for working poor families with children. Despite the EITC expansion, however, the anti-poverty effectiveness of government programs was no higher in 2008 than in the late 1970s.[2]

Four Decades of Anti-poverty Policy: Welfare Reform for Families with Children

It is beyond the scope of this chapter to review the evolution of the entire range of U.S. anti-poverty programs and policies. Instead, we focus on cash welfare policies for families with children. Welfare reform generated intense public and policy debates on the nature and goals of anti-poverty policy from the mid-1960s to the mid-1990s, even though, as noted above, most spending growth on income-tested programs since the mid-1970s was for health and medical care programs. Cash welfare spending declined as a percentage of all income-tested spending, but controversy about it increased exponentially.

The key goal of welfare reform proposals in the late 1960s was to reduce poverty by providing cash assistance to poor families with children, both non-working and working. These plans would have extended welfare eligibility limits and raised cash benefit levels. Later, as public dissatisfaction over the rising welfare rolls and rising government welfare spending increased, greater attention was paid to constraining budgetary costs and to promoting work incentives, and, since the mid-1990s, requiring work from non-disabled adult recipients of cash assistance. These policies came to be applied to mothers with children at increasingly younger ages. By the early 1980s, reforming welfare had little to do with reducing poverty; the goal was to reduce reliance on welfare and increase work among the poor, independent of the policy's effect on poverty.

By the mid-1990s, the United States had rejected the idea of fighting poverty by raising the incomes of the non-working poor, but it had not adopted an alternative policy to provide employment to those who seek work but cannot find jobs. It did implement an effective policy for supplementing the earnings of low-income working parents. Our review of major welfare reform proposals from the late 1960s to the mid-1990s emphasizes the rise and fall of poverty reduction as a welfare reform goal, and the rise of work among the poor as a goal in and of itself.

The War on Poverty

The anti-poverty policies proposed when the War on Poverty was launched did not include either a public jobs program or an increase in cash welfare benefits for the non-working poor (except for the aged and disabled). Employment programs were advocated at the outset of the War on Poverty by some policy makers, notably the Secretary of Labor. However, most of President Johnson's economic advisers were confident that stable economic growth could be maintained indefinitely, as it had been since the end of World War II; they expected that a sufficient number of jobs would be available. They emphasized strategies to raise the wages of the working poor. In a Special Message to Congress in March 1964 introducing the Economic Opportunity Act, the President emphasized that if the earnings of the working poor could be raised, welfare spending could be reduced: "If we can raise the annual earnings of 10 million among the poor by only $1000, we will have added 14 billion dollars a year to our national output. In addition, we can make important reductions in public assistance payments."

The centerpiece of the original anti-poverty strategy was a series of labor supply policies designed to raise the low labor market productivity of the poor. Employment and training programs were established or expanded to enhance individual skills, especially for young people, through classroom education and on-the-job training. Graduates of these programs were given job search assistance and launched into the labor market with little concern about the public provision of post-program jobs, as unemployment rates were then at historically low levels, even for less-skilled workers.

Little attention was focused on welfare dependency at that time because the total caseload of the Aid to Families with Dependent Children (AFDC) program was quite small, about 4 million recipients. In the aftermath of welfare program liberalizations brought on by the War on Poverty, caseloads increased to about 6 million by 1969, leading to the first of a long series of Presidential proposals to reform welfare.

The Family Assistance Plan and the Expansion of Welfare

In 1969, President Nixon proposed the Family Assistance Plan (FAP) as a replacement for AFDC. Its centerpiece was a national minimum welfare benefit, a guaranteed annual income that would be coupled with a work requirement for non-working families with no young children. The President stated that "a welfare mother with preschool children should not face benefit reductions if she decides to stay home. It is not our intent that mothers of preschool children must accept work." This view about maternal employment was consistent with both the original goal of AFDC and the conventional wisdom of the 1960s that mothers should stay home and care for their young children.

FAP and other negative income tax (NIT) plans proposed the extension of cash assistance to two-parent families (AFDC provided benefits primarily to single-parent families), the establishment of a national minimum welfare benefit (welfare benefit levels were set by the states and varied widely), the reduction of work disincentives arising from AFDC's high marginal tax rate on earnings, and the de-coupling of cash assistance and social services. These reform proposals sought to reduce poverty and provide work incentives by providing higher benefits to non-working welfare recipients and extending some cash assistance to the working poor who had previously been ineligible for welfare.

Neither the Family Assistance Plan nor any other cash negative income tax for all of the poor was ever approved by both houses of Congress. However, the Food Stamp program evolved into an NIT. By the mid-1970s, it provided a national benefit in food coupons that varied by family size, regardless of state of residence or living arrangements or marital status.

Income maintenance programs continued to expand between the late 1960s and mid-1970s as new programs (e.g. the Earned Income Tax Credit, discussed below, and the Supplemental Security Income) were introduced, benefit levels were increased, and eligibility requirements were liberalized. The number of AFDC recipients increased from about 6 million to 11 million, and the number of Food Stamp recipients increased from about 1 million to 19 million over this period.

As higher cash and in-kind benefits were claimed by a larger percentage of the poor, the work disincentives and high budgetary costs of welfare programs were increasingly challenged by the public and policy makers. A frequent assertion of critics of government programs was that anti-poverty programs subsidized dependency and encouraged idleness. The initial government response was to emphasize programs that could raise the employment and earnings of less-skilled workers.

The first public service employment (PSE) program since the 1930s Great Depression was enacted as part of the Emergency Employment Act in 1971, primarily as a counter-cyclical device to fund jobs with state and local governments. PSE slots were increased by the Comprehensive Employment and Training Act of 1973 (CETA) and became the largest component of the employment and training budget at that time. The 1976 CETA Amendments targeted PSE jobs for the disadvantaged, particularly the long-term unemployed and welfare recipients, and represented the most recent public response to inadequate labor demand for the disadvantaged. In 1978, there were about 750,000 PSE participants.

The Program for Better Jobs and Income: Extending Cash Assistance and Providing Jobs

President Carter's 1977 proposal, the Program for Better Jobs and Income (PBJI), integrated the expansion of cash assistance for both the non-working poor and the working poor via a negative income tax with the PSE jobs emphasis in employment and training policy. If PBJI had been enacted by Congress, it would have created up to 1.4 million minimum-wage public service jobs at an estimated cost of $8.8 billion in 1980 (about $23 billion in 2008 constant dollars). PBJI represents the first (and only) presidential welfare reform proposal since the New Deal in the 1930s to offer jobs to non-working welfare recipients who were expected to work as a condition of cash assistance.

PBJI was ahead of its time. Some elements were adopted two decades later by the 1996 welfare reform; other aspects foreshadowed the drive to "make work pay" that influenced the growth of the Earned Income Tax credit. Its concept of increasing cash assistance while promoting employment was also evident in Prime Minister Blair government's policies in the United Kingdom in the late 1990s.

As was the case with FAP, a single mother with a child age six or younger would have been exempted from the work requirement of PBJI. Those whose youngest child was between the ages of seven and fourteen would have been expected to work part-time; those whose youngest child was over age fourteen would have been expected to work full-time.

By providing jobs of last resort to parents who could not find regular employment and by supplementing low earnings, PBJI would have raised the family income of welfare recipients working at low wages, regardless of family composition or state of residence, and, in many cases would have taken them out of poverty. Of course, the plan would have increased total federal welfare spending substantially, which was a key reason for its rejection by Congress.

PBJI also called attention to insufficient employer demand for less skilled workers. It recognized that some recipients would seek work but would not find a job in the private or public sectors, and that a minimum-wage job of last resort was one way to deal with their involuntary unemployment and provide an alternative to welfare receipt. As we note below, one criticism of the 1996 welfare reform is that it neglected the demand side of the labor market when it ended the entitlement to cash assistance and implemented work requirements without implementing any work opportunity, such as an entitlement to work in exchange for welfare benefits.

PBJI marked the first time that welfare sanctions were proposed for recipients who were expected to work but refused to accept available jobs. For example, if a recipient who was expected to work did not find a part-time job on her own or refused the part-time job of last resort offered by PBJI, she would have lost her share of the family's welfare benefit—the family would have received benefits only for the children. Partial sanctions such as this one, and full-family sanctions, which terminate all benefits when a family does not comply with state rules, became federal mandates after passage of the 1996 welfare reform.

The Reagan Years and the Attack on Welfare Dependency and Welfare Spending

The Reagan Presidency signaled a profound change in welfare policy because the administration showed itself as "rare if not unique in American politics—truly an ideological one" (Glazer 1984). The Reagan administration sought to roll back the welfare programs that had expanded so much in the previous decade. Reducing welfare caseloads and cutting back welfare spending replaced poverty reduction as the primary anti-poverty goal. The emphasis on work intensified.

The Reagan administration opposed what had been a key goal of both FAP and PBJI—simultaneous receipt of wages and welfare benefits by working poor parents. It argued that work effort was best promoted by strict work requirements (proposed, but not enacted by Congress). Public employment was considered an unnecessary intrusion into the private labor market and CETA was abolished. Since the end of CETA more than two decades ago, no President has proposed a public jobs program, either for counter-cyclical purposes to help the unemployed during recessions or for structural purposes to help the long-term jobless or as an alternative to cash assistance.

The Omnibus Budget Reconciliation Act of 1981 reduced the welfare rolls by about 14 percent and eliminated work incentive provisions that had been in place since the late 1960s. This policy change contributed to increased public dissatisfaction with welfare because it made it very difficult for the working poor to receive cash welfare; most of those eliminated from welfare had been poor working parents. From this point on, the very high rate of non-workers among welfare recipients would become the key criticism of opponents of AFDC. Consider this conclusion from a task force convened at the American Enterprise Institute:

> Money alone will not cure poverty; internalized values are also needed.... The most disturbing element among a fraction of the contemporary poor is an inability to seize opportunity even when it is available and while others around them are seizing it.... Their need is less for job training than for meaning and order in their lives.... An indispensable resource in the war against poverty is a sense of personal responsibility. (Novak et al. 1987)

The War on Poverty had set a "modest goal" of eliminating income poverty. By the mid-1980s, personal responsibility had replaced income poverty as the primary concern of many advocates of welfare reforms.

The Earned Income Tax Credit: Expanding Cash Assistance for Working Poor Parents

Although increased cash assistance for non-working welfare recipients had been rejected by the mid-1980s, the last two decades have been marked by a dramatic increase in cash assistance to working poor and near-poor parents who receive the Earned Income Tax Credit (EITC). The EITC, enacted in 1975, was a legacy of the failure of Nixon's Family Assistance Plan. When Congress rejected the idea of raising cash welfare for non-workers, it adopted a program that included some elements of the NIT, but rejected others.

Under a negative income tax, the welfare payment is at a maximum for a family without work; then the welfare benefit falls at some fixed rate (the marginal tax rate or benefit reduction rate) as earnings rise. In contrast, EITC payments are zero for a non-worker. They increase instead at a fixed rate as earnings increase (the marginal tax rate is negative) and reach a maximum value at an earnings level that is similar to annual earnings for a full-time, full-year (about 2000 hours per year) minimum-wage worker. EITC payments stay at the maximum benefit over a small range of incomes and then fall at a fixed rate (here the marginal tax rate is positive, as it is for an NIT) as incomes rise beyond this range before phasing out at income levels at about twice the poverty line.

The EITC avoids the social stigma associated with welfare receipt in part because the Internal Revenue Service administers it. After the family files its income tax for the calendar year, it will receive a check if its EITC exceeds the income tax owed. The EITC is available to both one- and two-parent families and provides a benefit level that is constant across the nation. (About a dozen states have chosen to implement a state EITC on top of the federal one.) The maximum federal EITC for a family with two or more children (in current dollars) was $400 in 1975, $550 in 1986, $953 in 1991, and $4,824 in 2008.

The EITC was increased as part of tax reform legislation during the Reagan, G. H. W. Bush, and Clinton administrations. For the most part, it has had broad, bipartisan Congressional support, and has been mostly invisible to the public, even though the number of recipients and the total costs have increased substantially. The number of families benefiting from the EITC each year between 1975 and 1986 was between 5 and 7.5 million. This increased to about 11 million families by 1988 and to 23 million by 2005 (http://www.taxpolicycenter.org/taxfacts/displayafact.cfm?Docid=37).

In 1975, a family with one parent working full-time full-year at the minimum wage received an EITC payment that was about 10 percent of her annual earnings; by 1990, the EITC reached 15 percent of her earnings. By 2003, because of a large expansion implemented by the Clinton administration, the EITC was 40 percent of the annual earnings of a minimum-wage parent of two children. The EITC increases each year with inflation, whereas the minimum wage did not increase at all between 1997 and 2007. In 2005, federal expenditures for the EITC were $42.4 billion for about 22.7 million families, about twice the combined spending of the federal and state governments on about 2 million families who received benefits from the cash welfare program, Temporary Assistance to Needy Families. In contrast, in the mid-1970s, spending on cash welfare was about 10 times the spending on the EITC (Scholz, Moffitt and Cowan 2008, Appendix Table 1). Cash welfare benefits have not been raised in many states for more than 20 years.

The Family Support Act: Maintaining Welfare and Supporting Work

The Family Support Act (FSA) of 1988 reflected a bipartisan consensus crafted by Senator Daniel Patrick Moynihan in which liberals achieved a broader safety net and conservatives achieved stronger work requirements. The Act expanded the AFDC program for two-parent families, instituted transitional funding for childcare expenses and Medicaid for recipients leaving welfare for work, and required states to establish the Job Opportunities and Basic Skills Training Program (JOBS) to move greater numbers of welfare recipients into jobs.

Liberals and conservatives still disagreed on other goals of welfare-to-work programs and the bipartisan spirit of the FSA lasted for only a few years. Liberals thought welfare reform should provide greater opportunities for beneficiaries to receive training and work experiences to help them get "good jobs" at higher wages when they moved from welfare to work. Conservatives emphasized work requirements—obligations welfare mothers owed in return for government support whether or not their family incomes increased. They argued that any job was a good job that could provide labor force experience and set the stage for higher-paying jobs in the future.

During the welfare reform debate of the early 1990s, work requirements took center stage. One of the most successful JOBS programs, in terms of getting recipients into employment (Riverside, California), had developed a "work first" strategy. Work First programs adopt the philosophy "that any job is a good job and that the best way to succeed in the labor market is to join it, developing work habits and skills on the job rather than in a classroom" (Brown 1997, p. 2). A Work First approach reduces the need for government funds for education, training, or expanded support services and allows more recipients to be served with a fixed budget. In addition, the increased EITC subsidy for low-earners made it easier to justify placing recipients into any job, rather than training them for "good jobs."

JOBS also raised work expectations and provided partial sanctions for recipients who did not co-operate. It lowered the age of the recipient's child: once her youngest child reached age three, the mother had to participate for up to 20 hours per week; once that child reached age six, she could be required to participate for up to 40 hours per week. Participating meant agreeing to a reasonable "employability plan" the state devised, as long as the state provided childcare, transportation, and other work-related expenses.

JOBS reflected a commitment to mutual responsibility: recipients were required to exercise personal responsibility and take advantage of education, training, and work opportunities, which the government had the responsibility to provide. If a state did not provide a JOBS slot (and many states did not), the recipient was not sanctioned. Within a few years, however, personal responsibility would take center stage and such requirements on the states would be greatly reduced.

The 1996 Welfare Reform: The End of the Entitlement to Cash Assistance

Welfare rolls jumped in the late 1980s and early 1990s from about 11 to about 14 million recipients, in part because of a recession, giving rise to the perception that JOBS had failed and that the Family Support Act was flawed. During the 1992 Presidential campaign, candidate Clinton made welfare reform one of his top domestic priorities, pledging to "end welfare as we know it." A contentious welfare reform debate raged in the mid-1990s, and the President vetoed several bills put forward by the Republican Congress.

In 1996, however, he signed a bill that had initially been put forward by the Republicans, the Personal Responsibility and Work Opportunity Reconciliation Act of 1996 (PRWORA). The Act replaced AFDC with Temporary Assistance for Needy Families (TANF) and ended the entitlement to cash assistance that had been in place since AFDC was created by the Social Security Act in the 1930s. Under PRWORA, each state decided who receives cash assistance, subject only to a requirement that they receive "fair and equitable treatment." PRWORA reduced the total spending required from the federal and state governments. The federal contribution changed from a matching grant to a block grant that was capped for each state at its fiscal year 1994 spending level. Moreover, the states could reduce their spending by 25 percent from their 1994 spending levels.

Each state could pursue whatever kind of reform it chose, including reforms that would provide transitional public service jobs. In practice, however, most states have worked harder to cut welfare caseloads than to provide work opportunities and services to current recipients or those who left the rolls without finding employment.

The centerpiece of the Clinton reform was its time limit—states may not use federal funds to provide more than a lifetime total of 60 months of cash assistance to any welfare recipient; they have the option to set shorter time limits. States can grant exceptions to the lifetime limit and continue using federal funds for up to 20 percent of the caseload.

Work expectations were increased substantially. Single mothers with no child under age three were expected to work or participate in work-related activities at least 30 hours per week to maintain eligibility for cash assistance. States could require participation regardless of the age of the youngest child. Whereas President Nixon proposed exemptions for mothers of children under age six, some states exempt a mother for only 13 weeks following childbirth.

Lessons Learned from the PRWORA Experience

The 1996 welfare reform achieved a number of its goals—caseloads declined to the lowest levels in decades, more single mothers worked, child poverty fell modestly, and many states used funds previously spent on cash assistance for non-workers to increasingly supplement low earnings and subsidize childcare and other services for the working poor. However, a significant minority of welfare recipients have serious personal problems that have kept them from working steadily under these administrative rules even during the economic boom of the late 1990s, when unemployment rates fell to their lowest levels in 30 years. We draw several lessons from the PRWORA experience.

First, welfare no longer provides an alternative to working to support a family, as conservative critics of AFDC had been charging since the 1980s (Murray 1984). TANF has made it very unlikely that a single mother could "choose" to remain a non-working welfare recipient, even if the economic benefits of a minimum-wage job do not exceed the costs. Because cash assistance is conditional on the performance of work-related activities, those not searching for work or co-operating with the welfare agency can be sanctioned and can lose both cash assistance and Food Stamps. Other changes in regulations made it more difficult to qualify for welfare and harder to stay on the rolls.

Second, in response to pressures from welfare agencies and higher returns to work due to changes in other state and federal policies for the working poor (discussed next), greater numbers of single mothers entered the labor force after the mid-1990s. The percentage of single mothers with children under the age of 18 who worked at any time during the year was about 70 percent for most of the period from the late 1960s to the late 1980s. After the economic boom and welfare reform, this annual employment rate increased to 85 percent prior to the 2001 recession.

Third, the increase in poverty that critics of the 1996 law predicted did not happen even though most former recipients are working less than full-time, full-year, and earn relatively low wages. This result reflects changes in state and federal policies for the working poor that were also implemented in the mid-1990s (e.g., a minimum-wage increase in 1997, higher earnings disregards within TANF that allow workers to receive cash assistance, and the expansion of the EITC), which helped current/former recipients achieve higher net incomes.

The Reagan administration had reduced the extent of work among AFDC recipients by reducing income disregards. After four months at work, a recipient's benefit fell by about one dollar for each dollar earned (100 percent marginal tax rate), creating a "welfare trap." In response to PRWORA's granting them more autonomy, about two-thirds of the states eliminated this "welfare trap" by increasing earnings disregards that allow recipients to keep more of their welfare benefits as their earnings increase. States have also increased spending on childcare for current/former recipients—in some states, more is now being spent on childcare than on cash assistance and childcare subsidies are also available to many poor who have never received cash welfare.

Federal policy changes outside of welfare also increased the benefits of leaving welfare for work. The minimum wage increased from $4.25 to $5.15 in 1997. It remained at this level until it was raised by Congress to $5.85 in July 2007; it then increased to $6.55 in July 2008 and $7.25 in July 2009. As noted above, the 1993 EITC expansion increased the maximum annual credit for a full-time, full-year minimum-wage worker with two or more children from less than $1,000 in 1990 to $4,824 in 2008.

The State Child Health Insurance Program (SCHIP) of 1997 and changes in Medicaid policies expanded public health insurance coverage so that jobs not providing subsidized health coverage are now more attractive. By the end of the 1990s, leaving welfare for work was less likely to leave a mother and her children uninsured than in the past. However, the percentage of all Americans without insurance was higher in 2007 (16 percent) than in 1985 (13 percent).

Fourth, a minority of welfare recipients have worked very little in the aftermath of PRWORA. These women tend to have low levels of human capital, few specific job skills and work experiences, and high levels of health and mental health problems and experiences of domestic violence (Danziger and Seefeldt 2002). The Work First programs implemented after the 1996 reform by most states emphasized rapid labor force attachment and were based on the assumption that most recipients could quickly become job-ready. As a result, they did not typically screen recipients for these personal problems or offer services to address such problems (Danziger and Seefeldt 2000).

We think it is reasonable, given American preferences for work, that welfare recipients without serious personal impairments should have the personal responsibility to search diligently for work. However, if job search does not produce a job within a reasonable period, we think that government should assume more responsibility and not simply terminate cash assistance. For example, recipients who reach time limits without meeting work requirements could be offered a chance to work in community service jobs in return for cash assistance.

A more costly option, but one that would have a greater anti-poverty impact, would be to provide a transitional low-wage public service job of last resort to the long-term jobless. Welfare recipients who were willing to work could then combine wages with the EITC and support their families even when there was little demand by private employers for their skills. For recipients with extensive personal problems, there remains a need to expand social service and treatment programs and to experiment with supported work or other forms of transitional job assistance.

The 1996 welfare reform terminated the cash-based safety net that provided monthly checks for non-working poor families. However, if the modest success of welfare reform in reducing poverty (discussed below) is to be increased, additional funds will be needed to complete the task of creating a work-oriented safety net.

Trends in Poverty and the Anti-poverty Effects of Cash and Non-cash Transfers

What have been the effects of four decades of changes in social welfare spending and the policy changes discussed above on the trend in income poverty and the anti-poverty effects of government transfers? We address these issues by focusing on differences between the trends for the elderly and the trends for families with children.

Trends in Poverty Rates

As mentioned above, the safety net became much more effective for the elderly than for anyone else in the aftermath of the War on Poverty. As a result, over the last four decades their economic status increased relative to that of children and non-elderly adults.[3] Figure 1 shows a dramatic reduction in poverty among the elderly. In 1959, the official poverty rate of elderly persons was 35.2 percent, more than twice the 17.0 percent rate for adults 18 to 64. In 2006, the rate for the elderly had fallen to 9.4 percent, lower than the 10.8 percent rate for adults.[4]

Poverty declined for all age groups in the 1960s, when economic growth was rapid. Yet, between 1969 and 2006, there was no additional progress against poverty for adults or children. The poverty rate for adults was 8.7 percent in 1969 and 10.8 percent in 2006; for children, the rates were 14.0

percent in 1969 and 17.4 percent in 2006. The three decades following the early 1970s were characterized by slow economic growth, declining real wages for less-educated workers, falling inflation-adjusted cash welfare payments for families with children, declines in the percentage of the unemployed receiving unemployment insurance, and a declining real minimum wage.

In contrast, poverty fell for the elderly in each decade. Most of the decline in their poverty rate in the first two decades is attributable to increased government benefits. Between 1965 and 1973, Congress legislated seven across-the-board increases in Social Security benefits. For example, Congress increased benefits by 13 percent in 1968, by 15 percent in 1969, by 10 percent in 1971, and by 20 percent in 1972 (Derthick 1979, pp. 431–432). Then Congress passed the inflation-indexation of Social Security benefits to begin in 1975.

In addition, the Supplemental Security Program (SSI), enacted in 1972, is a negative income tax or guaranteed annual income for the elderly, blind, and disabled. SSI provides a non-contributory, income-tested cash welfare benefit to any elderly person who did not work enough to qualify for Social Security benefits; it also provides supplements to those who had low earnings and hence a low Social Security benefit. All of the poor elderly, but not all poor children or adults, are thus entitled to a monthly cash benefit.

From the early 1970s to the early 1990s, the earnings of workers failed to keep up with inflation. As a result, average Social Security benefits increased relative to average wages, relative to the poverty line, and relative to the government benefits available to the non-elderly. For example, in 1960, the mean annual Social Security benefit for an elderly married couple was 80 percent of their poverty line. The mean Social Security benefit rose to the same level as their poverty line in 1970 and to 34 percent more than that line in 1980 (Smolenksy, Danziger, and Gottschalk 1988). In 1964, the Social Security benefit for a single male retiree was 20 percent of the mean annual earnings of a non-supervisory production worker. By 1999, this ratio had increased to 45 percent.

Figure 2 compares trends in the extent to which families headed by an elderly person and one-parent families with children are supported by government programs. For each year from 1979 to 2006, we show the percentage of family income after taxes and transfers that results from government cash and near cash transfers (for example, Food Stamps, school lunch benefits, and housing benefits) and the earned income tax credit. These data are based on computations from the annual March Current

Population Surveys. They show little change in the extent to which elderly families rely on government support. The typical family headed by an elderly person received about 54 to 59 percent of its post-tax, post-transfer income from government programs in each of the years shown. In contrast, reliance on government support for single-parent families has dramatically fallen over this period. The typical one-parent family received about 25 percent of its income from government benefits in 1979, but only 13 percent in 2006. Given these trends, it will come as no surprise that the anti-poverty effectiveness of government transfers is much greater for the elderly than for families with children.

The Anti-poverty Effects of Government Transfers

We have shown that the U.S. safety net seems quite comprehensive for the elderly, but not for families with children. Rainwater and Smeeding (2004) show that other industrialized countries provide much more generous benefits to families with children than does the U.S. government. As a result, these countries do not have the wide difference between the poverty rates of children and the elderly that we showed in Figure 1.

We now turn to an analysis of how the anti-poverty effects of government transfers have evolved over the past several decades. Table 1 reports trends in the official poverty measure (which does not count non-cash benefits or the EITC) between 1967 and 1979 for elderly persons in the top panel, for families with children headed by males in the middle panel, and for families with children headed by females in the bottom panel. In each panel, we show the poverty rate before and after cash transfers.

Table 2 reports similar trends between 1979 and 2002 for elderly persons and for children, using a more comprehensive poverty measure that does include the receipt of non-cash transfers and the EITC and subtracts income and payroll taxes paid. The series in Table 2 provides a better picture of the anti-poverty effects of the safety net, but comparable data are not available for the years prior to 1979.

The top panel of Table 1 shows a dramatic increase in the anti-poverty effects of cash transfers for the elderly. In both 1967 and 1979, the poverty rate for the elderly would have been about 58 percent if they had relied entirely on their market income.[5] Cash transfers reduced poverty by 28.6 percentage points in 1967 and by 43.8 points in 1979. Thus, the entire decline in the official poverty rate for the elderly during this period was due to the anti-poverty effects of cash transfers.

The top panel of Table 2 shows that the entire decline in poverty among the elderly between 1979 and 2002 was due to their increasing market income, as their pretransfer poverty rate declined from 54.2 to 49.9 percent. In each year, transfers had a very large impact, reducing poverty by about 41 percentage points.

The bottom two panels of Table 1 show that much of the poverty reduction for families with children was due to growth in market incomes, not cash transfers. For families with male heads, poverty declined by 2.8 percentage points between 1967 and 1979 (from 10.0 to 7.2 percent), with 1.9 points due to declining pretransfer poverty (from 11.5 to 9.6 percent) and 0.9 points due to the increased anti-poverty effect of transfers (from 1.5 to 2.4 points).

For single-mother families, pretransfer poverty rates are higher than 50 percent, as high as the elderly pretransfer poverty rate; however, officially, the poverty rate for single-mother families is actually much higher than that of the elderly, because of the less-effective safety net for families with children. Between 1967 and 1979, their poverty rate fell by 5.8 percentage points (from 49.1 to 43.3 percent), with 5.3 points due to reduced pretransfer poverty (from 58.8 to 53.5 percent) and only 0.5 points due to the increased anti-poverty effects of transfers (from 9.7 to 10.2 points).

As mentioned, Table 1 does not account for the rapid growth in non-cash transfers and the EITC. Thus, for children, Table 2 provides a much better perspective on how changes in welfare policies and the EITC have affected child poverty over the last quarter century.

Consider the period from 1979 to 1996, an era of intense welfare reform debate, slow growth in real wages, falling welfare benefits, and rapidly rising EITC payments. Market income poverty among all children increased by 3.5 percentage points over these 17 years (from 20.1 to 23.6 percent). Cash and non-cash transfers reduced poverty by 6.8 percentage points in 1979 and by a bit less, 5.8 points in 1996 (for each year, subtract the rate in row 2 from that in row 1). However, the anti-poverty effects of the EITC became significant. In 1979, the Social Security and income taxes paid by the poor actually exceeded their EITC payments, so that the row 3 poverty rate was 0.3 points higher than the one in row 2. By 1996, the EITC reduced child poverty by 1.7 percentage points (17.8–16.1 percent); the anti-poverty effect of the EITC increased further to 2.2 percentage points by 2002 (14.8–12.6 percent).

Over the 23-year period from 1979 to 2002, market income poverty for families with children fell by only 0.4 points, the anti-poverty effect of cash and non-cash transfers fell by 1.9 points, and the anti-poverty effect of the EITC increased by 2.5 points. The net result was a child poverty rate that dropped by only one percentage point over a generation (from 13.6 to 12.6

percent). The EITC emerged as the primary anti-poverty policy for families with children when Americans rejected the notion of cash assistance for the non-working poor and turned instead to cash assistance for the working poor.

The anti-poverty effects of government programs can also be evaluated by measuring the percentage reduction in the pretransfer poverty gap due to government transfers. The poverty gap is the dollar amount needed to bring all poor persons up to the poverty line. Since it is a continuous measure, the poverty gap can show a different pattern than the trend in the percentage of persons taken out of poverty by transfers. For example, consider a family whose market income was $4,000 below their poverty line that received $4,200 from the maximum EITC. In this year, the family would be taken out of poverty by the EITC, and the EITC would have filled 100 percent of the poverty gap. Now assume that a recession occurs, pretransfer income falls to $5,000 below the poverty line, and the $4,200 EITC is still received. Now, this family is not taken out of poverty by transfers; however, the poverty gap is reduced by 84 percent ($4,200/5,000).

The poverty gap (U.S. House of Representatives, 2004) is reduced less by government programs for children than for the elderly in any year. For the elderly, this reduction was around 90 percent for every year between 1979 and 2002. The anti-poverty effects of the safety net on children follow a pattern that is consistent with the policy history reviewed above. In 1979, cash, non-cash transfers, and the EITC reduced their poverty gap by about 62 percent; after the Reagan budget cuts and the recession of the early 1980s, this effect declined to 57 percent in 1983. In the midst of an economic boom and after the 1993 EITC expansion, 62 percent of the pretransfer poverty gap for children was filled in 1996. After the 1996 welfare reductions and the recession of 2001, this declined to 54 percent.

The U.S. Experience Compared to Other Countries

While most presidents after Lyndon Johnson have given major addresses on welfare reform, we are not aware of any president who proposed a major anti-poverty initiative. Since the Nixon administration, poverty has fallen from the top of the public's agenda to the periphery. Despite its ideological commitment to providing equality of opportunity, the United States has in place a less-effective safety net than that of most other industrialized nations.

Poverty is not a high priority for the public either. A 2001 poll by the Henry J. Kaiser Family Foundation found that only 10 percent of the population considered poverty, welfare, or something similar as one of the top

two issues government should address, whereas 20 percent or more mentioned health care, education, and tax reform. The poll reported the following about the public's view of the 1996 welfare reform:

> Americans who know about the new welfare law like the way it is
> working.... And the most important reason they give for why it is
> working well is that it requires people to go to work. Americans
> appear to value work so strongly that they support welfare reform
> even if it leads to jobs that keep people in poverty. The vast major-
> ity of those who know there has been a major change in the wel-
> fare laws (73 %) *believes that people who have left the welfare rolls
> are still poor, despite having found jobs* [emphasis added].

Thus, it seems that poverty is higher in the United States than in other
industrialized countries in part because Americans want to increase work
among the poor more than they want to reduce income poverty. These
preferences are long-standing. Ladd and Bowman (1998) review opinion
polls from industrialized countries and conclude that Americans "are
inclined to the idea that opportunity is present to those who avail themselves of it. As a result, they are unsympathetic to government redistribution of wealth" (p. 115). They cite a 1992 poll that asked, "Do you agree or
disagree that it is the responsibility of the government to reduce the differences in income between people with high incomes and those with low
incomes?" and "Do you agree or disagree that the government should provide everyone with a guaranteed income?" The percentages reporting
"agree" plus "strongly agree" were lower in the United States (38 and 35
percent, respectively), than in Australia (43 and 51 percent), Sweden (53
and 46 percent), the United Kingdom (66 and 68 percent), and West Ger-
many (66 and 58 percent).

In contrast, U.K. Prime Minister Tony Blair made poverty a high priority for his administration in 1999, stating, "Our historic aim will be for
ours to be the first generation to end child poverty, and it will take a generation. It is a 20-year mission but I believe it can be done." The anti-
poverty policies put into place in the United Kingdom are based to a
significant extent on U.S. experiences and poverty policy research. The
broad categories in which significant new U.K. programs have been set up
and in which funding for existing programs has been increased are
designed to promote "work for those who can, security for those who cannot," to increase investments in children, and to expand opportunity and
intergenerational mobility.

A major departure from the U.S. experience is that the Blair government increased cash welfare benefits. In 2003, these benefits were 85 percent higher in real terms than in 1997. Universal child benefits also increased by 25 percent over this period. A Working Families Tax Credit was put into place that is similar to the structure of the EITC in that benefits rise with earnings and then fall. Moreover, the credits are more generous relative to the average wage and are paid to a greater percentage of families, including childless working adults. A minimum wage that is higher as a percentage of the average wage than is the U.S. minimum wage was also introduced.

Other U.K. programs have been modeled on the U.S. experience. The Sure Start program for early childhood enrichment is similar to the U.S. Head Start program. There are also expanded childcare funds to guarantee slots in preschool and expand access to childcare. They have expanded paid parental leave and are currently providing tax-free child savings accounts.

In total, U.K. spending on children increased by about 75 percent between 1997 and 2004, representing an additional 1 percent of GDP, and child poverty has fallen substantially (Hills and Waldfogel 2004). As this U.K. experience demonstrates, if there is a political will to reduce poverty, there are many public policies that can be put in place to achieve child poverty reduction.

Implications for Anti-poverty Policy in Mexico

An anti-poverty initiative in any country will have a hard time succeeding if that country does not achieve and maintain stable economic growth. In addition, the increasingly competitive globalized economy and continuing rapid technological changes require that substantial effort be given to raising the human capital and skills of the labor force. Globalization and labor-saving technological changes are exerting strong pressure in all countries, including the United States, to hold down labor costs. Thus, productivity increases are the best way to raise real wages. In the long run, this primarily requires an increase in access to schooling to raise the educational attainment of the labor force. Attention to both macroeconomic and education policies is a necessary component of successful poverty reduction strategies. These policies are discussed in other chapters in this volume.

The experiences of the United States in the 1960s and the United Kingdom since the late 1990s suggest that powerful political leadership and a willingness to devote additional resources to the problems of the poor are prerequisites for launching a major anti-poverty initiative. The U.S.

policies have been successful over the long run in reducing poverty among the elderly; the U.K. policy has succeeded in its newer comprehensive set of child poverty reduction programs. In both cases, government spending increased substantially.

What are the implications for Mexico, assuming that it can muster the political willingness to devote sufficient resources to an anti-poverty agenda? We consider it essential that the anti-poverty agenda promote both work and income security for the poor and increase the educational attainment of children from poor families. A daunting challenge of such programs is how best to fund them, given the problems of the tax base in Mexico and other economies where the rural sector and the informal sector account for a substantial share of total economic activity.

For example, earnings supplements for working poor families with children, such as the Earned Income Tax Credit or the Working Families Tax Credit, work well only in countries where most workers participate in the payroll tax and income tax systems, as these records are required to determine the amount of the poor family's credit. We realize that such programs are not feasible in many developing economies.

Instead, Mexico has demonstrated a creative new mechanism for helping poor families with children that has already spread to other developing economies—conditional cash transfer programs like the *Progresa/Oportunidades* program (Escobar 2009). It seems feasible for Mexico to expand cash assistance and other assistance to the poor through similar means-tested programs. Other Latin American countries are developing such conditional cash transfer programs with the expectation that they can not only reduce economic hardship but also lead to positive educational and health outcomes for recipients (Rawlings 2004; Gertler and Boyce 2001).

We think it is possible to build on both the U.S. experience and the *Progresa/Oportunidades* experience to develop a non-contributory, income-tested cash transfer for the Mexican elderly. Indeed, in 2005 the program did devise a new component specifically for the old, meant to allow them to maintain or increase their cash transfers. Since the 1970s, the United States has had such a program for the elderly, blind, and disabled poor—the Supplemental Security Income program. To the extent that the elderly share residences with their children and grandchildren in developing countries, cash payments to the elderly poor have spillover effects that also raise the living standards of substantial numbers of the non-elderly poor.

For example, Barrientos (2003) analyzed the anti-poverty effects of non-contributory pension programs for the elderly in Brazil and South

Africa and found that persons who reside in a household with a pension recipient have an 18 percent lower probability of being poor in Brazil and a 12 percent lower probability in South Africa than those whose households do not contain a pension recipient. He reviews other studies that show that such non-contributory pension programs enable physical and human capital investments within households, strengthen intergenerational transfers, and encourage local economic activity. Because these programs are targeted for the elderly, there is little concern about reduced work incentives, as there would be with a program that was not conditioned on old age.

Mexico has already put in place an administrative mechanism that seems to have successfully implemented the income-tested *Progresa/Oportunidades* program. It seems feasible to create a similar mechanism to distribute the benefits of a non-contributory pension program.

There are likely to be many other components to an anti-poverty strategy for the Mexican economy. However, poverty is likely to remain high if fighting poverty is not a top national priority. This is another lesson that can be learned from the U.S. experience of the last several decades—in the absence of anti-poverty policies, the poor are not likely to benefit fully from the GDP gains generated by a growing economy in the current global economic environment.

Tables and Figures

Table 1. Poverty Rates and Anti-Poverty Effects of Cash Income Transfers, 1967

Poverty Rate	1967	1979
Elderly Persons Age 65 and Older		
(1) Before Transfers	58.3	58.9
(2) After Cash Transfers	29.7	15.1
Percentage Point Reduction in Poverty (1) – (2)	28.6	43.8
Persons Living in Families with Children: Male Family Head		
(1) Before Transfers	11.5	9.6
(2) After Cash Transfers	10.0	7.2
Percentage Point Reduction in Poverty (1) – (2)	1.5	2.4
Persons Living in Families with Children: Female Family Head		
(1) Before Transfers	58.8	53.5
(2) After Cash Transfers	49.1	43.3
Percentage Point Reduction in Poverty (1) – (2)	9.7	10.2

Source: Danziger and Weinberg, 1994.

Table 2. Poverty Rates and Anti-Poverty Effects of All Income Transfers and Federal Tax Credits, Selected Years, 1979–2002

Poverty Rate	1979	1996	2002
Elderly Persons Age 65 and Older			
(1) Before Transfers	54.2	50.1	49.9
(2) After Cash and Non-cash Transfers	13.5	9.2	9.0
(3) After EITC and Less Taxes Paid	13.5	9.2	9.0
Percentage Point Reduction in Poverty (1) – (3)	40.7	40.9	40.9
Children Under 18			
(1) Before Transfers	20.1	23.6	19.7
(2) After Cash and Non-cash Transfers	13.3	17.8	14.8
(3) After EITC and Less Taxes Paid	13.6	16.1	12.6
Percentage Point Reduction in Poverty (1) – (3)	6.5	7.5	7.1

Source: U.S. House of Representatives, 2004 Green Book, Appendix H.

Figure 1. Poverty Rates by Age, 1959–2006

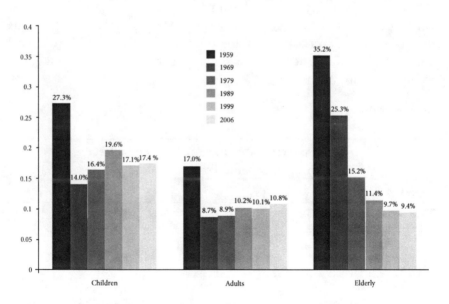

Source: Census Bureau (March CPS Historical Poverty Table 3)

Figure 2. Percentage of Post-tax, Post-transfer Income from Government Programs

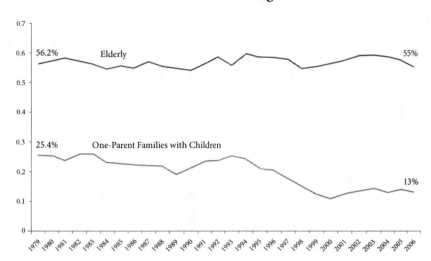

Note: Income from government programs includes cash transfers, near-cash transfers such as Food Stamps, and refundable tax credits net of federal, state, and local payroll and income taxes paid. Source: Authors' calculations from March CPS

Notes

1   This estimate is based on computations by the authors from the March Current Population Surveys.

2   Spending on medical programs for the elderly and the poor has increased dramatically since the introduction of Medicare and Medicaid in 1965. The official Census Bureau poverty measure does not consider benefits from these programs when measuring poverty or the anti-poverty effects of government programs.

3   For further discussion of trends in poverty for other demographic groups, see Danziger and Gottschalk (2005).

4   The official poverty rate is based on the sum of money income from all sources received by all family members. Non-cash transfers, such as Food Stamps, and refundable tax credits, such as the EITC, are not counted as money income.

5   The calculations reported here make the simplifying assumption that there are no labor-supply or savings responses to transfers that have caused market incomes to be lower, and hence the number of pre-transfer poor persons to be higher, than they would have been in the absence of transfers. Because

transfers do induce such behavioral changes, the anti-poverty effects shown in Tables 1 and 2 should be considered as upper bounds.

References

Barrientos, Armando. 2003. "What Is the Impact of Non-contributory Pensions on Poverty? Estimates from Brazil and South Africa." Manchester, U.K.: Institute for Development, Policy and Management, University of Manchester. http://idpm.man.ac.uk.

Blair, Tony. 1999. "Beveridge Revisited: A Welfare State for the 21st Century." In R. Walker, ed. *Ending Child Poverty: Popular Welfare for the 21st Century?* pp. 7–18. Bristol, U.K.: Policy Press.

Burke, Vee. 2003. *Cash and Noncash Benefits for Persons with Limited Income: Eligibility Rules, Recipient and Expenditure Data, FY2000–FY2002.* Washington, D.C.: Congressional Research Service, Order Code RL3223.

Brown, Amy. 1997. *Work First: How to Implement an Employment-focused Approach to Welfare Reform.* New York: Manpower Demonstration Research Corporation.

Danziger, Sandra K., and Kristin Seefeldt. 2000. "Ending Welfare through Work First: Manager and Client Views." *Families in Society.* 81/6: 593–604.

———. 2002. "Barriers to Employment and the Hard to Serve." *Focus.* Madison, WI: Institute for Research on Poverty.

Danziger, Sheldon. 2001. "Welfare Reform Policy from Nixon to Clinton." In D. Featherman and M. Vinovskis, eds. *Social Science and Policy Making.* pp. 137–164. Ann Arbor, MI: University of Michigan Press.

Danziger, Sheldon and Peter Gottschalk. 2005. "Diverging Fortunes: Trends in Poverty and Inequality." In R. Farley and J. Haaga, eds. *The American People, Census 2000.* pp. 49–75. New York: Russell Sage Foundation.

Danziger, Sheldon, and Robert Plotnick. 1986. "Anti-poverty Policy: Effects on the Poor and the Nonpoor." In S. Danziger and D. Weinberg, eds. *Fighting Poverty: What Works and What Doesn't.* pp. 50–77. Cambridge, MA: Harvard University Press.

Danziger, Sheldon and Daniel Weinberg. 1994. "The Historical Record: Trends in Family Income, Inequality, and Poverty." In S. Danziger, G. Sandefur and D. Weinberg, eds. *Confronting Poverty: Prescriptions for Change.* pp. 18–50. Cambridge, MA: Harvard University Press.

Derthick, Martha. 1979. *Policy Making for Social Security.* Washington, D.C.: Brookings Institution.

Escobar Latapí, Agustín. 2009. Chapter 7 in this book.

Gertler, Paul J., and Simone Boyce. 2001. "An Experiment in Incentive-based Welfare: The Impact of PROGRESA on Health in Mexico." unpublished, University of California-Berkeley, Haas School of Business.

Galbraith, John K. 1958. _The Affluent Society_. New York: New American Library.

Harrington, Michael. 1962. _The Other America: Poverty in the United States_. New York: Macmillan.

Henry J. Kaiser Family Foundation. 2001. National Survey on Poverty in America. http://www.kff.org.

Hills, John and Jane Waldfogel. 2004. "A 'Third Way' in Welfare Reform? Evidence from the United Kingdom." _Journal of Policy Analysis and Management_, 23/4: 765–788.

Ladd, Everett, and Karlyn Bowman. 1998. _Attitudes toward Economic Inequality_. Washington, D.C.: American Enterprise Institute.

Lampman, Robert. 1959. _The Low-income Population and Economic Growth_. U.S. Congress, Joint Economic Committee, Study Paper no. 12. Washington, DC: GPO.

Lampman, Robert. 1971. _Ends and Means of Reducing Income Poverty_. Chicago: Markham.

Murray, Charles. 1984. _Losing Ground: American Social Policy, 1950–1980_. New York: Basic Books.

Nixon, Richard M. 1969. Welfare Reform: A Message from the President of the United States. House Document No. 91–146, _Congressional Record_, Vol. 115, no. 136, The House of Representatives, 91st Congress, First Session, H7239–7241.

Novak, Michael et al. 1987. _The New Consensus on Family and Welfare: A Community of Self-reliance_. Milwaukee, WI: Marquette University.

Rawlings, Laura. 2004. "A New Approach to Social Assistance: Latin America's Experience with Conditional Cash Transfer Programs." Washington, D.C.: Social Protection Unit, Human Development Network. http://www.world-bank.org/sp.

Rainwater, Lee, and Timothy Smeeding. 2004. _Poor Kids in a Rich Country: America's Children in Comparative Perspective_. New York: Russell Sage Foundation.

Scholz, John Karl, Robert Moffitt, and Benjamin Cowan. 2008. "Trends in Income Support." Madison, WI: Institute for Research on Poverty.

Smolensky, Eugene, Sheldon Danziger, and Peter Gottschalk. 1988. "The Declining Significance of Age in the United States: Trends in the Well-being of Children and the Elderly since 1939." In J. Palmer, T. Smeeding, and B. Torrey, eds. _The Vulnerable_. pp. 29–54. Washington, D.C.: Urban Institute Press.

Social Security Bulletin. 2002. "Social Welfare Expenditures." _Annual Statistical Supplement, 2002_. Washington, D.C.: USGPO.

U.S. Council of Economic Advisers. 1964. _Economic Report of the President_. Washington, D.C.: USGPO.

U.S. House of Representatives, Committee on Ways and Means. 2004. _Background Material and Data on Programs within the Jurisdiction of the Committee on Ways and Means: Green Book_. Washington, D.C.: GPO.

Conclusions

Mary Jo Bane and René Zenteno

Take, for a moment, the imaginative leap of thinking of North America not as three countries but as one unit, or as an agglomeration of 92 separate states. Now imagine yourself in charge of developing a poverty alleviation strategy for this entity. How would you go about it?

This unit would have a population of about 442 million. Suppose we used a common definition of material poverty in analyzing living standards in this unit, appropriately adjusted for regional and urban/rural differences in the cost of living. Suppose we set the poverty line at the level of something like the current Mexican definition of basic needs. If the calculations we present in Chapter 1 of the volume give us a hint of the underlying reality (though we must note that those calculations suffer from a myriad of defects, including an inability to adjust well for true cost of living differences), we would likely find that something like 75 to 100 million people would be counted as poor.

Then imagine that we plotted the distribution of the poor on a map. We would find pockets of poverty north of the Rio Grande, with concentrations in Native American, First Nations, and Inuit communities, as well as in some inner city neighborhoods of the largest cities, in Appalachia and the Mississippi delta, and in a series of border communities just north of the Rio Grande. But at least half of the counted poor, and probably more like two thirds, would be found south of the Rio Grande. They would be heavily concentrated in the southern states of Mexico, with the densities decreasing as one moves north, but still showing much higher concentrations of poor people in the states just south of the Rio Grande and in the border communities on the southern shore than in the states and communities north of the river.

Economic Development and Migration

This thought experiment suggests that the first leg of poverty alleviation policy must be based on geography, and that it must take its cues from the well-documented association between poverty and economic development in geographically defined units. That means a focus on economic development in Mexico, and especially in the southern states of Mexico.

This leg of poverty alleviation policy should be grounded in the best current thinking and practice in development, which increasingly emphasize context-specific efforts to identify and overcome the binding constraints to growth. As Hernández and Székely argue in their chapter in this volume, increasing productivity is crucial to development in Mexico. If this assumption is correct, it leads to a focus on physical infrastructure and human capital that reflects an analysis of the development path best suited to the patterns of resources and opportunities in given areas. As Walton states in his chapter, development strategies must also pay attention to inequality if they are to alleviate poverty. Walton rightly emphasizes the importance of reforming institutions at the state and national levels, and of developing political mechanisms that ensure participation of the poor.

We emphasize development, recognizing that migration to more prosperous areas is also an option for poverty alleviation. But it is a very disruptive option, both for the families who move and for the villages, towns, cities, states, and regions that gain and lose population, and it cannot be the whole solution to the problem. Presumably the less prosperous subunits would like to keep their population and also become more prosperous. They should look for industries and services, including tourism, that build on their particular advantages and try to develop the physical and human assets that would make them more economically viable. They should build the institutions that both facilitate growth and ensure that the poor are full participants and beneficiaries.

Presumably it would also be in the best interests of the more prosperous areas to help the less prosperous areas solve their problems through growth rather than migration. This happened in the United States at mid-twentieth century, when the central government made massive investments in the infrastructure of the southern states, which promoted non-agricultural development and led to wage convergence and eventually a reversal of the south-to-north migration patterns. This does not necessarily mean trying to keep population on the farms. It may, however, mean, as it did in the U.S. south, investment in towns and small cities outside the major urban areas.

The combination of migration and economic development within the fifty U.S. states resulted in a fair amount of economic convergence and a relative dispersion, rather than concentration, of poverty. The migration of labor from south to north perhaps resulted in some lowering of northern wages, but because the whole economy was growing rapidly, it more likely meant slower growth in wages rather than absolute losses. If the same processes were to occur between Mexico and the states and provinces north of the Rio Grande, and even more importantly within Mexico, the same outcome might come to characterize North America as a whole.

Thinking about more open borders might be possible in a North America where the south began developing economically and building human capital. People tend to migrate from less prosperous to more prosperous localities and also from more extreme to less extreme climates. It might be possible to start a virtuous circle in which greater south-to-north migration is accompanied by economic development in the south, as happened in the U.S. south during the twentieth century, which saw increased agricultural productivity, the development of agriculture-related industries, service industries to serve the slightly smaller and slightly more prosperous population, and eventually the development of a prosperous mixed economy built on human capital contributed by people who prefer warm climates to New England winters.

Education

Now extend the thought experiment to education. None of the states or regions of North America wants to compete economically on the basis of low wages. Nor, frankly, could they, given the size and number of countries in the world with enormous, very low-wage workforces. Presumably states and regions will specialize, on the basis of existing natural and physical resources and on the constellation of industries already existing and thus available to build on. But all will want to increase their human capital, in order to compete in the higher-productivity and higher-wage sectors of the world economy. And of course not all the poverty in North America is geographically concentrated. Indeed, contemporary poverty in the 50 U.S. states and 11 Canadian provinces is much more highly correlated with education and skill levels than it is with geography.

So education seems to clearly be the second leg of poverty alleviation policy.

Both the quality of education and the quantity of education that children receive vary enormously from place to place in North America, and from sub-group to sub-group. In some places and for some groups, primary and high school completion rates remain low, and figuring out how to get children to school and keep them there remains a substantial challenge. In some parts of North America, for example, in the rural areas of the southern states of Mexico and the native peoples' reservations of the United States and Canada, schools still need to be built, teachers hired, and parents provided incentives, as is being done through the Mexican *Oportunidades* program, to send their children to school.

In general, however, the education problem is one of quality, not of quantity. In their own ways, the U.S. and the Mexican education systems fail to provide good compensatory education to children with poor socioeconomic backgrounds, making more likely the reproduction of social inequalities across ethnic and immigrant or indigenous lines. Even in prosperous areas, there is general agreement that levels of literacy and numeracy are not high enough, and that levels of sophisticated skills, both cognitive and social, are not consistent with the needs of a 21st century economy. Creativity, innovativeness, and problem-solving abilities, all crucial to economic and personal flourishing, are not enhanced and may even be stifled by the education system.

The bigger challenge, then, is to improve classroom instruction dramatically, to bring together well-nourished and motivated children, challenging content, and highly trained teachers in modes of classroom interaction that generate high-level learning. The specific problems to be addressed and the most appropriate policy instruments will vary by place: in some places physical infrastructure is crucial; in others, incentives for attendance; in some, development of curriculum materials; in many, intensive and specific teacher training.

Perhaps the notion of "binding constraints," which is proving so useful in thinking about economic development, might also be usefully put to work on problems of education. Detailed local analyses can reveal whether the binding constraints to student achievement are school buildings, teacher attendance, student attendance, student motivation, teacher skills, teacher effort, high-level curriculum materials, or other impediments. Such an analysis can then lead to an assessment of various policy instruments. Some may be directed at accountability: for example, transparent testing programs for students and teachers. Some may be directed at incentives: performance pay for teachers or performance funding for schools; structural changes such as the introduction of charter schools or vouchers to introduce competition; high-stakes testing of students. Others may be directed at capacities: curriculum materials and teacher training directed at high level skills.

The key to effective education policy, we propose, is to ground everything in the classrooms, and to examine whether the learning that takes place there is effective. What is enhancing or impeding effective teaching and learning? What very specific policies and practices will make it more effective? Answering these questions school by school and system by system will be the key to this aspect of poverty alleviation.

Social Safety Nets

Poverty alleviation policy in developed countries often focuses on safety nets and redistribution, to the neglect of policies that enhance growth. In the developing countries the focus is often the reverse, on growth with little attention to either distributional issues or safety nets. A more sophisticated approach recognizes both that appropriately designed safety-net programs can be growth-enhancing, and that the design of safety-net programs needs to address effects on growth.

The three countries of North America vary considerably in their conceptualization of the problems that safety-net programs need to address, and thus in the basic design parameters that they have chosen. All three countries recognize a need to provide basic levels of assistance for the needy and some form of social insurance. And all three countries recognize that a safety-net strategy needs to be consistent with an overall economic development strategy. In Mexico, that means tying the key safety program to human capital development, specifically school attendance and health services. In the United States, it means providing incentives for and supporting work, through an important program tied to earned income (the EITC) and through incentives and requirements in other programs. In Canada, it means more concern for providing an adequate safety net and for alleviating inequalities, and less obsession with incentives.

In all three countries, research on the effects of safety-net programs is ongoing and extensive, especially on two innovative design approaches, the EITC in the United States and *Oportunidades* in Mexico. Continued interaction and research about issues and findings has the potential to inform debates about modifications in these programs in important ways. The research coming out of Mexico's *Oportunidades* program, for example, led New York City to experiment with cash grants conditional on school and health-monitoring behaviors. At some point, Mexico will need to concern itself with the labor market implications of the program, perhaps supplementing it with something like the EITC. And perhaps both can learn from the example of Canada, which found that a relatively generous approach to social protection does not doom a country to economic stagnation.

An issue of common concern for the three countries is dealing with the migration implications, if any, of differences in the generosity and design of safety-net programs. This is an issue within each of the 50 U.S. states as well, since some important safety-net programs are funded and administered by the states and vary in their requirements and level of benefits. Research suggests that migration decisions are not unduly influenced by benefit packages, but they almost certainly have some effects, and are at any rate politically explosive. Some consistency in residency rules across states and countries would almost certainly be a good thing, as would some convergence of safety-net regimes.

Governance

Obviously, other policy areas relevant to poverty alleviation could have been discussed in this volume. Health and health services are among a number of omissions. But the three areas that we did focus on in the volume and in this conclusion—economic development, education, and social protection—provide plenty of material for policy debate. They also raise all the issues of governance that any poverty alleviation strategy must confront. What is the appropriate locus for policy development and implementation in the areas that have just been discussed? And how on earth might some level of coordination among policies be achieved? We are, after all, talking about three national governments, 92 state governments, plus hundreds of local governments and dozens of bi-lateral and multi-lateral agreements.

Thinking about each of the three areas individually suggests both the complexity of the problems and the opportunities for addressing them through policy action at various jurisdictional levels and through a variety of policy mechanisms. Policy development and coordination across national borders are especially challenging. In this arena, treaties, other types of compacts, and informal mechanisms for bringing groups together are likely to be very important.

Economic Development and Migration

Economic development work occurs most intensively on the ground at the local level. State, province, and national policies can affect it both directly and indirectly. Regulatory and trade regimes, crucial to economic development, are structured both at the state and at the national levels; some coordination of these regimes could be very productive. Some regions need serious infrastructure development, on a scale that they are unlikely to be able to finance from their own internal resources; it is in their interest to advocate for investment in infrastructure from outside, and to structure incentives for and financing of infrastructure that work to the general benefit of both private investors and governments. A crucial element here is the recognition that economic development in the southern states of Mexico is in everybody's interest, with the details of how that can be worked out at among the different levels.

Migration within the current national boundaries occurs without much management and sometimes without much recognition of the actual extent and patterning of migration flows. More research on and awareness of emerging migration patterns could help localities prepare and adjust. The management of migration across current national boundaries obviously requires treaty work. Such work might be considerably easier if it took place simultaneously with the kind of economic and human capital development that might limit migration.

Education

Education is traditionally and rightly mainly a state and local responsibility, but with a mix of both financing and control patterns. Thinking through what responsibilities are most appropriately vested where suggests roles for schools, localities, states, national, and even international bodies. For example, schools are appropriately managed at the school level, but equity may require financing at the state or national level, and accountability may rest on the development of measures and standards at the national or international level.

There is also much room for learning, knowledge-sharing, and technical assistance at all levels and between levels. In this arena, cross-national NGOs and private enterprises as well as government agencies and commissions may be in positions to make important contributions.

Safety Nets

The most important safety net programs, like the EITC in the United States and *Oportunidades* in Mexico, were designed and are operated at the national level. Because these are redistributive programs, and because redistribution logically takes place at a quite high level of aggregation, it makes sense that safety-net programs have moved upward from states and localities. Learning about design and incentive issues has also taken place at the level of the nation, and cross-border learning has improved the design and operation of programs in many countries.

If one were really concerned about inequality, and if one recognized universal needs, then redistributive safety-net programs should logically be operated at the level of the hemisphere or even the world; with, for example, U.S. taxpayers contributing to easing the severe poverty of some citizens in the southern states of Mexico. Implementation of this principle is highly unlikely to happen in our lifetime, needless to say. But perhaps some progress could be made at the international level to subsidize very basic needs through foreign aid for specific humanitarian purposes.

A Vision for North America

With immigration such a contentious issue in U.S. politics, and with NAFTA and talk of better relationships capable of generating a truly remarkable degree of paranoia, it no doubt seems wildly utopian and unrealistic to think about a vision for North America. We are not so naïve as to think that a "North American Union" is remotely possible, even if it were desirable. But we do think that governments at the various relevant levels would do well to keep in mind the broader picture of poverty in North America as they develop the programs and policies to address issues in their own locations. The sum of independently determined policy parts, all conceived in a broader context, could with some luck produce a greater whole. We have tried to make suggestions both in the separate chapters and in this conclusion for policy actions at various levels that could promote this larger agenda.

We also believe that bi- or tri-lateral coordinated policy actions of various sorts would be both possible and desirable; for example, joint efforts to increase investment in the poorer areas of the three countries; or efforts to harmonize the ways in which safety-net regimes deal with residency requirements. Migration policy is, of course, the most important and the most difficult. We do not underestimate the challenges. But we also find it hard to envision a poverty-free North America without taking this on.

LaVergne, TN USA
27 March 2010
177319LV00001BA/138/P